기출모의

TOEIC
Speaking

기출 변형 **실전모의고사 15회**

기출모의 TOEIC SPEAKING

지은이 장성진 · 넥서스콘텐츠개발팀
펴낸이 임상진
펴낸곳 (주)넥서스

초판 1쇄 발행 2011년 11월 15일
초판 8쇄 발행 2017년 3월 15일

출판신고 1992년 4월 3일 제311-2002-2호
10880 경기도 파주시 지목로 5
Tel (02)330-5500 Fax (02)330-5555

ISBN 978-89-5797-922-8 18740

www.nexusbook.com

기출모의
TOEIC
Speaking
장성진 · 넥서스콘텐츠개발팀 지음
기출 변형 실전모의고사 15회
넥서스

값비싼 토익 스피킹 시험, 꼭 봐야 하나?

대기업들이 영어말하기 능력을 평가하는 데 있어서 토익 스피킹 점수 제출을 의무화하면서 대학생들에게 토익 스피킹은 이제 필수 스펙이 되었다. 취업 시즌을 앞두고 토익 점수 올리기에도 급급한 취업 준비생들의 부담은 더욱 커져만 가고 있다. 경제적으로 넉넉하지 않은 대학생들이 값비싼 토익 스피킹 시험을 여러 번 보기엔 무리가 있으며 영어 면접도 준비해야 하는 상황에서 토익 스피킹 점수와 영어 면접이라는 두 마리 토끼를 모두 잡을 수 있는 방법이 절실하다.

회화에 자신 있으니 스피킹 공부는 필요 없다고?

토익 스피킹 시험은 시험 보기 전에 미리 준비를 해 두지 않으면 아무리 회화에 자신이 있다 할지라도 절대 좋은 점수를 기대할 수 없다. 토익 스피킹 테스트는 회화 능력을 평가하는 것이 아니다. 국제적인 업무상에서 영어를 사용하는 능력을 평가하는 것이므로 논리적으로 자신의 의견을 펼칠 수 있는 능력이 필요하다. 또한 각 파트별로 평가 기준이 다르기에 그에 맞게 준비하고 전략을 구상하는 것도 중요하다. 이러한 전략을 구상하는 데 바로 실전 연습만큼 중요한 것이 없다고 말할 수 있다.

국내 최초 기출 변형 15회분 실전 테스트

"기출모의 TOEIC SPEAKING"은 토익 스피킹 교재 최초로 최신 기출 문제를 변형한 15회분의 실전 Test를 제공하고 있다. 실제 시험에서는 어떤 문제가 나오는지 알기를 원하고, 충분한 실전 연습을 원하는 수험생들에게 가장 적합한 교재이다. 실전 연습만큼 중요한 것이 없으므로 CD-ROM에 수록된 온라인 실전 Test를 통하여 직접 체험하고, 말하고, 녹음하는 것이 무엇보다 중요하다. 각 Test가 끝난 후에는 자신이 말한 녹음을 들어보고 원어민의 음성 녹음과 비교해 보거나 다른 친구들에게 들어보게 해야 한다. 집에서 실제 환경과 똑같은 환경에서 15회분의 Test를 풀어본다면 충분히 실제 시험장에서도 당황하지 않고 자신감 있게 말할 수 있을 것이다.

그동안 막연히 토익 스피킹에 대한 두려움을 가진 수험생들이 있다면 이 교재를 통하여 충분한 연습을 하고 자신감을 가졌으면 한다. 15회분의 Test를 모두 풀어 본다면 최소 Level 6 이상은 받을 수 있을 것이다. 본 교재로 학습한 수험생들이 모두 원하는 등급을 얻고 취업, 승진하기를 간절히 바란다.

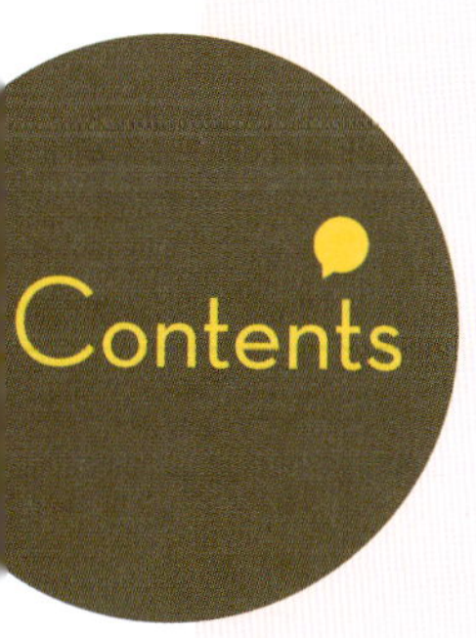

Contents

PREFACE

STRUCTURE & FEATURES

TOEIC SPEAKING이란?

토익 스피킹 유형 분석

*Actual Test 11~15회는 CD-ROM에 수록되어 있습니다.

토익 스피킹 유형 분석

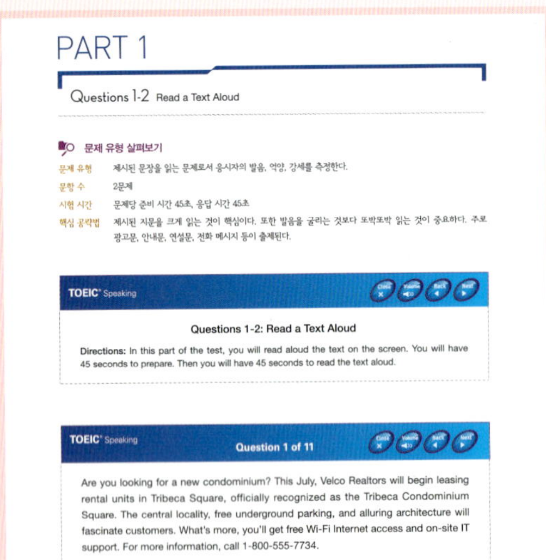

토익 스피킹의 문제 유형을 미리 살펴보고 체계적인 공략법을 학습할 수 있다.

문제집

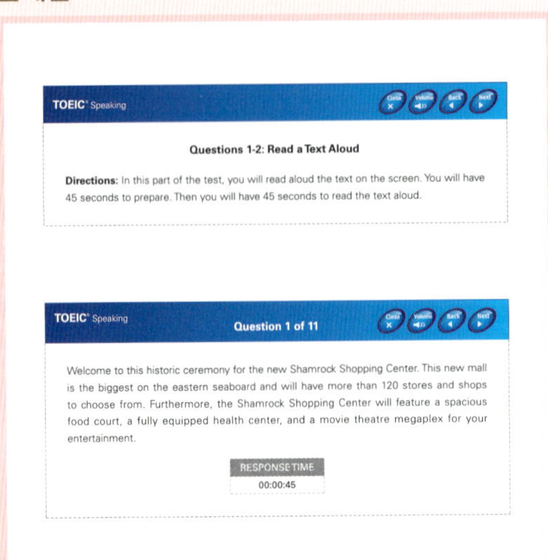

실제 토익 스피킹 시험의 키포인트를 살린 총 10회분의 기출 변형 문제를 풀어볼 수 있다. 추가 5회분은 CD-ROM에서 풀어볼 수 있다.

해설집

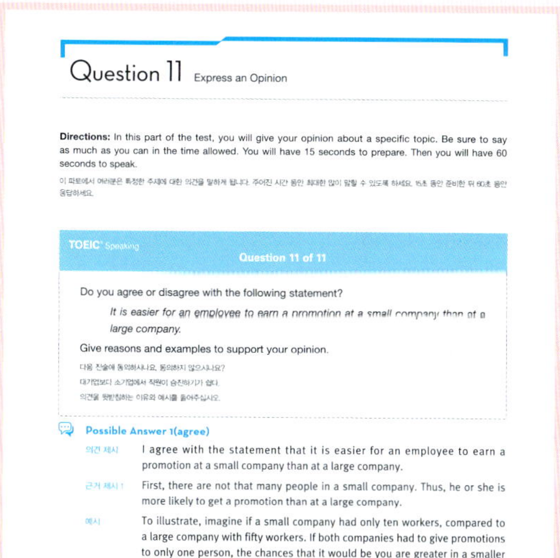

각 테스트의 Possible Answers를 제공함으로써
수험생들이 모법 답안을 확인할 수 있도록 하였다.
Test를 마친 후 발음 교정, 내용 구성 등 체계적인
모법 답안을 스스로 확인할 수 있다.

실전 테스트 CD-ROM

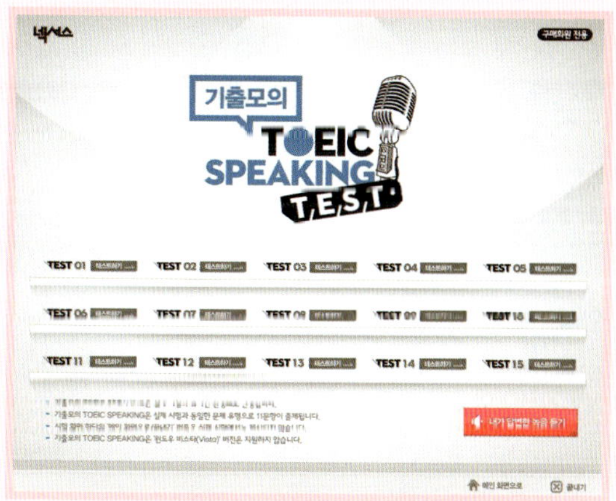

컴퓨터로 진행되는 토익 스피킹 실제 시험 환경을
그대로 CD-ROM에 구현하였다. 시험이 끝나고
녹음한 것을 바로 확인할 수 있으며 원어민의 발
음 및 정답과 자신의 것을 비교할 수 있다.

1. 시험 구성

6개 파트로 총 11문항이며 약 20분에 걸쳐서 시험이 진행됩니다.

구분	문제 유형	문항 수	준비 시간	답변 시간
Questions 1-2	Read a Text Aloud 문장 읽기	2	45초	45초
Question 3	Describe a Picture 사진 묘사	1	30초	45초
Questions 4-6	Respond to Questions 듣고, 질문에 답하기	3	없음	4-5 : 15초 6 : 30초
Questions 7-9	Respond to Questions Using Information Provided 제공된 정보를 사용하여 질문에 답하기	3	없음 (지문 읽는 시간 30초)	7-8 : 15초 9 : 30초
Question 10	Propose a Solution 해결책 제안하기	1	30초	60초
Question 11	Express an Opinion 의견 제시하기	1	15초	60초

2. 시험 평가 기준

답변은 ETS On-line Scoring Network로 보내지며, 수험자의 답안은 전문 Rater가 아래와 같은 기준으로 평가합니다.

구분	평가 기준
Questions 1-2	• 발음 • 억양과 강세
Question 3	위의 모든 항목들에 더하여 • 문법 • 어휘 • 일관성
Questions 4-6	위의 모든 항목들에 더하여 • 내용의 일관성 • 내용의 완성도
Questions 7-11	위의 모든 항목들

3. 시험 접수

시험 접수	http://exam.ybmsisa.com에서 온라인으로 접수
응시료	77,000원
시험 장소	ETS 인증 IBT 센터(전국 100여 개)

4. 시험 성적

싱직은 Score와 Level로 표시됩니다. Score는 최저 0점에서 최고 200점으로 구성되어 있으며, 10점 단위로 표시됩니다. Level은 최저 1에서 최고 8 Level로 표시됩니다.

등급	점수	등급	점수
Level 8	190~200	Level 4	80~100
Level 7	160~180	Level 3	60~70
Level 6	130~150	Level 2	40~50
Level 5	110~120	Level 1	0~30

5. 시험 성석 확인

성적 발표	응시일로부터 약 10일 후 오후 3시 (ETS의 사정에 의해 조정될 수 있음)
성적표 수령	온라인 또는 우편
성석표 수령 소요일	온라인 · 즉시, 우편 : 싱직 발표 후 7~10일
성적 유효기간	2년

TOEIC Speaking

기출모의

기출 변형 실전모의고사 15회

TOEIC

PART 1

Questions 1-2 Read a Text Aloud

🔍 문제 유형 살펴보기

문제 유형	제시된 문장을 읽는 문제로서 응시자의 발음, 억양, 강세를 측정한다.
문항 수	2문제
시험 시간	문제당 준비 시간 45초, 응답 시간 45초
핵심 공략법	제시된 지문을 크게 읽는 것이 핵심이다. 또한 발음을 굴리는 것보다 또박또박 읽는 것이 중요하다. 주로 광고문, 안내문, 연설문, 전화 메시지 등이 출제된다.

TOEIC® Speaking

Questions 1-2: Read a Text Aloud

Directions: In this part of the test, you will read aloud the text on the screen. You will have 45 seconds to prepare. Then you will have 45 seconds to read the text aloud.

TOEIC® Speaking
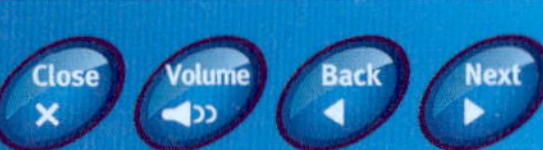

Question 1 of 11

Are you looking for a new condominium? This July, Velco Realtors will begin leasing rental units in Tribeca Square, officially recognized as the Tribeca Condominium Square. The central locality, free underground parking, and alluring architecture will fascinate customers. What's more, you'll get free Wi-Fi Internet access and on-site IT support. For more information, call 1-800-555-7734.

RESPONSE TIME
00:00:45

 모범 답안 (Test 9)

Are you looking for a new **condominium**? ↗(be동사 의문문 맨 끝) This **July**(시간/날짜/숫자 강세), ↗(계속 의미/쉼표 뒤 짧게 끊고) **Velco Realtors**(고유명사 강세) will begin leasing **rental units** in **Tribeca Square**(고유명사 강세), ↗(계속 의미/쉼표 뒤 짧게 끊고) officially **recognized** as the **Tribeca Condominium Square**(고유명사 강세). ↘(문장의 맨 끝) **The central locality** ↗, **free underground parking** ↗, and **alluring architecture** ↘(A ↗, B ↗ and C ↘) will **fascinate customers.** ↘(문장의 맨 끝) **What's more**(부가 강조), you'll get **free Wi-Fi Internet access**(주요 내용 강세) and **on-site IT support**(주요 내용 강세). For more information, call **1-800-555-7734**(시간/날짜/숫자 강세). ↘(문장의 맨 끝)

새로운 콘도를 찾고 계십니까? 이번 7월 Velco 부동산은 공식적으로 Tribeca Condominium Square로 명명된 Tribeca Square에서 건물을 임대하기 시작합니다. 중심지 소재, 무료 지하 주차장, 그리고 매력적 구조가 여러분을 매혹시킬 것입니다. 게다가 무료 와이파이 인터넷 접속 및 현장 IT 지원 서비스를 제공해 드립니다. 더 자세한 내용은 1-800-555-7734로 전화 주세요.

모범 답안 키포인트

1. 위의 지문은 광고문이다. 광고문은 Part 1에서 가장 많이 출제되므로 반드시 사전 준비가 필요하다. 광고문은 상품을 광고하는 글이므로 광고하는 물건은 강조해서 읽어야 하며 특징이니 장점 역시 부각시켜줘야 한다. 빨리 읽는 것이 중요한 것이 아니라 강조해야 하는 부분이 어디인지 미리 파악해 두고 또박또박 정확하게 읽는다.

2. 준비 시간에 고유명사를 자세하게 파악해 두는 것이 중요하다. Velco Realtors, Tribeca Square와 같이 미리 철자를 파악하지 않으면 실수를 할 수가 있기 때문이다.

3. 그냥 나온 지문을 읽기만 하면 된다고 Part 1을 쉽게 생각해선 안 된다. 평소에 영어로 된 글을 많이 접해야 하고 무엇보다도 크게 소리 내어 읽는 연습이 중요하다. 고득점을 목표로 하는 수험생들이라면 Part 1은 꼭 만점을 받아야 한다.

 **ETS 채점 키포인트**

무엇보다 중요한 것은 자신감이다. 자신감을 가지고 또박또박 읽고 본인이 녹음한 내용은 꼭 다시 들어보거나 다른 사람이 들어보도록 해야 한다. Part 1에서는 여러분들의 발음, 강세, 억양을 채점하는데, 끊어 읽기 또한 중요하니 유념해야 한다.

1. 강세

내용의 키워드는 강조하여 읽어야 정확하게 의미 전달을 할 수 있다.

강세 (○)	명사	고유명사
	복합명사 (앞 명사)	본동사
	이어동사 (뒷 단어)	축약형 (뒷 단어)
	부정어 (not, no, don't)	최상급 (highest)
	비교급 (more, better)	숫자 (기수, 서수)
	형용사	
	부사 (부가적으로 첨부하는 단어이므로 강세를 주든 주지 않든 상관 없음)	
강세 (×)	대명사	
	조동사	
	소유격	

2. 끊어 읽기

정확한 의미 전달을 위해서는 다음과 같은 부분에서 반드시 끊어 읽어야 한다.
⇨ 전치사 앞, 접속사 앞, 관계대명사 앞, 콤마 뒤, 마침표 뒤

Collin is / in the classroom.

Simon wakes up / in the morning.

Kelly is / at the grocery store.

I gave him a pen, / but he didn't have it.

3. 억양

음의 고저를 분명하게 해야 높은 점수를 받을 수 있다.

Antonio is a handsome man.

Wilson had a blind date.

Megan is very sweet.

This is well organized.

We say the street performance.

He drinks it.

Liz will make it happen.

Alica has a nice computer.

He seems ill.

Jinna teaches English.

I am taking Jinna's class.

Sarah is standing up.

MBC / KBS

It makes her happy.

PART 2

Question 3 Describe a Picture

🔍 문제 유형 살펴보기

문제 유형	주어진 사진을 묘사하는 문제로, 얼마나 적절한 단어를 사용하여 묘사할 수 있는지를 측정한다.
문항 수	1문제
시험 시간	문제당 준비 시간 30초, 응답 시간 45초
핵심 공략법	제시된 사진을 얼마나 잘 묘사하는지가 관건이다. 사무실, 쇼핑에 관한 사진이 주로 출제된다.

TOEIC® Speaking

Question 3: Describe a Picture

Directions: In this part of the test, you will describe the picture on your screen in as much detail as you can. You will have 30 seconds to prepare your response. Then you will have 45 seconds to speak about the picture.

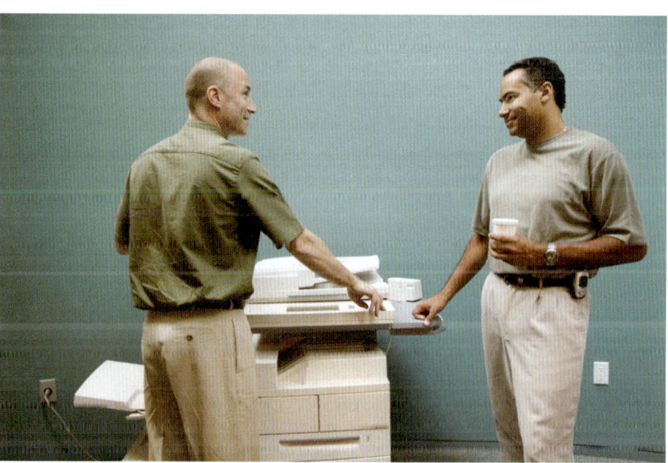

 **모법 답안** (Test 3)

There are two men in a blue-colored room, looking at one another in this picture. They are both wearing light-colored khakis and standing in front of a photocopier. The man on the left is bald and is wearing a short-sleeved collared shirt. The man on the right is wearing a T-shirt and is holding a cup in his left hand. Both men are smiling at each other.

사진에서 청색으로 칠해진 방에 두 남자가 서로 마주보고 있습니다. 이들은 둘 다 밝은 카키색 계열의 옷차림으로 복사기 앞에 서 있습니다. 왼쪽에 있는 남성은 대머리이고 칼라가 달린 반팔 셔츠를 입었습니다. 오른쪽에 있는 남성은 티셔츠를 입고 왼손에 컵을 들고 있습니다. 둘 다 서로를 보며 미소 짓고 있습니다.

모법 답안 키포인트

1. Part 2에서는 먼저 사진을 보고 관련 단어들을 생각해 두는 것이 중요하다. 위의 사진에서는 two men, a photocopier, a short-sleeved collared shirt, a cup 등 지문에서 쉽게 볼 수 있는 인물, 사물 위주로 생각해 둔다.

2. 사람이 등장하는 사진에서는 사람을 중심으로 묘사한다. 먼저 사람을 묘사하고 나서 가까이에 있는 배경, 멀리 있는 배경 순으로 묘사한다.

3. 사람이 등장하는 사진에서는 눈에 보이는 사물 외에도 사람의 동작을 표현할 수 있도록 standing, wearing, holding, smiling과 같은 동사를 떠올린다.

4. 평소에 토익 Part 1의 사진들을 살펴보고 스크립트를 적극 활용하면 도움이 된다.

ETS 채점 키포인트

준비 시간 30초, 답변 시간 45초로 구성된 Part 2는 토익 시험에서도 많이 접했던 문제다. Part 2에서는 과거 시제를 쓰는 것보다 대부분 사람은 현재, 현재 진행형으로, 사물은 수동태 표현을 써야 고득점을 받을 수 있다. 또한 준비 시간을 최대한 활용하고 갑자기 떠오르지 않는 단어가 있다면 유사하게라도 표현해야 한다.

Part 2에서 고득점을 받기 위해서는 정확한 문법을 사용하여 말해야 한다. 또한 그림 묘사 시, 눈에 띄는 것부터 먼저 설명하고 자세한 것은 나중에 말하는 General to Detail의 원칙을 지켜서 설명해야 한다. 또한 and, also, as, because, since, who, which 등 문장의 연결어를 적절하게 사용하는 것도 중요하다.

⚤ PART 2 빈출 상황 핵심 표현

1. 사무실

회의 테이블 주위에 앉아 있는	sitting around the meeting table
프레젠테이션을 하고 있는	giving a presentation
회의에 참석하고 있는	attending (participating in) a meeting
서류를 건네고 있는	handing in (giving) the documents
컴퓨터 타이핑을 하고 있는	typing on the computer
책상에 쌓여 있는 문서들	documents piled up on the desk
필기를 하고 있는	taking notes
스크린을 가리키고 있는	pointing at the screen
회의를 하고 있는	having a meeting
서류를 검토하고 있는	reviewing (examining) documents
서류를 철하고 있는	filing documents
통화를 하고 있는	talking on (over) the telephone
명함을 주고받는	exchanging business cards
책상 청소를 하고 있는	cleaning up the desk
책꽂이에 단정하게 놓여 있는	neatly placed on the bookshelf
컴퓨터를 끄고 있는	turning off the computer

2. 건물 / 도로 / 거리 / 도시

길을 건너고 있는	walking across the road
사람들로 붐비고 있는	crowded with people
자전거를 타고 있는	riding on a bicycle
트럭에 짐을 싣고 있는	loading a truck
도로를 막고 있는	blocking the road
신호를 기다리고 있는	waiting for the signal
길을 따라 걷고 있는	walking along (down) the street
길가에 주차되어 있는	parked along the street
버스정류장을 지나가고 있는	passing by the bus stop
버스에 올라타고 있는	getting on the bus
신호등 앞에 서 있는	standing in front of the traffic signal (light)
주차장에 주차되어 있는	parked in the parking lot
교통 표지판	a road (traffic) sign
보행자 / 보행도로	pedestrian / sidewalk
파라솔 / 차단막	a parasol / a sun shade (canopy)

3. 공원 / 여행지 / 정원

산책을 하고 있는	taking a walk
울타리로 둘러싸여 있는	surrounded with (by) the fences
항구에 정박되어 있는 배	a boat docked at a port
노를 젓고 있는	paddling a boat (sailing a boat with paddles)
기둥에 묶여 있는	tied to a pole
포즈를 취하고 있는	posing for a photograph
바닥을 쓸고 있는	sweeping the floor

4. 식당 및 레스토랑

메뉴판에서 고르고 있는	selecting the food from the menu
음식을 나르고 있는	serving the food (plates)
간판 / 가로등	a sign / a street lamp (light)
진열대에 진열된 와인들	wines displayed on the shelves
음식을 함께 먹는	sharing the food
비닐봉투 / 포장 판매 음식	a plastic bag / take-out food
주문을 받고 있는	taking orders

5. 공사장 / 작업장 / 공장

공사 중인	under construction
사다리를 오르고 있는	climbing up the ladder
기계를 작동시키고 있는	operating the machine
삽질을 하고 있는	shoveling
기계를 고치고 있는	repairing the machine
박스를 싣고 있는 (내리고 있는)	loading (unloading) the boxes
안전장비를 착용하고 있는	wearing safety gear
통나무에 톱질을 하는	sawing the log

PART 3

Questions 4-6 Respond to Questions

🔍 문제 유형 살펴보기

문제 유형   일상생활에서 자주 접하는 주제에 대한 간단한 질문에 답변하는 문제로, 신속하고 정확하게 응답하는 능력을 평가한다.

문항 수   3문제

시험 시간   준비 시간 없이 4, 5번은 15초, 6번은 30초의 응답 시간

핵심 공략법   전화 설문조사라는 것을 유념에 두고 전화 통화를 하듯이 자연스럽게 말하는 것이 핵심이다.

TOEIC® Speaking

Questions 4-6: Respond to Questions

Directions: In this part of the test, you will answer three questions. For each question, begin responding immediately after you hear a beep. No preparation time is provided. You will have 15 seconds to respond to Questions 4 and 5 and 30 seconds to respond to Question 6.

TOEIC® Speaking

Question 4 of 11

Close ✕   Volume ◀))   Back ◀   Next ▶

Imagine that a British marketing firm is doing research in your country. You have agreed to participate in a telephone interview about restaurants.

What kinds of restaurants are close to your home?

 ## 모범 답안 (Test 13)

어느 영국 마케팅 회사가 여러분의 나라에서 조사를 하고 있다고 가정해 봅시다. 여러분은 음식점에 관한 전화 인터뷰 참여를 승낙했습니다. 댁에서 가까운 곳에 어떤 음식점들이 있나요?

Possible Answer

There are many restaurants close to my home, such as a Korean food restaurant, a luxurious Chinese food restaurant as well as an Indian food restaurant.

저희 집 가까이에는 많은 음식점들이 있습니다. 한국 음식점, 고급스러운 중국 음식점, 또 인도 음식점 등 말이죠.

 ## 모범 답안 키포인트

1. 답변 문장을 만들 때에는 최대한 질문을 활용하는 것이 좋다. 위의 질문 What kinds of restaurants are close to your home?에서 restaurants are close to your home을 응용하여 답변을 만드는 것이 가장 좋다.

2. 개인적인 의견을 묻는 질문의 답변에는 I would ~, I'd like to ~ 등의 문장으로 시작하는 것이 좋다.

3. 다른 Part와는 달리 준비 시간이 없기 질문에 대해 바로 답변하는 순발력이 중요하다.

ETS 채점 키포인트

일상적인 대화를 적절하게 해낼 수 있는 능력이 있는 지, 친숙한 화제에 관한 특정 정보를 묻는 질문에 신속하고 정확하게 응답할 수 있는 능력이 있는 지를 측정하는 Part 3에서 고득점을 받기 위해서는 최대한 자연스럽게 말해야하며, 응답을 빨리 시작해야 한다. 또한 4, 5, 6번은 연결되는 내용이므로 가능한 한 긍정적으로 답변해야 고득점을 받을 수 있다.

의견에 대한 근거를 제시할 때 유용한 표현

1. This is the reason why ~ (= That's because)

I love spicy food. This is the reason why I eat Kimchi everyday.

저는 매운 음식을 좋아합니다. 매일 김치를 먹는 것도 그러한 이유 때문입니다.

2. For example

My neighborhood promotes recycling by making it convenient for people to recycle their waste. For example, recycling bins are available in most buildings and stores.

제 주변에는 사람들이 쓰레기를 재활용하기 쉽게 함으로써 재활용을 권장합니다. 예를 들어, 재활용 (분리수거) 휴지통은 대부분의 건물이나 상점에서 이용할 수 있습니다.

3. On the other hand

Taking an airplane is very fast, convenient and comfortable. On the other hand, it is very expensive to travel by air.

비행기를 타는 것은 매우 빠르고, 편리하며 편안하기까지 합니다. 하지만 비행기로 여행하는 것은 매우 비쌉니다.

4. As for me

As for me, I jog every morning. Jogging every morning is a good way to stay healthy.

저 같은 경우에는 매일 아침 조깅을 합니다. 매일 아침 조깅을 하는 것은 건강을 지키기에 매우 좋습니다.

5. Personally

Personally, I enjoy sleeping in and staying up late.

개인적으로, 늦게 자고 늦게 일어나는 것을 좋아합니다.

6. In my opinion

In my opinion, capital punishment should not be legal.

저는 사형 제도를 합법화해서는 안 된다고 생각합니다.

7. My opinion is that ~

My opinion is that drinking coffee once a day is good for health.

제 생각에는 하루에 한 잔 커피를 마시는 것은 건강에 좋다고 생각합니다.

8. In my case

In my case, I usually find the information on the Internet.

저 같은 경우에는 정보를 인터넷에서 찾습니다.

 ## 장·단점을 묻는 질문에 유용한 표현

Internet

Q. 인터넷의 장점과 단점을 알려주세요.

Advantages 장점	**Disadvantages** 단점
I can check my e-mail. 이메일을 확인할 수 있다.	I can be addicted to the Internet. 인터넷에 중독될 수 있다.
I can take a class online. 온라인 강좌를 수강할 수 있다.	Viruses may be contained in the e-mail. 이메일에 바이러스가 포함되어 있을 수 있다.
I can chat with my family and friends. 가족과 친구들과 채팅을 할 수 있다.	
I can shop online. 온라인 쇼핑을 할 수 있다.	
I can download music and movies. 음악과 영화를 다운로드할 수 있다.	

Internet Shopping

Q. 인터넷 쇼핑의 장점과 단점을 알려주세요.

Advantages 장점	**Disadvantages** 단점
It much cheaper than offline shopping. 오프라인 쇼핑보다 훨씬 저렴하다.	I can't try things on. 실제로 입어볼 수가 없다.
I can save time and money. 시간과 돈을 절약할 수 있다.	It needs access to the Internet and computer necessary. 인터넷 접속과 컴퓨터가 필요하다.
No need for vendors and no pressure to buy. 판매자가 필요 없고 구매 압박감이 없다.	There are too many choices. 선택의 폭이 지나치게 넓다.
I am able to compare product prices and features. 상품 가격과 사양을 비교할 수 있다.	I could buy a wrong item by misinterpretation or misunderstanding. 오인과 오해로 인해 잘못된 상품을 구매할 수 있다.

Public Transportation

Q. 대중교통의 장점과 단점을 알려주세요.

Advantages 장점	**Disadvantages** 단점
I can save money for gas and the insurance. 연료 및 보험 비용을 절감할 수 있다.	I can't go directly to destination. 목적지로 바로 갈 수 없다.
I can reduce CO_2 (=cárbon dióxide). CO_2(=이산화탄소) 배출을 줄일 수 있다.	It is not under my control. 통제 하에 있지 않다.
I can reduce traffic and energy consumption. 교통량 및 에너지 소비를 줄일 수 있다.	It is difficult for old people, pregnant and sick people to travel. 노인, 임산부, 병약자가 이용하기에 불편하다.
I don't have to find parking space. 주차 공간을 찾을 필요가 없다.	

Eating Out

Q. 외식하는 것의 장점과 단점을 알려주세요.

Advantages 장점	**Disadvantages** 단점
I can save time to cook. 요리할 시간을 절약할 수 있다.	It is not good for health. 건강에 좋지 않다.
Restaurants provide people with jobs. 레스토랑이 사람들에게 일자리를 제공한다.	It is more expensive than eating at home. 집에서 식사하는 것보다 돈이 많이 든다.
I can try many different meals. 다양한 음식을 접할 수 있다.	

Watching TV

Q. TV 시청의 장점과 단점을 알려주세요.

Advantages 장점	**Disadvantages** 단점
I can follow the latest trends. 최신 경향을 감지할 수 있다.	I can see some of the harmful ideas, frightening and scary films. 일부 유해한 생각에 물들게 되거나, 끔찍하고 무서운 장면을 보게 될 수 있다.
I can learn about different people and places. 다양한 사람과 다양한 지역에 대해 알게 된다.	It is unhealthy for my eyes. 눈 건강에 해롭다.
It can be educational and informative. 교육적이고 유익하다.	

Driving a Car

Q. 차를 운전하는 것의 장점과 단점을 알려주세요.

Advantages 장점	**Disadvantages** 단점
I can go anywhere even very late at night. 매우 늦은 야간일지라도 어디든지 갈 수 있다.	I need a lot of money to own a car(insurance fees and the gas money). 차를 소유하려면 많은 돈이 필요하다(보험비 및 주유비).
I can go directly to the destination (so it takes less time). 목적지로 바로 갈 수 있다(따라서 시간이 덜 든다).	I have to find parking space. 주차 공간을 찾아야 한다.

Having a Pet

Q. 애완동물을 기르는 것의 장점과 단점을 알려주세요.

Advantages 장점	Disadvantages 단점
I can have more friendship. 더 많은 친밀감을 가질 수 있다.	It needs care (look after them). 돌봄을 필요로 한다(애완동물을 돌본다).
It can be home security. 안전 지킴이가 될 수 있다.	I have to spend my money for food, veterinarian, and emergencies. 먹이, 수의사, 응급상황에 비용을 지불해야 한다.
It can raise their mood. 화목한 분위기를 자아낼 수 있다.	

Working for a Part-time Job

Q. 시간제 일을 하는 것의 장점과 단점을 알려주세요.

Advantages 장점	Disadvantages 단점
I can learn how to arrange time. 시간 일정을 짜는 법을 배울 수 있다.	I can't focus on my school work. 학업에 집중할 수 없다.
I can earn money for living expense. 생활비를 위한 돈을 벌 수 있다.	I can be less committed to my jobs. 본업에 덜 전념하게 된다.
I can expand my social and support network. 사회 및 지지 인맥을 확장할 수 있다.	It is lower social security benefits. 사회 보장 혜택이 낮다.
I can be financially independent of my parents. 부모로부터 재정적으로 독립할 수 있다.	It is lower incomes (due to shorter hours and lower hourly wages). 수입이 적다(짧은 근무 시간과 낮은 시급으로 인해).

Using a Cell Phone

Q. 휴대폰 사용의 장점과 단점을 알려주세요.

Advantages 장점	Disadvantages 단점
I can communicate with others (wherever I am). 타인과 의사소통을 할 수 있다 (내가 어디에 있든지).	It is harmful to my health (electromagnetic waves). 나의 건강에 해롭다(전자파).
It helps us organize our daily plans. 일일 계획을 관리하도록 돕는다.	Everybody can find me so it's sometimes very annoying. 누구나 나를 찾을 수 있기에 휴대폰은 때때로 나를 매우 성가시게 한다.
I can play games with my cell phone. 휴대폰으로 게임을 할 수 있다.	

PART 3 완벽 대비 답안

Part 3는 Part 6와 연동된 문제들이 많이 나오기 때문에 답안을 외우는 것도 필요하다.

예를 들어, Part 3에서의 빈출 문제인

1. How often ~?

2. When was the last time ~?

3. Where can you buy ~?

4. Where can you get information ~?

5. What is the most important thing ~?

등의 문제가 나올 때 모범 답안을 외우고 있으면 빨리 답변을 시작할 수 있다.

1. How often do you go shopping? -> 무조건 한 달에 한 번
얼마나 자주 쇼핑하러 가십니까?

In my case, I go shopping once a month. I am normally busy with my studies, so it is really hard to go shopping often.

저의 경우에는, 한 달에 한 번 쇼핑하러 갑니다. 대체로 저는 학업 때문에 바쁩니다. 따라서 자주 쇼핑하러 가는 것은 정말 여의치 않습니다.

2. When was the last time you went to a theater? -> 무조건 지난주
마지막으로 영화관에 갔었던 때는 언제입니까?

As for me, the last time I went to a theater was last week. I watched *X-man* and it was awesome.

제 경우에, 마지막으로 영화관에 갔던 때는 지난주였습니다. 엑스맨을 관람했는데 아주 인상적이었습니다.

3. In your country, where can you buy bottled water? -> 무조건 백화점 또는 마트
여러분의 나라에서는 어디에서 휴대용 용기에 든 생수를 구매할 수 있습니까?

In my country, we can buy bottled water at department stores. They have everything that I want to buy.

우리나라의 경우, 백화점에서 휴대용 용기에 든 생수를 구매할 수 있습니다. 그곳에는 제가 사고 싶은 모든 것이 다 구비되어 있습니다.

4. Where can you get information on buying a car? -> 무조건 인터넷으로부터
자동차 구매 정보를 어디에서 구할 수 있습니까?

Personally, I get information about buying a car from the Internet. The Internet has much information, and downloading is easy.

개인적으로 저는 인터넷에서 정보를 구합니다. 인터넷에는 많은 정보가 있습니다. 그리고 그것은 다운로드하기가 쉽습니다.

5. What is the most important thing when buying a computer—price, design or feature?
-> 무조건 가격이 중요
컴퓨터를 구매할 때 가장 중요한 점은 무엇인가요? 가격인가요, 아니면 디자인 또는 사양인가요?

As for me, the most important thing when buying a computer is the price. This is because I am a still student and I can't afford an expensive one.

제 경우에, 가격이 컴퓨터를 구매할 때 가장 중요한 점입니다. 왜냐하면 저는 아직 학생이기 때문에 값이 비싼 것을 구매할 여유가 없습니다.

PART 4

Questions 7-9 Respond to Questions Using Information Provided

🔍 문제 유형 살펴보기

문제 유형	제시된 정보를 보고 질문에 답하는 문제로서 정보를 신속히 분석하고 답하는 능력을 평가한다.
문항 수	3문제
시험 시간	정보 파악 시간 30초, 준비 시간 없이 7, 8번은 15초, 9번은 30초의 응답 시간
핵심 공략법	주어진 표를 정확히 분석하는 능력도 중요하지만 질문 역시 잘 들어야 한다. 회의, 세미나, 강연에 대한 표가 가장 많이 출제된다.

TOEIC® Speaking

Questions 7-9: Respond to Questions Using Information Provided

Directions: In this part of the test, you will answer three questions based on the information provided. You will have 30 seconds to read the information before the questions begin. For each question, begin responding immediately after you hear a beep. No additional preparation time is provided. You will have 15 seconds to respond to Questions 7 and 8 and 30 seconds to respond to Question 9.

Cooking Meals from Coast to Coast

Fall Course List

- Classes: Two times per week for 4 weeks
- Price: $75
- Size limit: 12 students per class

SEPTEMBER

Mon./Wed.	6:00 - 8:30 P.M.	Vegan and Vegetarian meals (Class filled)
Tue./ Thurs.	5:30 - 8:00 P.M.	Breakfast Beginnings

OCTOBER

Mon./Wed.	7:30 - 9:30 P.M.	Barbeque Techniques (Class filled)
Tue./Thurs.	5:30 - 7:00 P.M.	Diverse Dinner Delights

NOVEMBER

Mon./Wed.	6:30 - 8:00 P.M.	Dessert Design and Decorations (Materials - $35)
Tue./Thurs.	4:30 - 6:00 P.M.	Easy to Prepare Meals

RESPONSE TIME

00:00:30

Hi. I was talking to a friend about your cooking classes and she told me that you came out with your new course list. I was wondering if I could ask you a few questions.

Q7. Which months does the course list cover?

 ## 모범 답안 (Test 3)

전역을 아우르는 요리

가을 수업 목록

- 수업: 4주 동안 주 2회
- 가격: 75달러
- 정원 제한: 수업 당 12명

9월

월/수요일	오후 6시~8시 30분	엄격한 채식주의자와 채식주의자 음식 (정원 마감)
화/목요일	오후 5시 30분~오후 8시	조식 시작

10월

월/수요일	오후 7시 30분~9시 30분	바비큐 요리법 (정원 마감)
화/목요일	오후 5시 30분~7시	다양한 저녁식사의 즐거움

11월

월/수요일	오후 6시 30분~8시	디저트 디자인 및 꾸미기 (재료비 – 35달러)
화/목요일	오후 4시 30분~6시	쉽게 준비하는 음식

안녕하세요. 저는 친구와 선생님의 요리 수업에 대해 이야기하고 있었습니다. 그리고 친구 말로는 선생님께서 새로운 수업 목록으로 수업을 진행하실 것이라고 하더군요. 몇 가지 여쭤볼까 합니다.

Q7. 수업 목록은 몇 개월에 걸쳐 진행되나요?

Possible Answer

The course list covers the fall months from September to November.

수업 목록은 9월에서 11월까지의 가을 동안 진행됩니다.

 ## 모범 답안 키포인트

1. 간단하게 정답만을 말하지 말고 문장으로 말해야 한다. 보통 부사구나 전치사구를 사용해서 답변을 하면 가장 좋은 문장이 된다.

2. Part 3와 마찬가지로 질문을 적극 활용해서 답변하는 것이 좋다. 질문에 나온 the course list cover를 사용한 후 뒤에 전치사로 정답을 말하면 가장 자연스럽게 답변할 수 있다.

3. 위의 표에서처럼 시간과 가격이 많이 나오므로 이를 정확히 읽을 수 있도록 연습해 두어야 한다.

ETS 채점 키포인트

일정에 관한 특정 정보를 요구하는 질문에 신속하고 정확하게 응답할 수 있는 능력이 있는지 측정하는 Part 4에서 고득점을 얻기 위해서는 지문에서 정보를 빨리 찾아내는 연습이 필요하다. 또한 지문에 없는 내용을 질문할 수도 있다. 그럴 때는 지문에 없는 내용을 지어내려 애쓰지 말고 정보가 없다, 또는 잘못된 정보를 가지고 있다 등 지문에 나오는 대로 말해야 한다.

Part 4에서는 agenda / schedule / program의 앞으로 일어날 일에 대해 물으므로 will, be going to로 대답해야 하며 Question 7에서는 누가, 언제의 질문을, Question 8에서는 잘못된 정보의 질문을, Question 9에서는 전체 내용에 대한 자세한 정보를 묻고 있으므로 미리 표현과 전치사들을 익혀두면 더욱 좋다.

▶ 일정 표현
The conference **will be held at** 시간 / **in (at)** 장소.
The seminar **will be conducted by** 연설자.

▶ 도표에 없는 정보를 묻는 경우, 잘못된 정보를 언급해주면서 다시 정정하기
Well, I'm afraid you have the wrong information.
The agenda says the movie starts on 31st, not on 30th.

Wh–Question 질문에 유용한 표현

Who에 대한 질문 Who will make the speech ~ ?

~가 ~을 진행할 것입니다	The orientation The workshop The tour of the factory The discussion	will be led by	Mr. Kim.
~가 ~을 말할 것입니다	The speech The introduction The presentation The announcement	will be given by	Mr. Kim.
~가 ~을 줄 것입니다	The award The annual report	will be presented by	Mr. Kim.
~가 ~을 소개할 것입니다	The new manager	will be introduced by	Mr. Kim.

When / Where에 대한 질문   When (= What time) is ~ ?

~은 ~때 열립니다	It will	take place on 요일/날짜. be held at 장소.

PART 5

Question 10 Propose a Solution

🔍 문제 유형 살펴보기

문제 유형	어떤 특정 문제점을 인식하고 이에 대한 해결책을 제시하는 문제로 서론, 본론, 결론으로 나누어 일관성 있게 제시하는 능력을 평가한다.
문항 수	1문제
시험 시간	준비 시간 30초, 응답 시간 60초
핵심 공략법	문제 인식과 해결책을 제시하라는 요구 사항이 있으므로 이 두 가지 사항은 반드시 포함해야 한다.

TOEIC® Speaking

Question 10: Propose a Solution

Directions: In this part of the test, you will be presented with a problem and asked to propose a solution. You will have 30 seconds to prepare. Then you will have 60 seconds to speak.

In your response, be sure to

· show that you recognize the problem, and
· propose a way of dealing with the problem.

TOEIC® Speaking **Question 10 of 11** Close ✕ Volume ◀›› Back ◀ Next ▶

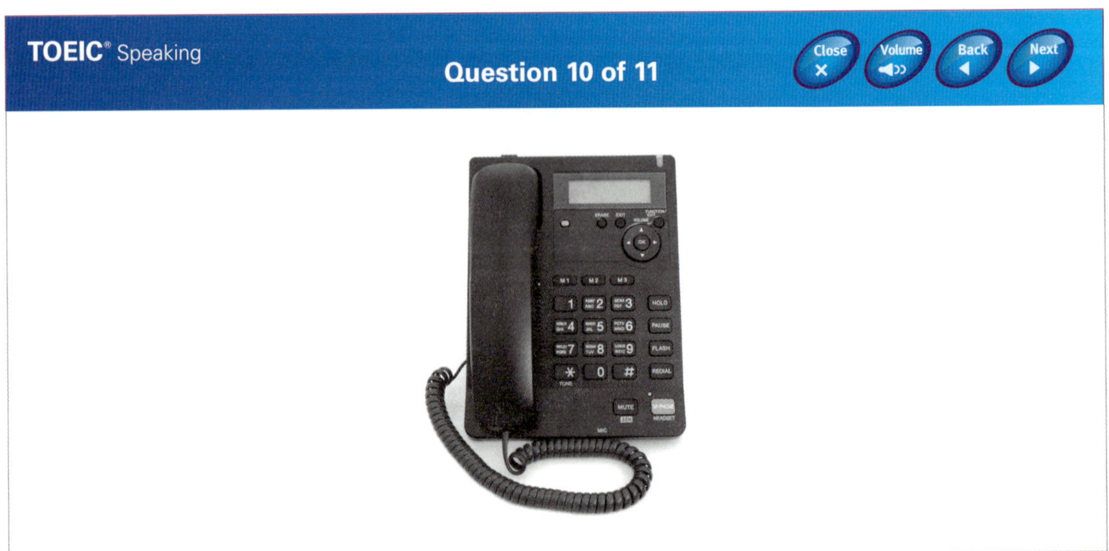

 **모범 답안** (Test 15)

1. 문제

Hello. This is Adam Smith calling from the Tower Green Corporation. This is a message for the hotel manager. I'll be checking in at your hotel on Saturday with a group of 15 people from our Human Resources department. I saw on your hotel's brochure that your check-in time is 1 P.M., but our group's flight arrives at 8 A.M. so we don't know what we should do until our rooms are ready at 1. Also, we'll have all of our baggage with us so it is not easy for us to get around the city. Please call me and let me know what we should do to check our baggage and any ideas for what we can do in town until our rooms are ready. Again it's Adam Smith, and my number is 417-555-1234.

안녕하세요. 저는 Tower Green 조합의 Adam Smith입니다. 호텔 매니저님께 메시지를 남겨 드립니다. 저는 토요일에 저희 인사 부서의 직원 15명과 귀 호텔에 체크인할 것입니다. 제가 호텔의 전단지에서 확인한 바에 따르면 귀 호텔에 체크인하는 시각은 오후 1시입니다. 하지만 저희 일행의 비행기는 아침 8시에 도착합니다. 그래서 저희는 객실이 준비되는 오후 1시까지 무엇을 해야 할지 모르겠습니다. 또한 저희는 모든 짐을 가지고 있을 것이므로 도시를 구경하는 것도 쉽지 않습니다. 세세 전화하셔서 짐을 맡기려면 무엇을 해야 할지 알려 주시겠어요? 또 객실이 준비되기 전까지 무엇을 할 수 있는지 아이디어가 있으시다면 알려 주세요. 저는 Adam Smith이고 제 전화번호는 417–555–1234입니다.

2. 답변 제시 맵

Start a message

Good day, Mr. Smith. I am Cathy from the Hilton Hotel. First of all, thank you for making a reservation with our hotel.

Explain your situation

Its seems that you would be arriving at 8 A.M., quite a bit earlier than the hotel check-in time which is 1 P.M. and you are not sure how you would spent the time with all your luggage before the hotel rooms are ready for check-in.

Propose a solution

Do not worry, Mr. Smith. We will take care of your problems, assuring you of the best of our services. We have a locker facility free of cost for our customers, operating 24 hours a day. So you can keep your luggage in the locker rooms and move around the city freely. We provide city tours every morning starting at 7:30 A.M., at 30 minute intervals, in air-conditioned limousine buses accompanied by a talented tour guide and covering all the best places, museums, art galleries and shopping malls in the city. Also, there are other options for spending fruitful time and we will be there to assist you once you arrive at our hotel.

Ending

Thank you once again for allowing us to serve you. For more assistance, you can call our customer care line at 1-800-3344-5567. Thank you, and we wish you a safe journey.

메시지 시작

안녕하세요, Smith 님. 저는 Hilton 호텔의 Cathy입니다. 우선, 저희 호텔에 예약해 주신 것을 감사드립니다.

문제 상황 설명

고객님은 오후 1시인 호텔 체크인 시각보다 훨씬 이른 오전 8시에 도착하시므로, 객실이 준비되기 전에 모든 짐을 지닌 채 시간을 어떻게 보내야 할지 걱정하시는 것으로 보입니다.

해결책 제시

Smith 님, 걱정하지 마십시오. 저희는 최선의 서비스로 고객님의 문제를 처리해 드리겠습니다. 저희는 고객님을 위해 하루 24시간 운영되며 비용이 무료인 사물함 시설을 갖추고 있습니다. 그래서 고객님은 사물함에 짐을 넣어 두실 수 있으며, 자유롭게 도시를 관광하실 수 있습니다. 저희는 매일 아침 시티 투어를 제공합니다. 오전 7시 30분에 시작하여 30분 간격으로 운행하는 에어컨이 설치된 리무진 버스에는 재능 있는 관광 가이드가 동승합니다. 시티 투어는 이 도시의 모든 최고의 장소, 박물관, 아트 갤러리, 쇼핑몰을 아우릅니다. 유익한 시간을 보낼 수 있는 다른 선택도 있습니다. 고객님이 저희 호텔에 도착하면 저희가 도와 드릴 것입니다.

마무리

고객님께 서비스를 제공해 드릴 수 있음에 감사드립니다. 그 외 제가 도와드릴 일이 있다면 1–800–3344–5567 고객 센터로 연락주시기를 바랍니다. 감사합니다. 여러분의 안전한 여행을 기원합니다.

모법 답안 키포인트

1. Hello라고 인사를 하며 자신의 소속과 이름을 가장 먼저 밝혀야 한다.

2. 배경 상황을 먼저 설명한 후, 반드시 문제점을 언급해줘야 한다. I understand, You said that 등의 표현을 사용하여 문제점을 인식했다는 것을 말해준다.

3. 해결책 제시는 First of all, Finally와 같은 표현을 사용해서 제시한다.

4. 해결책을 제시하고 나서 그냥 끝내지 말고 마무리 인사로 끝맺는다.

ETS 채점 키포인트

전화 메시지를 통해 제시되는 60초 내외의 지문을 통해 문제의 상황을 듣고 그에 해당하는 해결책을 제시하여야 하는 Part 5에서 고득점을 받기 위해서는 Listening을 통해 들은 내용을 이해했음을 보여주는 내용을 일부 포함하여 내용을 체계적으로 갖춘 답변을 완성해야 하며 도입부 → 문제점 요약 → 해결책 제시의 구성으로 답변해야 한다.

Part 5의 문제 유형으로는 크게 물건의 환불 요청, 업무상 도움 요청, 지인의 조언 요청 등 생활 속에서 접할 수 있는 상황들로 이루어진다.

PART 6

Question 11 Express an Opinion

🔍 문제 유형 살펴보기

문제 유형   특정 주제에 대해서 의견을 제시하는 문제로서 적절한 근거를 제시했는지가 중요하며 전체적인 완성도를 평가한다.

문항 수   1문제

시험 시간   준비 시간 15초, 응답 시간 60초

핵심 공략법   항상 두괄식으로 먼저 의견을 제시한 후 근거를 일관성 있게 제시하는 것이 중요하다. 평소에 다양한 주제에 대한 의견을 표현하는 연습을 해두면 좋다.

TOEIC® Speaking

Question 11: Express an Opinion

Directions: In this part of the test, you will give your opinion about a specific topic. Be sure to say as much as you can in the time allowed. You will have 15 seconds to prepare. Then you will have 60 seconds to speak.

TOEIC® Speaking

Question 11 of 11

Close ✕   Volume ◀»   Back ◀   Next ▶

When you go on a trip, do you usually make a precise plan before you leave or do you usually go on a trip without a plan?

Which do you prefer and why?

Give reasons and examples to support your answer.

1. 문제

<table>
<tr><td>TOEIC Speaking</td><td>Question 11 of 11</td></tr>
</table>

여행을 떠날 때, 대체로 출발에 앞서 세심한 계획을 짜십니까? 아니면 계획 없이 떠나십니까?

어느 쪽이 바람직하다고 보십니까? 그 이유가 무엇입니까?

여러분의 의견을 뒷받침하는 이유와 예시를 들어주십시오.

2. 답변 제시 맵

Express an opinion

When I go on a trip, I like to make a precise plan before I leave, for several reasons.

Supporting sentence 1

Most importantly, I do not have much vacation time so I need to maximize my time. I only get five days off a year, so I shouldn't waste my time off researching about interesting things to do.

Supporting sentence 2

Another reason why I like to make a precise plan is that I have had bad experiences in the past when I did not make any plans.

Give an example

A few years ago, I went to New York City. I wanted to see some of the shows on Broadway, but a lot of them were sold out. The shows that I could get tickets for only had undesirable seats far from the stage, and I couldn't see the stage that well. I could have bought tickets to better seats for some of the sold-out shows from scalpers, but they were charging almost five times the cost of the original ticket. I just could not afford those prices.

Conclusion

Thus, I have learned my lesson that it is better to make a precise plan before I leave on a trip than not to make any plans.

의견 제시

저는 여행을 떠날 때 여러 가지 이유로 인해 출발에 앞서 세심한 계획을 짜는 것을 좋아합니다.

근거 제시 1

가장 중요한 이유는 제 휴가가 길지 않으므로 시간을 최대로 활용해야 한다는 점입니다. 저는 일 년에 단 5일의 휴가를 얻습니다. 따라서 흥미 있는 것을 궁리하느라 시간을 허비해서는 안 됩니다.

근거 제시 2

제가 세심한 계획을 짜는 것을 좋아하는 또 다른 이유는 아무런 계획을 짜지 않았다가 과거에 좋지 않은 경험을 했었다는 것입니다.

예시

몇 년 전, 저는 뉴욕 시에 갔었습니다. 저는 브로드웨이의 쇼를 보고 싶었습니다. 그러나 거의 대부분 쇼는 매진이었습니다. 제가 그나마 표를 구할 수 있던 쇼는 무대가 잘 보이지 않는 멀리 떨어진 좋지 않은 좌석만 남아 있었습니다. 암표상으로부터 매진된 쇼를 관람할 수 있는 더 좋은 좌석의 표를 구할 수 있었지만 그것은 본래 표보다 거의 다섯 배나 비쌌습니다. 저는 그러한 값을 지불할 형편이 안 되었습니다.

마무리

따라서 저는 여행 시 출발에 앞서 세심한 계획을 짜는 것이 아무런 계획을 짜지 않는 것보다 바람직하다는 것을 배웠습니다.

모범 답안 키포인트

1. 처음에 의견을 제시할 때는 I think ~, I like to ~로 시작하는 것이 좋다.

2. Part 6는 자신의 의견을 주장하는 것이므로 논리적이고 구체적인 근거를 제시해야 한다. 근거를 제시할 때는 First, Second를 사용해서 차례대로 이야기하면 좋다.

3. 마지막에 마무리를 할 때는 Thus, Therefore 등을 사용해서 말하면 좋다.

ETS 채점 키포인트

질문을 듣고(또한 화면상으로도 제시됨) 의견을 말하는 Part 6에서는 내용의 완성도와, 일관성, 문법, 발음 등을 체크한다. 먼저 서론, 본론, 결론의 문장을 구상하는 것이 중요하다. 그러기 위해서는 논제가 제시되면 본인의 입장을 분명히 밝히고 키워드 위주로 살을 덧붙여 말한 후 입장을 재확인하는 것으로 마쳐야 한다. 그러나 입장을 밝히고 근거나 이유를 말할 때 시험장에서 당황하여 말하지 못하는 경우가 많으므로 다양한 문제를 풀고 준비하는 것이 무엇보나 중요하다

기출모의
TOEIC
Speaking
기출 변형 실전모의고사 15회

문제집
Speaking

Actual Test 1

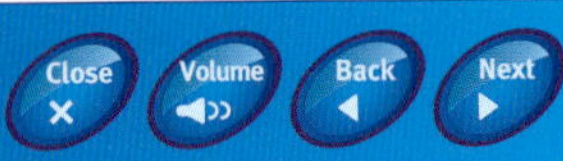

Speaking Test Directions

This is the TOEIC Speaking Test. This test includes eleven questions that measure different aspects of your speaking ability. The test lasts approximately 20 minutes.

Question	Task	Evaluation criteria
1-2	Read a text aloud	• pronunciation • intonation and stress
3	Describe a picture	all of the above, plus • grammar • vocabulary • cohesion
4-6	Respond to questions	all of the above, plus • relevance of content • completeness of content
7-9	Respond to questions using information provided	all of the above
10	Propose a solution	all of the above
11	Express an opinion	all of the above

For each type of question, you will be given specific directions, including the time allowed for preparation and speaking.

It is to your advantage to say as much as you can in the time allowed. It is also important that you speak clearly and that you answer each question according to the directions.

Click on **Continue** to go on.

Questions 1-2: Read a Text Aloud

Directions: In this part of the test, you will read aloud the text on the screen. You will have 45 seconds to prepare. Then you will have 45 seconds to read the text aloud.

Welcome to this historic ceremony for the new Shamrock Shopping Center. This new mall is the biggest on the eastern seaboard and will have more than 120 stores and shops to choose from. Furthermore, the Shamrock Shopping Center will feature a spacious food court, a fully equipped health center, and a movie theatre megaplex for your entertainment.

RESPONSE TIME

00:00:45

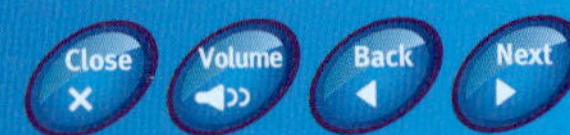

All passengers, please listen to the following two announcements. First, departures to Orlando, New Orleans, and Nashville will now begin boarding at Gate 78. Please proceed to Gate 78 for boarding if you already have checked in with security and have your boarding pass. Second, Flight 411 to San Diego is now departing from Gate 19. Thank you.

RESPONSE TIME

00:00:45

TOEIC® Speaking

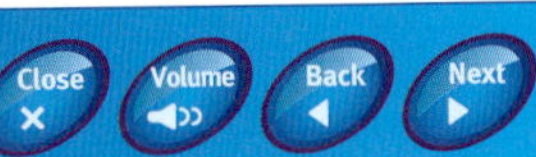

Question 3: Describe a Picture

Directions: In this part of the test, you will describe the picture on your screen in as much detail as you can. You will have 30 seconds to prepare your response. Then you will have 45 seconds to speak about the picture.

RESPONSE TIME

00:00:45

Questions 4-6: Respond to Questions

Directions: In this part of the test, you will answer three questions. For each question, begin responding immediately after you hear a beep. No preparation time is provided. You will have 15 seconds to respond to Questions 4 and 5 and 30 seconds to respond to Question 6.

Imagine that an Australian marketing firm is doing research in your country. You have agreed to participate in a telephone interview about books.

How many novels have you read in the last six months?

RESPONSE TIME
00:00:15

Imagine that an Australian marketing firm is doing research in your country. You have agreed to participate in a telephone interview about books.

Where do you usually get the novels you read?

RESPONSE TIME

00:00:15

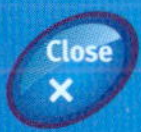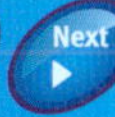

Imagine that an Australian marketing firm is doing research in your country. You have agreed to participate in a telephone interview about books.

Would you read the same novel more than once? Why or why not?

RESPONSE TIME

00:00:30

Questions 7-9: Respond to Questions Using Information Provided

Directions: In this part of the test, you will answer three questions based on the information provided. You will have 30 seconds to read the information before the questions begin. For each question, begin responding immediately after you hear a beep. No additional preparation time is provided. You will have 15 seconds to respond to Questions 7 and 8 and 30 seconds to respond to Question 9.

Summer Solstice Celebration

Sunny Willows Invites You

Details: June 21, 5:30-10:30 P.M.	Responses:
Lemonheads Bar and Grille (321) 555-8762	21 Attending
Contact: Chuck Lee - extension 412 (call for questions)	3 Not attending 0 Awaiting reply

Not Attending :	Comments:
Barb Sharky:	Great idea, but already have plans.
Melissa Puentes:	Sorry, friend's wedding that day. Have fun!
Suzy Scott:	Wow, sounds fun... unfortunately, out of town that weekend.

RESPONSE TIME

00:00:15

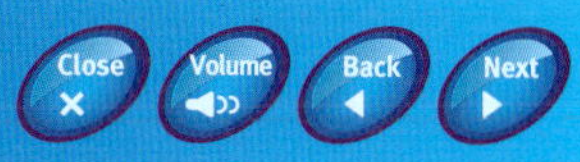

Summer Solstice Celebration

Sunny Willows Invites You

Details: June 21, 5:30-10:30 P.M.	Responses:
Lemonheads Bar and Grille (321) 555-8762	21 Attending
Contact: Chuck Lee - extension 412	3 Not attending
(call for questions)	0 Awaiting reply

Not Attending :	Comments:
Barb Sharky:	Great idea, but already have plans.
Melissa Puentes:	Sorry, friend's wedding that day. Have fun!
Suzy Scott:	Wow, sounds fun... unfortunately, out of town that weekend.

RESPONSE TIME

00:00:15

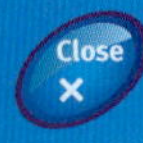   

Summer Solstice Celebration

Sunny Willows Invites You

Details: June 21, 5:30-10:30 P.M.

Lemonheads Bar and Grille (321) 555-8762

Contact: Chuck Lee - extension 412

(call for questions)

Responses:

21 Attending

3 Not attending

0 Awaiting reply

Not Attending :	Comments:
Barb Sharky:	Great idea, but already have plans.
Melissa Puentes:	Sorry, friend's wedding that day. Have fun!
Suzy Scott:	Wow, sounds fun... unfortunately, out of town that weekend.

RESPONSE TIME

00:00:30

Question 10: Propose a Solution

Directions: In this part of the test, you will be presented with a problem and asked to propose a solution. You will have 30 seconds to prepare. Then you will have 60 seconds to speak.

In your response, be sure to

- show that you recognize the problem, and
- propose a way of dealing with the problem.

In your response, be sure to

- show that you recognize the problem, and
- propose a way of dealing with the problem.

RESPONSE TIME
00:01:00

Question 11: Express an Opinion

Directions: In this part of the test, you will give your opinion about a specific topic. Be sure to say as much as you can in the time allowed. You will have 15 seconds to prepare. Then you will have 60 seconds to speak.

Do you agree or disagree with the following statement?

> *It is easier for an employee to earn a promotion at a small company than at a large company.*

Give reasons and examples to support your opinion.

RESPONSE TIME
00:01:00

Actual Test 2

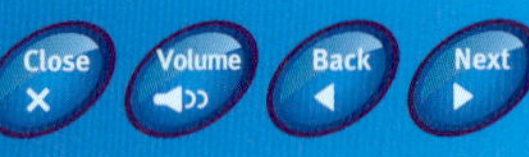

Speaking Test Directions

This is the TOEIC Speaking Test. This test includes eleven questions that measure different aspects of your speaking ability. The test lasts approximately 20 minutes.

Question	Task	Evaluation criteria
1-2	Read a text aloud	• pronunciation • intonation and stress
3	Describe a picture	all of the above, plus • grammar • vocabulary • cohesion
4-6	Respond to questions	all of the above, plus • relevance of content • completeness of content
7-9	Respond to questions using information provided	all of the above
10	Propose a solution	all of the above
11	Express an opinion	all of the above

For each type of question, you will be given specific directions, including the time allowed for preparation and speaking.

It is to your advantage to say as much as you can in the time allowed. It is also important that you speak clearly and that you answer each question according to the directions.

Click on **Continue** to go on.

Questions 1-2: Read a Text Aloud

Directions: In this part of the test, you will read aloud the text on the screen. You will have 45 seconds to prepare. Then you will have 45 seconds to read the text aloud.

Question 1 of 11

Welcome to the Muskoka Museum of Cultural Arts. Our collection features more than 700 artifacts, including Native American relics, totem poles, and prints. In addition, our musical studio highlights independent music from local musicians. After we finish the tour today, you are encouraged to visit our gift shop beside the front entrance.

RESPONSE TIME
00:00:45

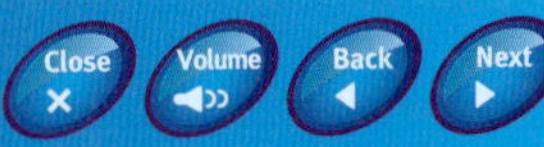

Hello and thank you for calling the Buffalo Bed and Breakfast. Regrettably, we are currently closed for repairs. This means that our rooms, gift shops and tour service centers will be closed until next Thursday. If you have any questions, stay on the line and an operator will be with you shortly. Thank you, and have a wonderful day.

RESPONSE TIME
00:00:45

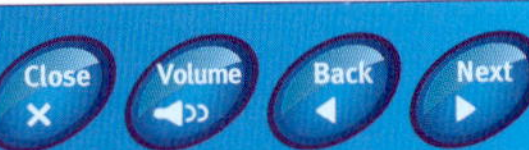

Question 3: Describe a Picture

Directions: In this part of the test, you will describe the picture on your screen in as much detail as you can. You will have 30 seconds to prepare your response. Then you will have 45 seconds to speak about the picture.

RESPONSE TIME

00:00:45

Questions 4-6: Respond to Questions

Directions: In this part of the test, you will answer three questions. For each question, begin responding immediately after you hear a beep. No preparation time is provided. You will have 15 seconds to respond to Questions 4 and 5 and 30 seconds to respond to Question 6.

Imagine that a U.S. marketing firm is doing research in your country. You have agreed to participate in a telephone interview about cooking.

When was the last time you invited guests to your home for dinner?

RESPONSE TIME
00:00:15

Imagine that a U.S. marketing firm is doing research in your country. You have agreed to participate in a telephone interview about cooking.

How long does it usually take you to prepare dinner for visitors, and why?

RESPONSE TIME

00:00:15

Imagine that a U.S. marketing firm is doing research in your country. You have agreed to participate in a telephone interview about cooking.

Do you think it is important to prepare a healthy and nutritious meal for your guests? Why, or why not?

RESPONSE TIME

00:00:30

Questions 7-9: Respond to Questions Using Information Provided

Directions: In this part of the test, you will answer three questions based on the information provided. You will have 30 seconds to read the information before the questions begin. For each question, begin responding immediately after you hear a beep. No additional preparation time is provided. You will have 15 seconds to respond to Questions 7 and 8 and 30 seconds to respond to Question 9.

Question 7 of 11

Itinerary Dante Shells

Monday, April 24

8:30 A.M.	Depart Tacoma (Seattle-Tacoma International Airport, Sharp Jet flight #S28)
12:45 P.M.	Arrive San Antonio (Hotel accommodations, Drake Hotel)

Tuesday, April 25

10:00 A.M. - 4:30 P.M.	Psychiatric Association Conference (Day 1)
5:00 P.M. - 7:00 P.M.	Give a lecture at Palo Alto College

Wednesday, April 26

10:00 A.M. - 3:30 P.M.	Psychiatric Association Conference (Day 2)

Thursday, April 27

11:10 A.M.	Depart San Antonio (San Antonio International Airport, Sharp Jet flight #S49)
2:25 P.M.	Arrive Tacoma (Tony's Limousine Services, 2:45 P.M. pickup)

RESPONSE TIME
00:00:15

Itinerary Dante Shells

Monday, April 24

8:30 A.M.	Depart Tacoma (Seattle-Tacoma International Airport, Sharp Jet flight #S28)
12:45 P.M.	Arrive San Antonio (Hotel accommodations, Drake Hotel)

Tuesday, April 25

10:00 A.M. - 4:30 P.M.	Psychiatric Association Conference (Day 1)
5:00 P.M. - 7:00 P.M.	Give a lecture at Palo Alto College

Wednesday, April 26

10:00 A.M. - 3:30 P.M.	Psychiatric Association Conference (Day 2)

Thursday, April 27

11:10 A.M.	Depart San Antonio (San Antonio International Airport, Sharp jet Flight #S49)
2:25 P.M.	Arrive Tacoma (Tony's Limousine Services, 2:45 P.M. pickup)

RESPONSE TIME
00:00:15

Itinerary Dante Shells

Monday, April 24

8:30 A.M.	Depart Tacoma (Seattle-Tacoma International Airport, Sharp Jet flight #S28)
12:45 P.M.	Arrive San Antonio (Hotel accommodations, Drake Hotel)

Tuesday, April 25

10:00 A.M. - 4:30 P.M.	Psychiatric Association Conference (Day 1)
5:00 P.M. - 7:00 P.M.	Give a lecture at Palo Alto College

Wednesday, April 26

10:00 A.M. - 3:30 P.M.	Psychiatric Association Conference (Day 2)

Thursday, April 27

11:10 A.M.	Depart San Antonio (San Antonio International Airport, Sharp Jet flight #S49)
2:25 P.M.	Arrive Tacoma (Tony's Limousine Services, 2:45 P.M. pickup)

RESPONSE TIME

00:00:30

Question 10: Propose a Solution

Directions: In this part of the test, you will be presented with a problem and asked to propose a solution. You will have 30 seconds to prepare. Then you will have 60 seconds to speak.

In your response, be sure to

- show that you recognize the problem, and
- propose a way of dealing with the problem.

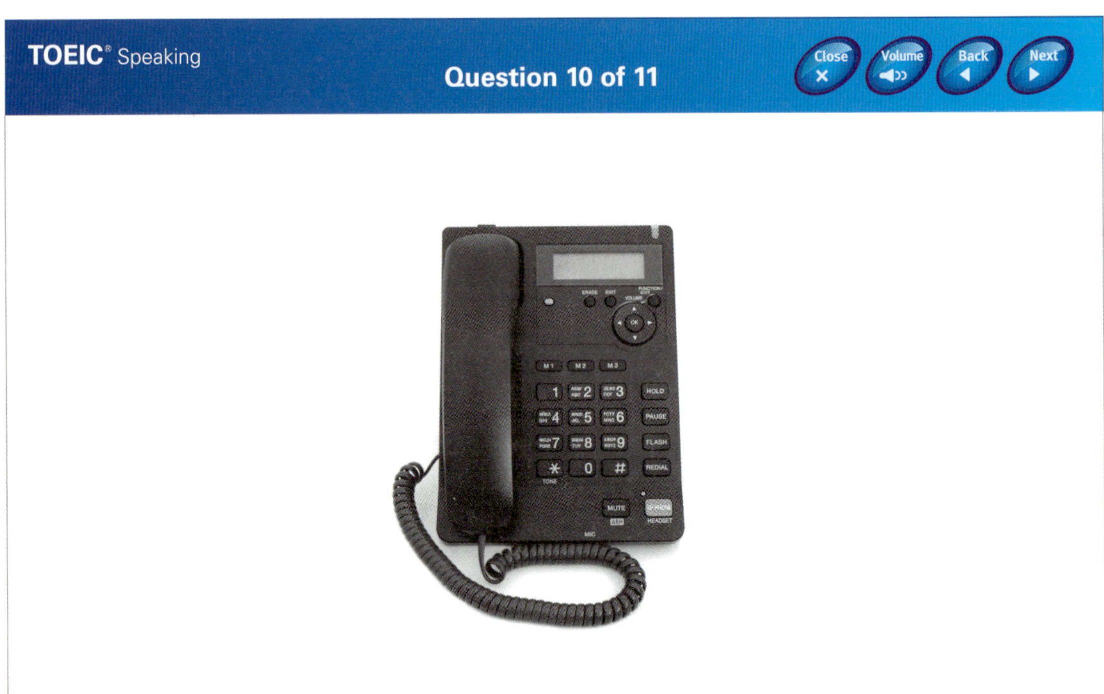

In your response, be sure to

- show that you recognize the problem, and
- propose a way of dealing with the problem.

RESPONSE TIME
00:01:00

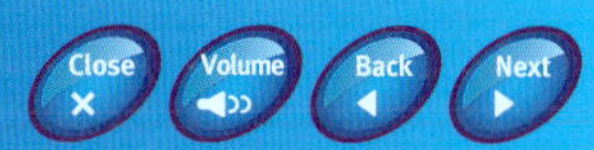

Question 11: Express an Opinion

Directions: In this part of the test, you will give your opinion about a specific topic. Be sure to say as much as you can in the time allowed. You will have 15 seconds to prepare. Then you will have 60 seconds to speak.

Do you agree or disagree with the following statement?

> *Memorizing facts and information is the most important part of a high school student's education.*

Use specific reasons and examples to support your opinion.

RESPONSE TIME
00:01:00

Actual Test 3

Speaking Test Directions

This is the TOEIC Speaking Test. This test includes eleven questions that measure different aspects of your speaking ability. The test lasts approximately 20 minutes.

Question	Task	Evaluation criteria
1-2	Read a text aloud	• pronunciation • intonation and stress
3	Describe a picture	all of the above, plus • grammar • vocabulary • cohesion
4-6	Respond to questions	all of the above, plus • relevance of content • completeness of content
7-9	Respond to questions using information provided	all of the above
10	Propose a solution	all of the above
11	Express an opinion	all of the above

For each type of question, you will be given specific directions, including the time allowed for preparation and speaking.

It is to your advantage to say as much as you can in the time allowed. It is also important that you speak clearly and that you answer each question according to the directions.

Click on **Continue** to go on.

Questions 1-2: Read a Text Aloud

Directions: In this part of the test, you will read aloud the text on the screen. You will have 45 seconds to prepare. Then you will have 45 seconds to read the text aloud.

Do you need office supplies for your office? Midland Depot offers photocopy machines, scanners, color printers, and paper. Furthermore, we can design a paper plan for you that will meet the specific needs of your office. So call Midland Depot, where office supplies are our business.

RESPONSE TIME

00:00:45

 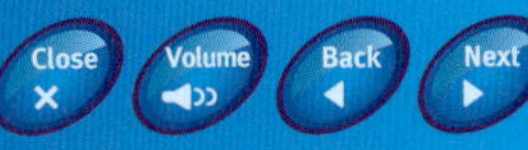

In business news, automotive sales increased between September and November, which is usually not a very active time for car buying. Industry experts say that more people have been purchasing smaller, compact vehicles instead of larger, utility vehicles. Sales have been mostly from car manufacturers that provide affordable vehicles rather than luxury or high-end car manufacturers. Next, we'll speak to a local car salesman.

RESPONSE TIME
00:00:45

Question 3: Describe a Picture

Directions: In this part of the test, you will describe the picture on your screen in as much detail as you can. You will have 30 seconds to prepare your response. Then you will have 45 seconds to speak about the picture.

RESPONSE TIME

00:00:45

Questions 4-6: Respond to Questions

Directions: In this part of the test, you will answer three questions. For each question, begin responding immediately after you hear a beep. No preparation time is provided. You will have 15 seconds to respond to Questions 4 and 5 and 30 seconds to respond to Question 6.

Question 4 of 11

Imagine that a U.S. marketing firm is doing research in your country. You have agreed to participate in a telephone interview about handwritten letters.

For what special occasions do you send cards or handwritten letters to family and friends?

RESPONSE TIME
00:00:15

Imagine that a U.S. marketing firm is doing research in your country. You have agreed to participate in a telephone interview about handwritten letters.

Other than cards or letters, how else do you congratulate family and friends for special occasions?

RESPONSE TIME

00:00:15

TOEIC® Speaking

Question 6 of 11

Imagine that a U.S. marketing firm is doing research in your country. You have agreed to participate in a telephone interview about handwritten letters.

Would you be interested in a service to send online greeting cards? Why, or why not?

RESPONSE TIME

00:00:30

Questions 7-9: Respond to Questions Using Information Provided

Directions: In this part of the test, you will answer three questions based on the information provided. You will have 30 seconds to read the information before the questions begin. For each question, begin responding immediately after you hear a beep. No additional preparation time is provided. You will have 15 seconds to respond to Questions 7 and 8 and 30 seconds to respond to Question 9.

Cooking Meals from Coast to Coast

Fall Course List

- Classes: Two times per week for four weeks
- Price: $75
- Size limit: 12 students per class

SEPTEMBER

| Mon./Wed. | 6:00 - 8:30 P.M. | Vegan and Vegetarian Meals (Class filled) |
| Tue./Thurs. | 5:30 - 8:00 P.M. | Breakfast Beginnings |

OCTOBER

| Mon./Wed. | 7:30 - 9:30 P.M. | Barbeque Techniques (Class filled) |
| Tue./Thurs. | 5:30 - 7:00 P.M. | Diverse Dinner Delights |

NOVEMBER

| Mon./Wed. | 6:30 - 8:00 P.M. | Dessert Design and Decorations (Materials - $35) |
| Tue./Thurs. | 4:30 - 6:00 P.M. | Easy-to-Prepare Meals |

RESPONSE TIME
00:00:15

Cooking Meals from Coast to Coast

Fall Course List

- Classes: Two times per week for four weeks
- Price: $75
- Size limit: 12 students per class

SEPTEMBER

| Mon./Wed. | 6:00 - 8:30 P.M. | Vegan and Vegetarian Meals (Class filled) |
| Tue./Thurs. | 5:30 - 8:00 P.M. | Breakfast Beginnings |

OCTOBER

| Mon./Wed. | 7:30 - 9:30 P.M. | Barbeque Techniques (Class filled) |
| Tue./Thurs. | 5:30 - 7:00 P.M. | Diverse Dinner Delights |

NOVEMBER

| Mon./Wed. | 6:30 - 8:00 P.M. | Dessert Design and Decorations (Materials - $35) |
| Tue./Thurs. | 4:30 - 6:00 P.M. | Easy-to-Prepare Meals |

RESPONSE TIME
00:00:15

Cooking Meals from Coast to Coast

Fall Course List

- Classes: Two times per week for four weeks
- Price: $75
- Size limit: 12 students per class

SEPTEMBER

| Mon./Wed. | 6:00 - 8:30 P.M. | Vegan and Vegetarian Meals (Class filled) |
| Tue./Thurs. | 5:30 - 8:00 P.M. | Breakfast Beginnings |

OCTOBER

| Mon./Wed. | 7:30 - 9:30 P.M. | Barbeque Techniques (Class filled) |
| Tue./Thurs. | 5:30 - 7:00 P.M. | Diverse Dinner Delights |

NOVEMBER

| Mon./Wed. | 6:30 - 8:00 P.M. | Dessert Design and Decorations (Materials - $35) |
| Tue./Thurs. | 4:30 - 6:00 P.M. | Easy-to-Prepare Meals |

RESPONSE TIME
00:00:30

Question 10: Propose a Solution

Directions: In this part of the test, you will be presented with a problem and asked to propose a solution. You will have 30 seconds to prepare. Then you will have 60 seconds to speak.

In your response, be sure to

- show that you recognize the problem, and
- propose a way of dealing with the problem.

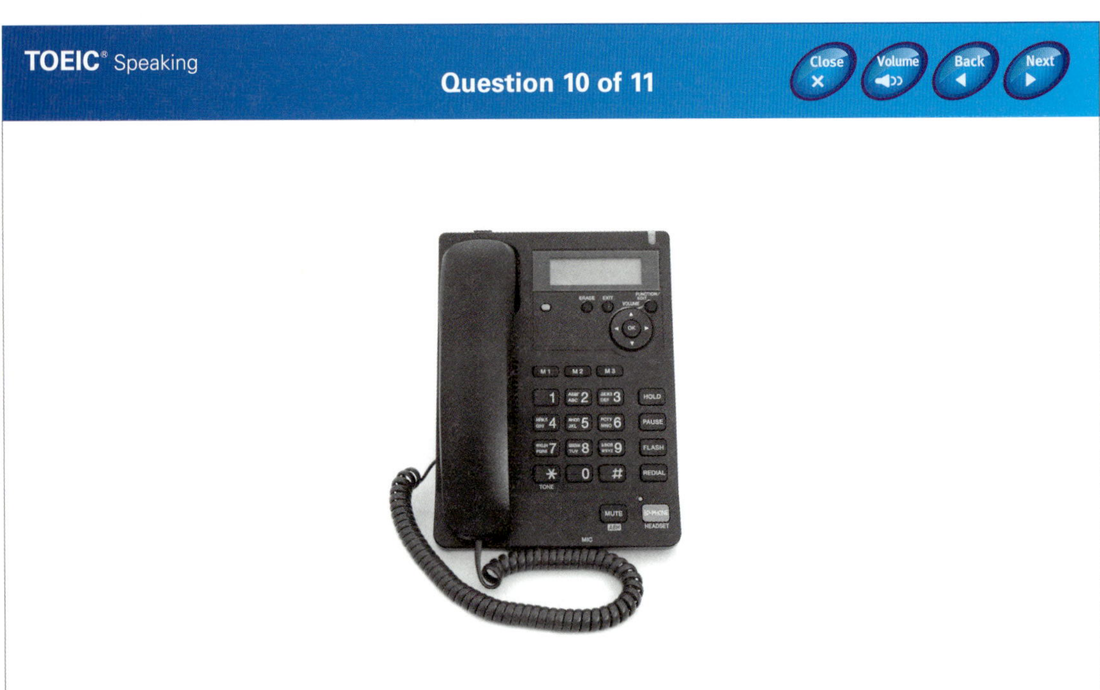

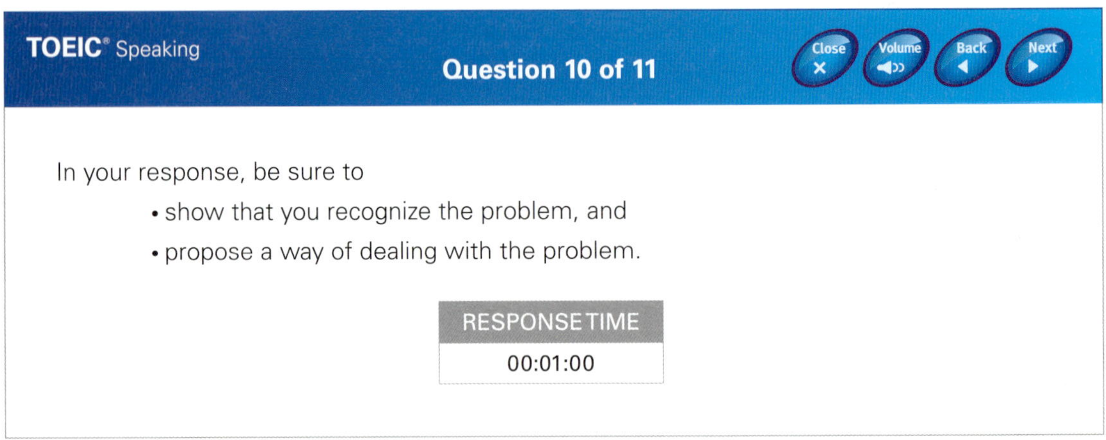

In your response, be sure to
• show that you recognize the problem, and
• propose a way of dealing with the problem.
RESPONSE TIME
00:01:00

Question 11: Express an Opinion

Directions: In this part of the test, you will give your opinion about a specific topic. Be sure to say as much as you can in the time allowed. You will have 15 seconds to prepare. Then you will have 60 seconds to speak.

Some people think success is mainly the result of intelligence. Other people think success is mainly the result of hard work. Which do you think is more important to success?

Intelligence or hard work?

Give reasons or examples to support your opinion.

RESPONSE TIME
00.01.00

Actual Test 4

Speaking Test Directions

This is the TOEIC Speaking Test. This test includes eleven questions that measure different aspects of your speaking ability. The test lasts approximately 20 minutes.

Question	Task	Evaluation criteria
1-2	Read a text aloud	• pronunciation • intonation and stress
3	Describe a picture	all of the above, plus • grammar • vocabulary • cohesion
4-6	Respond to questions	all of the above, plus • relevance of content • completeness of content
7-9	Respond to questions using information provided	all of the above
10	Propose a solution	all of the above
11	Express an opinion	all of the above

For each type of question, you will be given specific directions, including the time allowed for preparation and speaking.

It is to your advantage to say as much as you can in the time allowed. It is also important that you speak clearly and that you answer each question according to the directions.

Click on **Continue** to go on.

Questions 1-2: Read a Text Aloud

Directions: In this part of the test, you will read aloud the text on the screen. You will have 45 seconds to prepare. Then you will have 45 seconds to read the text aloud.

Question 1 of 11

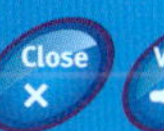

Welcome to Shakespeare's Theatre Company. This is a reminder to deactivate your cellular phones, pagers, or other electronic devices. If you would like to purchase snacks or drinks, they are available at the refreshment booth on the main floor. Finally, please be considerate of other audience members by refraining from talking during the performance.

RESPONSE TIME

00:00:45

Thank you for calling Lakeheed Waterworks. Regrettably, all our operators are currently busy. Please be advised that emergency crews are working to restore water to the downtown, midtown, and uptown neighborhoods. If you are calling to inform us of another emergency, please stay on the line. Someone will be with you shortly.

RESPONSE TIME
00:00:45

Question 3: Describe a Picture

Directions: In this part of the test, you will describe the picture on your screen in as much detail as you can. You will have 30 seconds to prepare your response. Then you will have 45 seconds to speak about the picture.

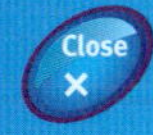   

RESPONSE TIME

00:00:45

Questions 4-6: Respond to Questions

Directions: In this part of the test, you will answer three questions. For each question, begin responding immediately after you hear a beep. No preparation time is provided. You will have 15 seconds to respond to Questions 4 and 5 and 30 seconds to respond to Question 6.

Imagine that a British marketing firm is doing research in your country. You have agreed to participate in a telephone interview about giving gifts to coworkers.

Why do you give gifts to your coworkers?

RESPONSE TIME
00:00:15

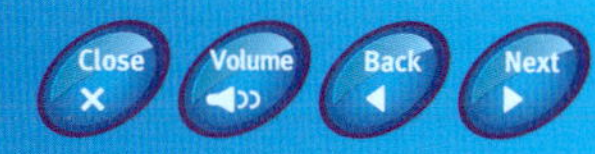

Imagine that a British marketing firm is doing research in your country. You have agreed to participate in a telephone interview about giving gifts to coworkers.

How much time do you tend to spend deciding on gifts for coworkers?

RESPONSE TIME

00:00:15

Imagine that a British marketing firm is doing research in your country. You have agreed to participate in a telephone interview about giving gifts to coworkers.

What do you take into account when you are choosing gifts for coworkers, and why?

RESPONSE TIME

00:00:30

Questions 7-9: Respond to Questions Using Information Provided

Directions: In this part of the test, you will answer three questions based on the information provided. You will have 30 seconds to read the information before the questions begin. For each question, begin responding immediately after you hear a beep. No additional preparation time is provided. You will have 15 seconds to respond to Questions 7 and 8 and 30 seconds to respond to Question 9.

Moonwalker Savings & Loans

Yearly Convention: Friday, May 11

Center of Operations, Philadelphia, Pennsylvania

8:30 A.M.	Welcome Address	Bobby Mack, President
9:00 A.M.	Customer Satisfaction Evaluations	Gordon Light, Market Research
10:30 A.M.	Restructuring of the Loans Division	Tonto Reynolds, Regional Manager
11:45 A.M.	Paris & Hong Kong Branch Openings	Lauren Reed, Branch Officer
12:30 P.M.	Lunch Buffet	
1:30 P.M.	New International Policies	Walter Williams, Legal Division
2:15 P.M.	New Products: Online Investing	Michael Meyers, Information Technology
3:00 P.M.	General Inquiries	All members
4:30 P.M.	Closing Notes	Bobby Mack, President

RESPONSE TIME

00:00:15

Moonwalker Savings & Loans

Yearly Convention: Friday, May 11

Center of Operations, Philadelphia, Pennsylvania

8:30 A.M.	Welcome Address	Bobby Mack, President
9:00 A.M.	Customer Satisfaction Evaluations	Gordon Light, Market Research
10:30 A.M.	Restructuring of the Loans Division	Tonto Reynolds, Regional Manager
11:45 A.M.	Paris & Hong Kong Branch Openings	Lauren Reed, Branch Officer
12:30 P.M.	Lunch Buffet	
1:30 P.M.	New International Policies	Walter Williams, Legal Division
2:15 P.M.	New Products. Online Investing	Michael Meyers, Information Technology
3:00 P.M.	General Inquiries	All members
4:30 P.M.	Closing Notes	Bobby Mack, President

RESPONSE TIME

00:00:15

Moonwalker Savings & Loans

Yearly Convention: Friday, May 11
Center of Operations, Philadelphia, Pennsylvania

8:30 A.M.	Welcome Address	Bobby Mack, President
9:00 A.M.	Customer Satisfaction Evaluations	Gordon Light, Market Research
10:30 A.M.	Restructuring of the Loans Division	Tonto Reynolds, Regional Manager
11:45 A.M.	Paris & Hong Kong Branch Openings	Lauren Reed, Branch Officer
12:30 P.M.	Lunch Buffet	
1:30 P.M.	New International Policies	Walter Williams, Legal Division
2:15 P.M.	New Products: Online Investing	Michael Meyers, Information Technology
3:00 P.M.	General Inquiries	All members
4:30 P.M.	Closing Notes	Bobby Mack, President

RESPONSE TIME

00:00:30

TOEIC® Speaking

Question 10: Propose a Solution

Directions: In this part of the test, you will be presented with a problem and asked to propose a solution. You will have 30 seconds to prepare. Then you will have 60 seconds to speak.

In your response, be sure to

- show that you recognize the problem, and
- propose a way of dealing with the problem.

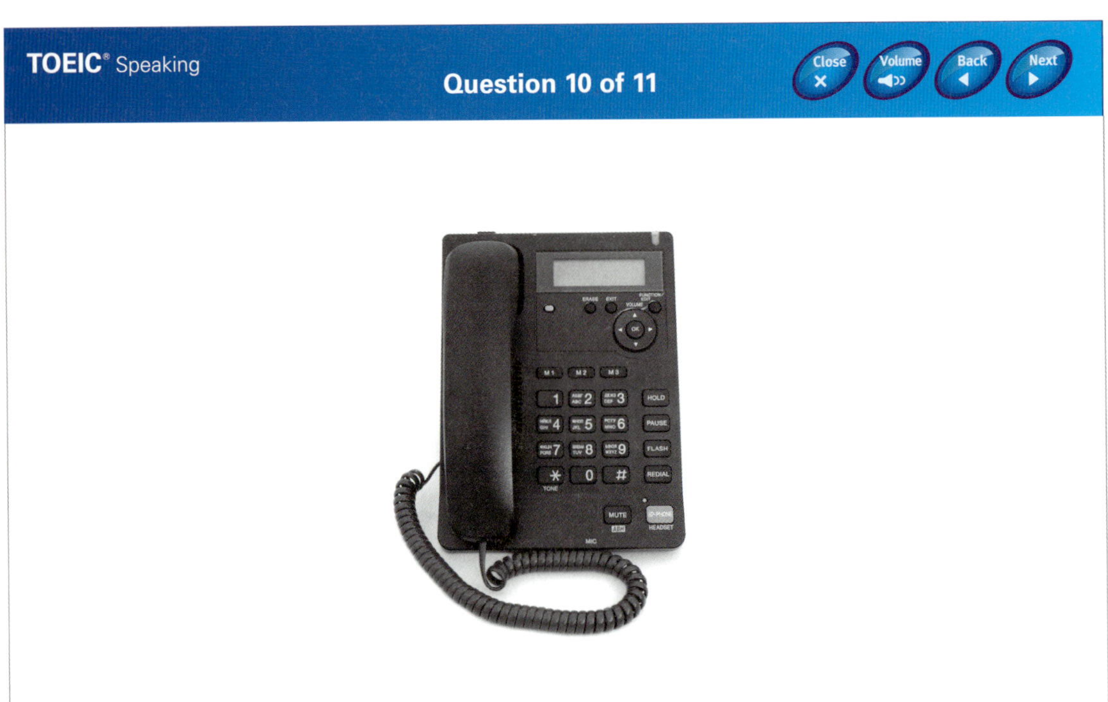

In your response, be sure to

- show that you recognize the problem, and
- propose a way of dealing with the problem.

RESPONSE TIME
00:01:00

Question 11: Express an Opinion

Directions: In this part of the test, you will give your opinion about a specific topic. Be sure to say as much as you can in the time allowed. You will have 15 seconds to prepare. Then you will have 60 seconds to speak.

Do you agree or disagree with the following statement?

Eating home-cooked meals is the best way to maintain a healthy diet.

Give reasons and examples to support your answer.

RESPONSE TIME
00:01:00

Actual Test 5

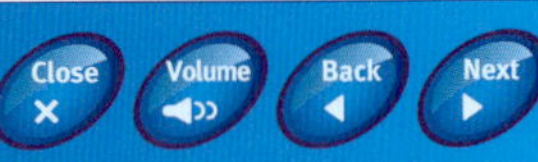

Speaking Test Directions

This is the TOEIC Speaking Test. This test includes eleven questions that measure different aspects of your speaking ability. The test lasts approximately 20 minutes.

Question	Task	Evaluation criteria
1-2	Read a text aloud	• pronunciation • intonation and stress
3	Describe a picture	all of the above, plus • grammar • vocabulary • cohesion
4-6	Respond to questions	all of the above, plus • relevance of content • completeness of content
7-9	Respond to questions using information provided	all of the above
10	Propose a solution	all of the above
11	Express an opinion	all of the above

For each type of question, you will be given specific directions, including the time allowed for preparation and speaking.

It is to your advantage to say as much as you can in the time allowed. It is also important that you speak clearly and that you answer each question according to the directions.

Click on **Continue** to go on.

Questions 1-2: Read a Text Aloud

Directions: In this part of the test, you will read aloud the text on the screen. You will have 45 seconds to prepare. Then you will have 45 seconds to read the text aloud.

Thank you for joining us on Fashion Forward. Today, our guest is Giovanni Carlo who is the owner of Milan Mode. He'll tell us about the latest styles in suits, ties, and dress shoes. After that, one of the lucky audience members will get a free style over. You will want to stay tuned!

RESPONSE TIME
00:00:45

Your attention please, Toronto Transit commuters. Because of a major construction project, the Bathurst Subway Station will be closed during the months of September, October, and November. During these months, there will be a temporary shuttle-bus service available for commuters who wish to go to Bathurst Street. We apologize for the inconvenience.

RESPONSE TIME
00:00:45

Question 3: Describe a Picture

Directions: In this part of the test, you will describe the picture on your screen in as much detail as you can. You will have 30 seconds to prepare your response. Then you will have 45 seconds to speak about the picture.

RESPONSE TIME

00:00:45

 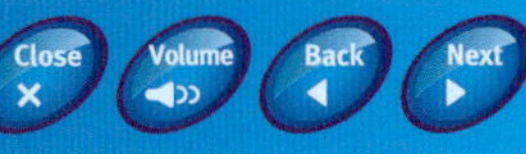

Questions 4-6: Respond to Questions

Directions: In this part of the test, you will answer three questions. For each question, begin responding immediately after you hear a beep. No preparation time is provided. You will have 15 seconds to respond to Questions 4 and 5 and 30 seconds to respond to Question 6.

Imagine that an Australian marketing firm is doing research in your country. You have agreed to participate in a telephone interview about alarm clocks.

When was the last time you bought an alarm clock, and where did you buy it?

RESPONSE TIME
00:00:15

Imagine that an Australian marketing firm is doing research in your country. You have agreed to participate in a telephone interview about alarm clocks.

When do you usually use the alarm clock?

RESPONSE TIME

00:00:15

Imagine that an Australian marketing firm is doing research in your country. You have agreed to participate in a telephone interview about alarm clocks.

What are the most important features that you look for in an alarm clock, and why?

RESPONSE TIME

00:00:30

Questions 7-9: Respond to Questions Using Information Provided

Directions: In this part of the test, you will answer three questions based on the information provided. You will have 30 seconds to read the information before the questions begin. For each question, begin responding immediately after you hear a beep. No additional preparation time is provided. You will have 15 seconds to respond to Questions 7 and 8 and 30 seconds to respond to Question 9.

Maple Recreation Center
Children's Story Book Celebration

Title	Date	Time	Location
Around the World	February 14	10:30 A.M.	Rec. Room 7
Surfer's Paradise	February 28	6:30 P.M.	Rec. Room 8
The Banana Boat	March 4	1:30 P.M.	Rec. Room 7
A Secret Agent	March 12	10:30 A.M.	Rec. Room 8
Barbarella's Ball	April 6	3:00 P.M.	Rec. Room 7
Samurai Versus Santa	April 21	9:30 A.M.	Rec. Room 8
One Thousand Pianos	May 7	6:30 P.M.	Rec. Room 7

RESPONSE TIME

00:00:15

Maple Recreation Center
Children's Story Book Celebration

Title	Date	Time	Location
Around the World	February 14	10:30 A.M.	Rec. Room 7
Surfer's Paradise	February 28	6:30 P.M.	Rec. Room 8
The Banana Boat	March 4	1:30 P.M.	Rec. Room 7
A Secret Agent	March 12	10:30 A.M.	Rec. Room 8
Barbarella's Ball	April 6	3:00 P.M.	Rec. Room 7
Samurai Versus Santa	April 21	9:30 A.M.	Rec. Room 8
One Thousand Pianos	May 7	6:30 P.M.	Rec. Room 7

RESPONSE TIME

00.00.15

Maple Recreation Center
Children's Story Book Celebration

Title	Date	Time	Location
Around the World	February 14	10:30 A.M.	Rec. Room 7
Surfer's Paradise	February 28	6:30 P.M.	Rec. Room 8
The Banana Boat	March 4	1:30 P.M.	Rec. Room 7
A Secret Agent	March 12	10:30 A.M.	Rec. Room 8
Barbarella's Ball	April 6	3:00 P.M.	Rec. Room 7
Samurai Versus Santa	April 21	9:30 A.M.	Rec. Room 8
One Thousand Pianos	May 7	6:30 P.M.	Rec. Room 7

RESPONSE TIME

00:00:30

Question 10: Propose a Solution

Directions: In this part of the test, you will be presented with a problem and asked to propose a solution. You will have 30 seconds to prepare. Then you will have 60 seconds to speak.

In your response, be sure to

- show that you recognize the problem, and
- propose a way of dealing with the problem.

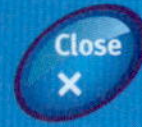   

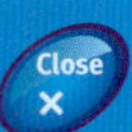  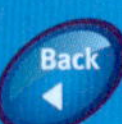 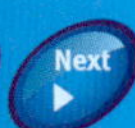

In your response, be sure to

- show that you recognize the problem, and
- propose a way of dealing with the problem.

RESPONSE TIME
00:01:00

Question 11: Express an Opinion

Directions: In this part of the test, you will give your opinion about a specific topic. Be sure to say as much as you can in the time allowed. You will have 15 seconds to prepare. Then you will have 60 seconds to speak.

Some people prefer to do all of their shopping at one large store. Others prefer to go to several smaller specialty stores.

Which do you think is better?

Give specific reasons or examples to support your opinion.

RESPONSE TIME
00:01:00

Actual Test 6

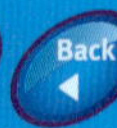

Speaking Test Directions

This is the TOEIC Speaking Test. This test includes eleven questions that measure different aspects of your speaking ability. The test lasts approximately 20 minutes.

Question	Task	Evaluation criteria
1-2	Read a text aloud	• pronunciation • intonation and stress
3	Describe a picture	all of the above, plus • grammar • vocabulary • cohesion
4-6	Respond to questions	all of the above, plus • relevance of content • completeness of content
7-9	Respond to questions using information provided	all of the above
10	Propose a solution	all of the above
11	Express an opinion	all of the above

For each type of question, you will be given specific directions, including the time allowed for preparation and speaking.

It is to your advantage to say as much as you can in the time allowed. It is also important that you speak clearly and that you answer each question according to the directions.

Click on **Continue** to go on.

Questions 1-2: Read a Text Aloud

Directions: In this part of the test, you will read aloud the text on the screen. You will have 45 seconds to prepare. Then you will have 45 seconds to read the text aloud.

Thank you for selecting the new Traveling Global Positioning System from Kent Technologies. Once you've charged and installed the battery, getting started is very simple. First, input the address of your destination. Then merely follow the step-by-step directions to get you there. You can also use the "search" menu to locate rest stops, restaurants, and tourist attractions along the way.

RESPONSE TIME
00:00:45

This is Ernie's Diner. Today, our visitor is Ray Kwon, the chef from Macao. His new cookbook is full of organic recipes that add variety to your meals. It will help you cook food that is healthy, easy to prepare, and most important, delectable. Now, let's welcome Ray to the program.

RESPONSE TIME

00:00:45

Question 3: Describe a Picture

Directions: In this part of the test, you will describe the picture on your screen in as much detail as you can. You will have 30 seconds to prepare your response. Then you will have 45 seconds to speak about the picture.

RESPONSE TIME

00:00:45

Questions 4-6: Respond to Questions

Directions: In this part of the test, you will answer three questions. For each question, begin responding immediately after you hear a beep. No preparation time is provided. You will have 15 seconds to respond to Questions 4 and 5 and 30 seconds to respond to Question 6.

Imagine that an American marketing firm is doing research in your country. You have agreed to participate in a telephone interview about cellular phones.

What kind of cellular phone do you use, and where did you get it?

RESPONSE TIME

00:00:15

TOEIC Speaking

Question 5 of 11

Imagine that an American marketing firm is doing research in your country. You have agreed to participate in a telephone interview about cellular phones.

What do you normally use your cellular phone for, and what did you do with your cellular phone most recently?

RESPONSE TIME

00:00:15

TOEIC Speaking

Question 6 of 11

Imagine that an American marketing firm is doing research in your country. You have agreed to participate in a telephone interview about cellular phones.

What is the most important feature you consider when buying a cellular phone?

RESPONSE TIME

00:00:30

 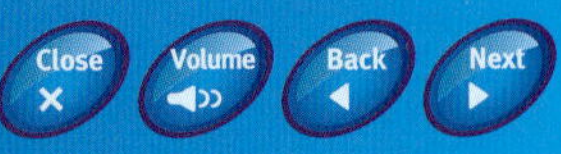

Questions 7-9: Respond to Questions Using Information Provided

Directions: In this part of the test, you will answer three questions based on the information provided. You will have 30 seconds to read the information before the questions begin. For each question, begin responding immediately after you hear a beep. No additional preparation time is provided. You will have 15 seconds to respond to Questions 7 and 8 and 30 seconds to respond to Question 9.

The Catsup Chalet
Lakeridge, North York, Ontario
555-3321

Availability: June 1-7   X: reserved

	Rate	June 1	June 2	June 3	June 4	June 5	June 6	June 7
Basil (2 rooms)	$95	X			X	X	X	X
Moonrise (2 rooms)	$109		X			X	X	X
Tulip (3 rooms)	$159			X		X	X	
Oak (4 rooms)	$179			X		X	X	

RESPONSE TIME

00:00:15

The Catsup Chalet
Lakeridge, North York, Ontario
555-3321

Availability: June 1-7   X: reserved

	Rate	June 1	June 2	June 3	June 4	June 5	June 6	June 7
Basil (2 rooms)	$ 95	X			X	X	X	X
Moonrise (2 rooms)	$ 109		X			X	X	X
Tulip (3 rooms)	$ 159			X		X	X	
Oak (4 rooms)	$ 179			X		X	X	

RESPONSE TIME

00:00:15

The Catsup Chalet
Lakeridge, North York, Ontario
555-3321

Availability: June 1-7   X: reserved

	Rate	June 1	June 2	June 3	June 4	June 5	June 6	June 7
Basil (2 rooms)	$ 95	X			X	X	X	X
Moonrise (2 rooms)	$ 109		X			X	X	X
Tulip (3 rooms)	$ 159			X		X	X	
Oak (4 rooms)	$ 179			X		X	X	

RESPONSE TIME
00:00:30

Question 10: Propose a Solution

Directions: In this part of the test, you will be presented with a problem and asked to propose a solution. You will have 30 seconds to prepare. Then you will have 60 seconds to speak.

In your response, be sure to

- show that you recognize the problem, and
- propose a way of dealing with the problem.

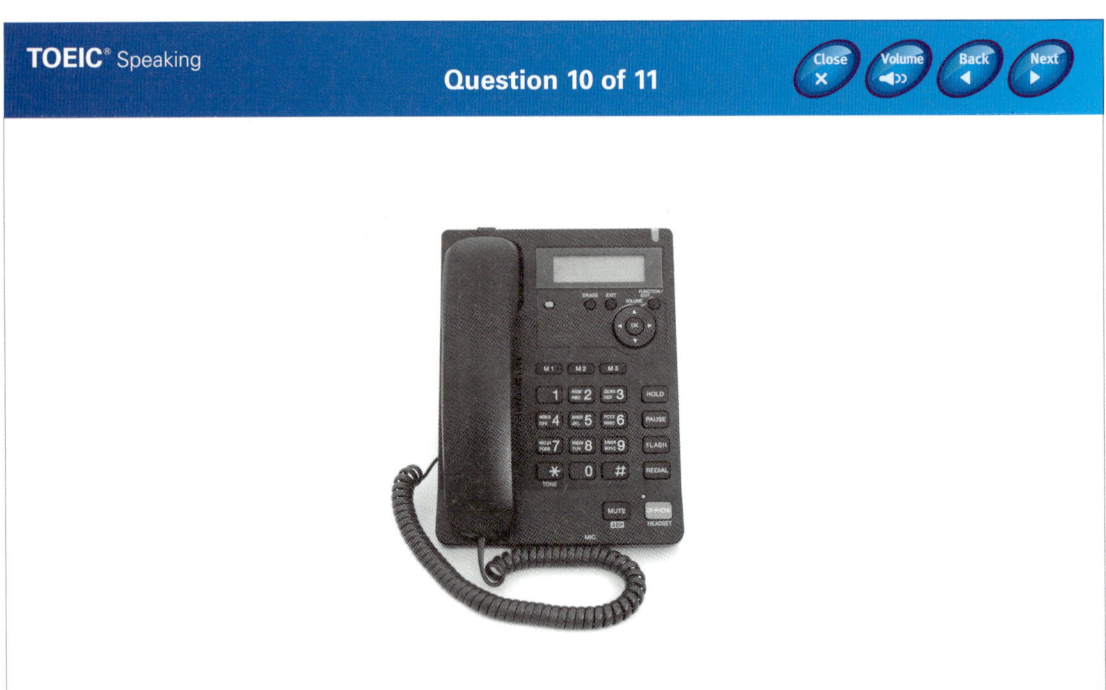

In your response, be sure to

- show that you recognize the problem, and
- propose a way of dealing with the problem.

RESPONSE TIME
00:01:00

TOEIC® Speaking

Question 11: Express an Opinion

Directions: In this part of the test, you will give your opinion about a specific topic. Be sure to say as much as you can in the time allowed. You will have 15 seconds to prepare. Then you will have 60 seconds to speak.

TOEIC® Speaking

Question 11 of 11

Do you think it is better to grow up in a city than to grow up in the country?

Why or why not?

Give specific reasons and details to support your answer.

RESPONSE TIME

00:01:00

Actual Test 7

TOEIC® Speaking

Speaking Test Directions

This is the TOEIC Speaking Test. This test includes eleven questions that measure different aspects of your speaking ability. The test lasts approximately 20 minutes.

Question	Task	Evaluation criteria
1-2	Read a text aloud	• pronunciation • intonation and stress
3	Describe a picture	all of the above, plus • grammar • vocabulary • cohesion
4-6	Respond to questions	all of the above, plus • relevance of content • completeness of content
7-9	Respond to questions using information provided	all of the above
10	Propose a solution	all of the above
11	Express an opinion	all of the above

For each type of question, you will be given specific directions, including the time allowed for preparation and speaking.
It is to your advantage to say as much as you can in the time allowed. It is also important that you speak clearly and that you answer each question according to the directions.

Click on **Continue** to go on.

TOEIC® Speaking

Questions 1-2: Read a Text Aloud

Directions: In this part of the test, you will read aloud the text on the screen. You will have 45 seconds to prepare. Then you will have 45 seconds to read the text aloud.

TOEIC® Speaking

Question 1 of 11

Hello. You've reached the St. Luis Society Information Line. Because of predictions of heavy precipitation, the folk fiesta has been delayed at Rainbow Courtyard until next Friday. On Friday, the features are a singing quartet, a comical performance, and games. On Saturday, the town rock band will perform at High Park at 7 P.M. The entrance cost is $4.

RESPONSE TIME
00:00:45

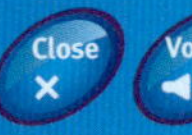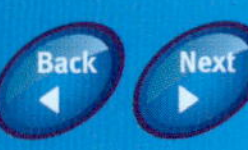

If your children need extra help with reading, writing, mathematics or the sciences, consider Goheen Education Institution. Our personnel of passionate and qualified educators will construct personalized lesson plans to meet your children's precise needs. What's more, improvements in academic performance are guaranteed. So what are you waiting for? Phone us today at 555-5981!

RESPONSE TIME
00:00:45

Question 3: Describe a Picture

Directions: In this part of the test, you will describe the picture on your screen in as much detail as you can. You will have 30 seconds to prepare your response. Then you will have 45 seconds to speak about the picture.

RESPONSE TIME

00:00:45

Questions 4-6: Respond to Questions

Directions: In this part of the test, you will answer three questions. For each question, begin responding immediately after you hear a beep. No preparation time is provided. You will have 15 seconds to respond to Questions 4 and 5 and 30 seconds to respond to Question 6.

Imagine that an Australian marketing firm is doing research in your country. You have agreed to participate in a telephone interview about drinks.

How often do you drink coffee or tea during the day, and when do you usually drink it?

RESPONSE TIME
00:00:15

Imagine that an Australian marketing firm is doing research in your country. You have agreed to participate in a telephone interview about drinks.

Where can you usually buy coffee or tea in your country?

RESPONSE TIME

00:00:15

Imagine that an Australian marketing firm is doing research in your country. You have agreed to participate in a telephone interview about drinks.

Do you prefer to drink coffee or tea at home? Why or why not?

RESPONSE TIME

00:00:30

Questions 7-9: Respond to Questions Using Information Provided

Directions: In this part of the test, you will answer three questions based on the information provided. You will have 30 seconds to read the information before the questions begin. For each question, begin responding immediately after you hear a beep. No additional preparation time is provided. You will have 15 seconds to respond to Questions 7 and 8 and 30 seconds to respond to Question 9.

Revival Game Corporation
Conference Call

Local Starting Times (Friday, August 30)

Call Access Information

Portland: 9:00 A.M. (Pacific time) Call-in number: (800) 555-1982

Memphis: 11:00 A.M. (Central time) Conference code: 3864

Schedule

1. Sales for May to July: Kent Payne (Memphis)

2. Customer complaints: Yo-Yo Min Koo Ahn (Portland)

3. New merchandise: Explaining remote boomerang, Sera Stevens (Memphis)

4. Future campaigns: Winter sports, Wanda Fish (Memphis)

5. Market research: Leonard Bradley (Portland)

RESPONSE TIME
00:00:15

Revival Game Corporation
Conference Call

Local Starting Times (Friday, August 30)

Call Access Information

Portland: 9:00 A.M. (Pacific time) Call-in number: (800) 555-1982

Memphis: 11:00 A.M. (Central time) Conference code: 3864

Schedule

1. Sales for May to July: Kent Payne (Memphis)

2. Customer complaints: Yo-Yo Min Koo Ahn (Portland)

3. New merchandise: Explaining remote boomerang, Sera Stevens (Memphis)

4. Future campaigns: Winter sports, Wanda Fish (Memphis)

5. Market research: Leonard Bradley (Portland)

RESPONSE TIME
00:00:15

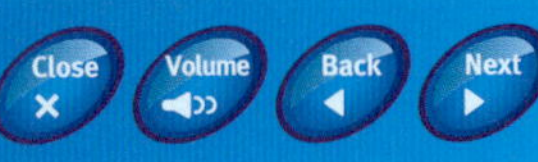

Revival Game Corporation
Conference Call

Local Starting Times (Friday, August 30)

Call Access Information

Portland: 9:00 A.M. (Pacific time) Call-in number: (800) 555-1982

Memphis: 11:00 A.M. (Central time) Conference code: 3864

Schedule

1. Sales for May to July: Kent Payne (Memphis)

2. Customer complaints: Yo-Yo Min Koo Ahn (Portland)

3. New merchandise: Explaining remote boomerang, Sera Stevens (Memphis)

4. Future campaigns: Winter sports, Wanda Fish (Memphis)

5. Market research: Leonard Bradley (Portland)

RESPONSE TIME
00:00:30

Question 10: Propose a Solution

Directions: In this part of the test, you will be presented with a problem and asked to propose a solution. You will have 30 seconds to prepare. Then you will have 60 seconds to speak.

In your response, be sure to

- show that you recognize the problem, and
- propose a way of dealing with the problem.

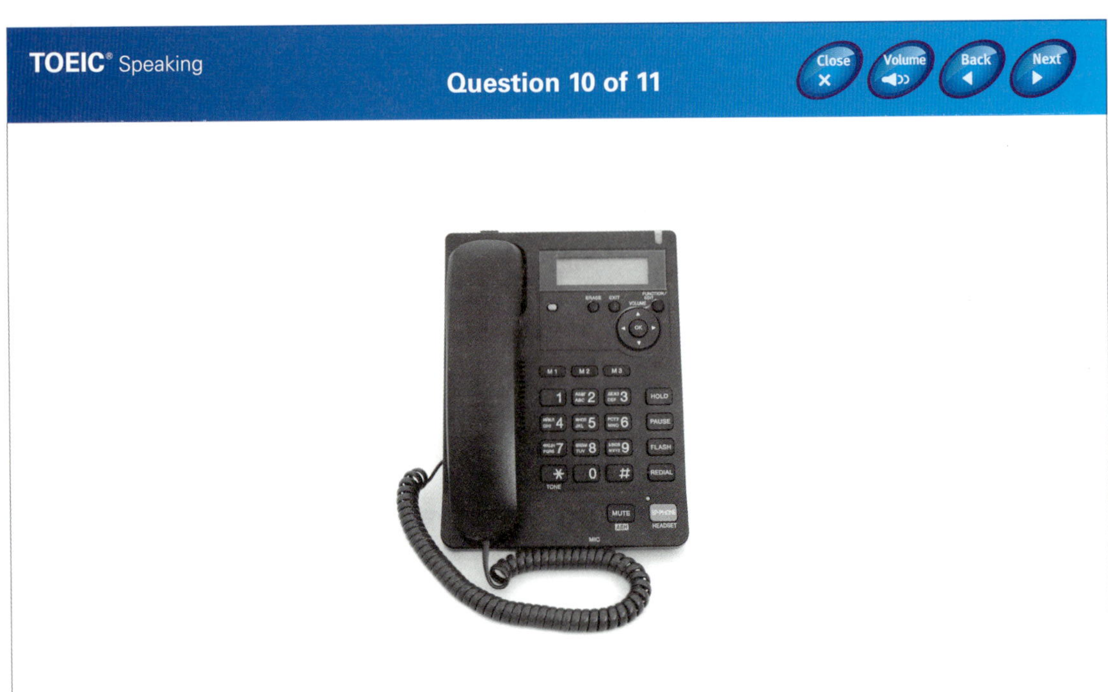

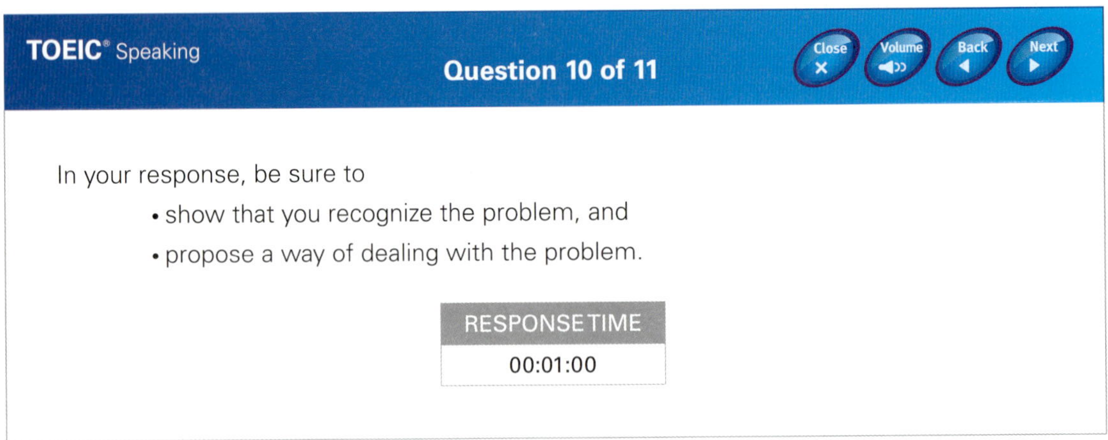
In your response, be sure to
• show that you recognize the problem, and
• propose a way of dealing with the problem.
RESPONSE TIME
00:01:00

Question 11: Express an Opinion

Directions: In this part of the test, you will give your opinion about a specific topic. Be sure to say as much as you can in the time allowed. You will have 15 seconds to prepare. Then you will have 60 seconds to speak.

Do you agree or disagree with the following statement?

> *The best way to reward hard-working employees is to give them extra vacation time.*

Use specific reasons or examples to support your answer.

RESPONSE TIME

00:01:00

Actual Test 8

Speaking Test Directions

This is the TOEIC Speaking Test. This test includes eleven questions that measure different aspects of your speaking ability. The test lasts approximately 20 minutes.

Question	Task	Evaluation criteria
1-2	Read a text aloud	• pronunciation • intonation and stress
3	Describe a picture	all of the above, plus • grammar • vocabulary • cohesion
4-6	Respond to questions	all of the above, plus • relevance of content • completeness of content
7-9	Respond to questions using information provided	all of the above
10	Propose a solution	all of the above
11	Express an opinion	all of the above

For each type of question, you will be given specific directions, including the time allowed for preparation and speaking.

It is to your advantage to say as much as you can in the time allowed. It is also important that you speak clearly and that you answer each question according to the directions.

Click on **Continue** to go on.

Questions 1-2: Read a Text Aloud

Directions: In this part of the test, you will read aloud the text on the screen. You will have 45 seconds to prepare. Then you will have 45 seconds to read the text aloud.

TOEIC® Speaking

Question 1 of 11

The Furniture Corporation is having a closing sale this Thursday and Friday. Assorted dining sets, desks, and all oil paintings must be sold. Because it is forty to seventy percent off, you'll be sure to get awesome discounts. Everything is the lowest price in our store's history for these two days only. You can reach us at 555-6578.

RESPONSE TIME

00:00:45

Today's speaker is Norma Bosk from New Entrepreneurs Incorporated and Sisko Manufacturing. Under her supervision, Sisko factories have been opened in France, Belgium, and Austria. In addition, another branch opening is being planned. Now, her talk is about "Your company and your direction." Please welcome Mrs. Bosk.

RESPONSE TIME

00:00:45

Question 3: Describe a Picture

Directions: In this part of the test, you will describe the picture on your screen in as much detail as you can. You will have 30 seconds to prepare your response. Then you will have 45 seconds to speak about the picture.

Actual Test 8

RESPONSE TIME

00:00:45

Questions 4-6: Respond to Questions

Directions: In this part of the test, you will answer three questions. For each question, begin responding immediately after you hear a beep. No preparation time is provided. You will have 15 seconds to respond to Questions 4 and 5 and 30 seconds to respond to Question 6.

TOEIC® Speaking   **Question 4 of 11** 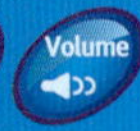

Imagine that a U.S. marketing firm is doing research in your country. You have agreed to participate in a telephone interview about watching news programs on television.

In a typical week, how many times do you watch the weather report on television?

RESPONSE TIME

00:00:15

Imagine that a U.S. marketing firm is doing research in your country. You have agreed to participate in a telephone interview about watching news programs on television.

When you watch the weather report on television, what kinds of information interest you the most?

RESPONSE TIME

00:00:15

Imagine that a U.S. marketing firm is doing research in your country. You have agreed to participate in a telephone interview about watching news programs on television.

Do you prefer to get your weather report from the television or from another source, such as the Internet, radio, or newspapers? Why?

RESPONSE TIME

00:00:30

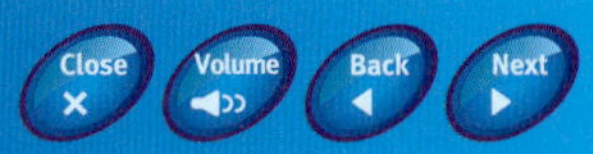

Questions 7-9: Respond to Questions Using Information Provided

Directions: In this part of the test, you will answer three questions based on the information provided. You will have 30 seconds to read the information before the questions begin. For each question, begin responding immediately after you hear a beep. No additional preparation time is provided. You will have 15 seconds to respond to Questions 7 and 8 and 30 seconds to respond to Question 9.

Speedy Stylish Garments Distributor

Customer Invoice

Ordered: December 12
Ship to: Fashion Outlet, 965 Tobermory Avenue, Detroit, MI
Shipped: January 3

Item #	Amount	Description	Total Price
23-456	40	Checkered cardigans: black/red	782.20
11-909	36	Men's polo's: 18 light, 18 dark	456.00
56-001	16	Women's skirts: 7 purple, 9 pink	375.64
92-411	20	Overcoats: 5 gray, 15 charcoal	915.50
			$2,529.34

For information, please call 888-555-7654.

RESPONSE TIME

00:00:15

Speedy Stylish Garments Distributor

Customer Invoice

Ordered: December 12

Ship to: Fashion Outlet, 965 Tobermory Avenue, Detroit, MI

Shipped: January 3

Item #	Amount	Description	Total Price
23-456	40	Checkered cardigans: black/red	782.20
11-909	36	Men's polo's: 18 light, 18 dark	456.00
56-001	16	Women's skirts: 7 purple, 9 pink	375.64
92-411	20	Overcoats: 5 gray, 15 charcoal	915.50
			$2,529.34

For information, please call 888-555-7654.

RESPONSE TIME
00:00:15

Speedy Stylish Garments Distributor

Customer Invoice

Ordered: December 12

Ship to: Fashion Outlet, 965 Tobermory Avenue, Detroit, MI

Shipped: January 3

Item #	Amount	Description	Total Price
23-456	40	Checkered cardigans: black/red	782.20
11-909	36	Men's polo's: 18 light, 18 dark	456.00
56-001	16	Women's skirts: 7 purple, 9 pink	375.64
92-411	20	Overcoats: 5 gray, 15 charcoal	915.50
			$ 2,529.34

For information, please call 888-555-7654.

RESPONSE TIME
00:00:30

TOEIC® Speaking

Question 10: Propose a Solution

Directions: In this part of the test, you will be presented with a problem and asked to propose a solution. You will have 30 seconds to prepare. Then you will have 60 seconds to speak.

In your response, be sure to

- show that you recognize the problem, and
- propose a way of dealing with the problem.

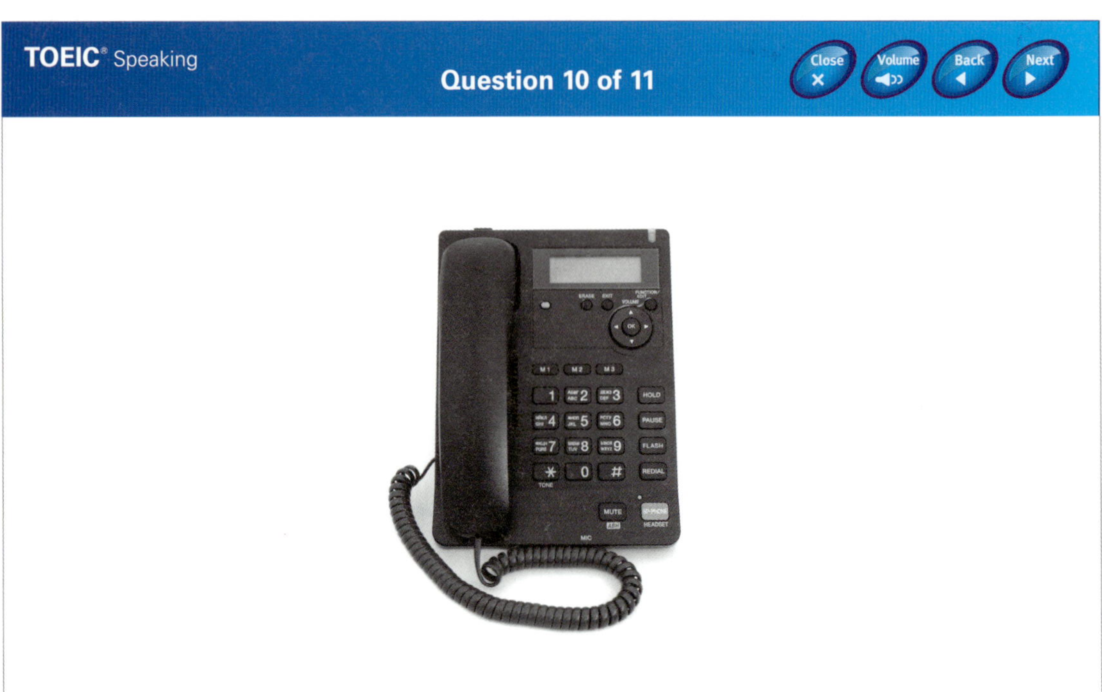

In your response, be sure to

- show that you recognize the problem, and
- propose a way of dealing with the problem.

RESPONSE TIME
00:01:00

Question 11: Express an Opinion

Directions: In this part of the test, you will give your opinion about a specific topic. Be sure to say as much as you can in the time allowed. You will have 15 seconds to prepare. Then you will have 60 seconds to speak.

Some people like to work with people who have similar interests and backgrounds. Others prefer to work with people who have different interests and backgrounds.

Which do you think is better? Why or why not?

RESPONSE TIME
00:01:00

Actual Test 9

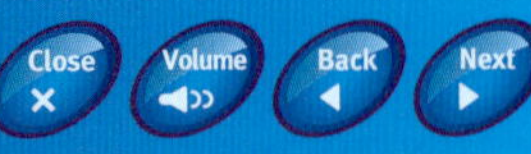

Speaking Test Directions

This is the TOEIC Speaking Test. This test includes eleven questions that measure different aspects of your speaking ability. The test lasts approximately 20 minutes.

Question	Task	Evaluation criteria
1-2	Read a text aloud	• pronunciation • intonation and stress
3	Describe a picture	all of the above, plus • grammar • vocabulary • cohesion
4-6	Respond to questions	all of the above, plus • relevance of content • completeness of content
7-9	Respond to questions using information provided	all of the above
10	Propose a solution	all of the above
11	Express an opinion	all of the above

For each type of question, you will be given specific directions, including the time allowed for preparation and speaking.

It is to your advantage to say as much as you can in the time allowed. It is also important that you speak clearly and that you answer each question according to the directions.

Click on **Continue** to go on.

Questions 1-2: Read a Text Aloud

Directions: In this part of the test, you will read aloud the text on the screen. You will have 45 seconds to prepare. Then you will have 45 seconds to read the text aloud.

Are you looking for a new condominium? This July, Velco Realtors will begin leasing rental units in Tribeca Square, officially recognized as the Tribeca Condominium Square. The central locality, free underground parking, and alluring architecture will fascinate customers. What's more, you'll get free Wi-Fi Internet access and on-site IT support. For more information, call 1-800-555-7734.

RESPONSE TIME
00:00:45

This is Robert Thornson with Daybreak Traffic Watch. Because of last night's severe hailstorms, many areas of the city have no electricity. This situation will make the morning drive especially difficult. At the present time, the traffic lights on Yonge, Bay and St. George streets are not functioning. So you may want to steer clear of these areas.

RESPONSE TIME

00:00:45

Question 3: Describe a Picture

Directions: In this part of the test, you will describe the picture on your screen in as much detail as you can. You will have 30 seconds to prepare your response. Then you will have 45 seconds to speak about the picture.

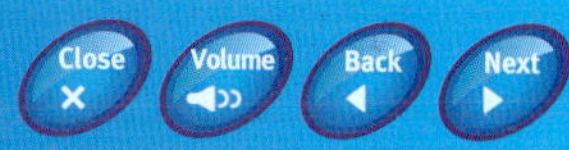

RESPONSE TIME

00:00:45

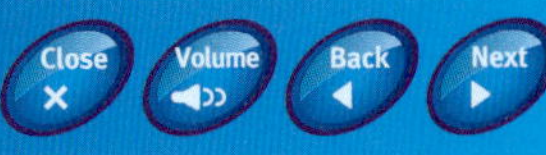

Questions 4-6: Respond to Questions

Directions: In this part of the test, you will answer three questions. For each question, begin responding immediately after you hear a beep. No preparation time is provided. You will have 15 seconds to respond to Questions 4 and 5 and 30 seconds to respond to Question 6.

Imagine that an American marketing firm is doing research in your country. You have agreed to participate in a telephone interview about clothes.

What kind of attire do people wear at your school or work?

RESPONSE TIME

00:00:15

Imagine that an American marketing firm is doing research in your country. You have agreed to participate in a telephone interview about clothes.

How often do you buy outfits for your school or work?

RESPONSE TIME

00:00:15

Imagine that an American marketing firm is doing research in your country. You have agreed to participate in a telephone interview about clothes.

What kind of features should a good clothing store have?

RESPONSE TIME

00:00:30

Questions 7-9: Respond to Questions Using Information Provided

Directions: In this part of the test, you will answer three questions based on the information provided. You will have 30 seconds to read the information before the questions begin. For each question, begin responding immediately after you hear a beep. No additional preparation time is provided. You will have 15 seconds to respond to Questions 7 and 8 and 30 seconds to respond to Question 9.

New Music Releases – Sam's Disc Superstore

Title	Date Released	Genre
The Jetsons	June 12	Alternative

*** Monthly Special – 15% discount on all New Releases (Members only!)**

Title	Date Released	Genre
~~Fantastic Seven~~	~~July 21~~	~~Trance~~
American Sweets	July 24	Disco
Samsonites	July 26	Rock and Roll

*** Monthly Special – Buy 3 albums and get 1 free**

Title	Date Released	Genre
Bach's Greatest Hits	August 3	Classical

*** Monthly Special – To be announced in July**

RESPONSE TIME
00:00:15

New Music Releases – Sam's Disc Superstore

Title	Date Released	Genre
The Jetsons	June 12	Alternative

*** Monthly Special – 15% discount on all New Releases (Members only!)**

Title	Date Released	Genre
~~Fantastic Seven~~	~~July 21~~	~~Trance~~
American Sweets	July 24	Disco
Samsonites	July 26	Rock and Roll

*** Monthly Special – Buy 3 albums and get 1 free**

Title	Date Released	Genre
Bach's Greatest Hits	August 3	Classical

*** Monthly Special – To be announced in July**

RESPONSE TIME
00:00:15

New Music Releases – Sam's Disc Superstore

Title	Date Released	Genre
The Jetsons	June 12	Alternative

*** Monthly Special – 15% discount on all New Releases (Members only!)**

Title	Date Released	Genre
~~Fantastic Seven~~	~~July 21~~	~~Trance~~
American Sweets	July 24	Disco
Samsonites	July 26	Rock and Roll

*** Monthly Special – Buy 3 albums and get 1 free**

Title	Date Released	Genre
Bach's Greatest Hits	August 3	Classical

*** Monthly Special – To be announced in July**

RESPONSE TIME
00:00:30

Question 10: Propose a Solution

Directions: In this part of the test, you will be presented with a problem and asked to propose a solution. You will have 30 seconds to prepare. Then you will have 60 seconds to speak.

In your response, be sure to

- show that you recognize the problem, and
- propose a way of dealing with the problem.

In your response, be sure to

- show that you recognize the problem, and
- propose a way of dealing with the problem.

RESPONSE TIME
00:01:00

Question 11: Express an Opinion

Directions: In this part of the test, you will give your opinion about a specific topic. Be sure to say as much as you can in the time allowed. You will have 15 seconds to prepare. Then you will have 60 seconds to speak.

Do you agree or disagree with the following statement?

> *The best employees are those who finish their duties in the shortest amount of time.*

Give reasons and examples to support your answer.

RESPONSE TIME
00:01:00

Actual Test 10

Speaking Test Directions

This is the TOEIC Speaking Test. This test includes eleven questions that measure different aspects of your speaking ability. The test lasts approximately 20 minutes.

Question	Task	Evaluation criteria
1-2	Read a text aloud	• pronunciation • intonation and stress
3	Describe a picture	all of the above, plus • grammar • vocabulary • cohesion
4-6	Respond to questions	all of the above, plus • relevance of content • completeness of content
7-9	Respond to questions using information provided	all of the above
10	Propose a solution	all of the above
11	Express an opinion	all of the above

For each type of question, you will be given specific directions, including the time allowed for preparation and speaking.

It is to your advantage to say as much as you can in the time allowed. It is also important that you speak clearly and that you answer each question according to the directions.

Click on **Continue** to go on.

TOEIC® Speaking

Questions 1-2: Read a Text Aloud

Directions: In this part of the test, you will read aloud the text on the screen. You will have 45 seconds to prepare. Then you will have 45 seconds to read the text aloud.

The Butterfly Spectators' Association is delighted to present Randy Desouza who is currently a professor at Victoria College. Randy has been researching butterflies living in the wilderness for more than 15 years. And now Randy will be joining us to enlighten us about the places to watch the butterflies such as outdoor gardens, zoos other than in urban areas, and nearby parks.

RESPONSE TIME

00:00:45

Are you planning an event? Marty's Merrymaking Rental Shop has everything you need to make your celebration a sensation. We offer a large assortment of tables, chairs and tents, and even provide free delivery. Whether you are planning a cafe event or a created event, Marty's Merrymaking Rental Shop can be of assistance. Plus this weekend only, we will take twenty percent off our usual prices.

RESPONSE TIME

00:00:45

Question 3: Describe a Picture

Directions: In this part of the test, you will describe the picture on your screen in as much detail as you can. You will have 30 seconds to prepare your response. Then you will have 45 seconds to speak about the picture.

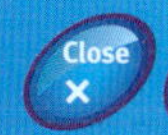

RESPONSE TIME

00:00:45

Questions 4-6: Respond to Questions

Directions: In this part of the test, you will answer three questions. For each question, begin responding immediately after you hear a beep. No preparation time is provided. You will have 15 seconds to respond to Questions 4 and 5 and 30 seconds to respond to Question 6.

Imagine that a U.S. marketing firm is doing research in your country. You have agreed to participate in a telephone interview about hair salons.

When was the last time you went to a barber or hair stylist?

RESPONSE TIME
00:00:15

Close ✕ Volume ◀》 Back ◀ Next ▶

Imagine that a U.S. marketing firm is doing research in your country. You have agreed to participate in a telephone interview about hair salons.

How far is your home from your barber shop or hair salon?

RESPONSE TIME

00:00:15

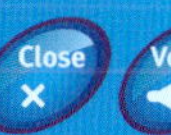

Close ✕ Volume ◀》 Back ◀ Next ▶

Imagine that a U.S. marketing firm is doing research in your country. You have agreed to participate in a telephone interview about hair salons.

What do you like most about going to your barber shop or hair salon?

RESPONSE TIME

00:00:30

Questions 7-9: Respond to Questions Using Information Provided

Directions: In this part of the test, you will answer three questions based on the information provided. You will have 30 seconds to read the information before the questions begin. For each question, begin responding immediately after you hear a beep. No additional preparation time is provided. You will have 15 seconds to respond to Questions 7 and 8 and 30 seconds to respond to Question 9.

Exhibition for Cafés
at the Convention Center

Preparation Checklist for Expo

Due dates	Materials to be submitted
☐ January 11	Display booth application (available on homepage or at Convention Center)
☐ February 15	Signed display booth contract
☐ March 3	Outline of your company for program brochure
☐ March 31	Advertisement for program brochure (non-compulsory)
☐ April 1	Payment closing date
☐ April 19	Leaflet inserts for program brochure (non-compulsory)

RESPONSE TIME
00:00:15

Exhibition for Cafés
at the Convention Center

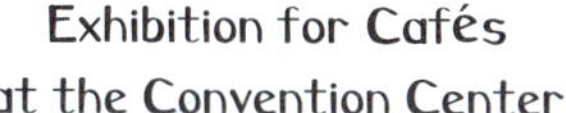

Preparation Checklist for Expo

Due dates	Materials to be submitted
☐ January 11	Display booth application (available on homepage or at Convention Center)
☐ February 15	Signed display booth contract
☐ March 3	Outline of your company for program brochure
☐ March 31	Advertisement for program brochure (non-compulsory)
☐ April 1	Payment closing date
☐ April 19	Leaflet inserts for program brochure (non-compulsory)

RESPONSE TIME

00:00:15

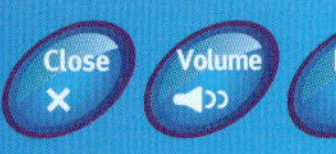

Exhibition for Cafés
at the Convention Center

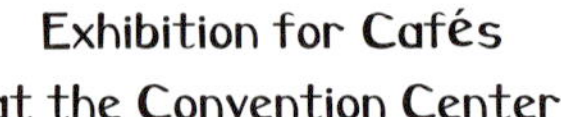
Preparation Checklist for Expo

Due dates	Materials to be submitted
☐ January 11	Display booth application (available on homepage or at Convention Center)
☐ February 15	Signed display booth contract
☐ March 3	Outline of your company for program brochure
☐ March 31	Advertisement for program brochure (non-compulsory)
☐ April 1	Payment closing date
☐ April 19	Leaflet inserts for program brochure (non-compulsory)

RESPONSE TIME

00:00:30

Question 10: Propose a Solution

Directions: In this part of the test, you will be presented with a problem and asked to propose a solution. You will have 30 seconds to prepare. Then you will have 60 seconds to speak.

In your response, be sure to

- show that you recognize the problem, and
- propose a way of dealing with the problem.

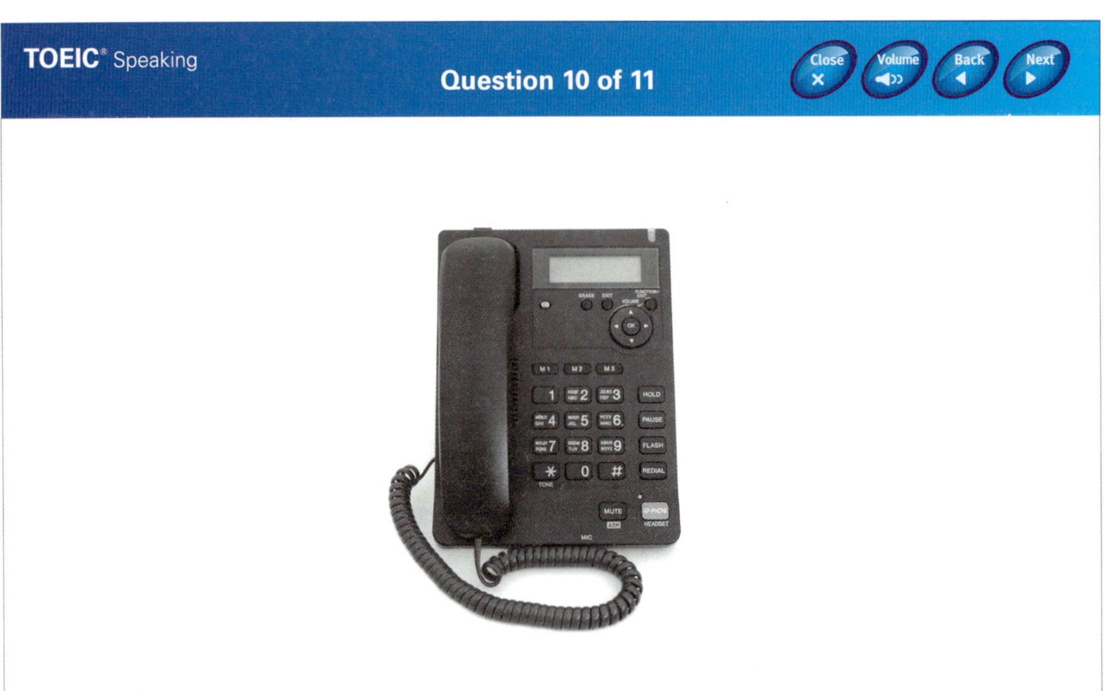

TOEIC® Speaking

Question 10 of 11

Close ×   Volume ◀))   Back ◀   Next ▶

In your response, be sure to

- show that you recognize the problem, and
- propose a way of dealing with the problem.

RESPONSE TIME

00:01:00

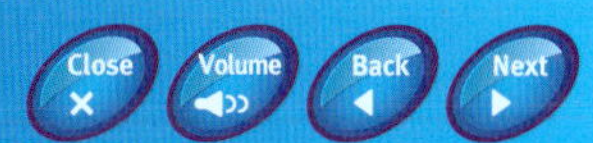

Question 11: Express an Opinion

Directions: In this part of the test, you will give your opinion about a specific topic. Be sure to say as much as you can in the time allowed. You will have 15 seconds to prepare. Then you will have 60 seconds to speak.

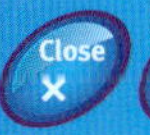

When you go on a trip, do you usually make a precise plan before you leave or do you usually go on a trip without a plan?

Which do you prefer and why?

Give reasons and examples to support your answer.

RESPONSE TIME

00:01:00

기출모의
TOEIC
Speaking
기출 변형 실전모의고사 15회

해설집
Speaking

Questions 1-2 Read a Text Aloud

Directions: In this part of the test, you will read aloud the text on the screen. You will have 45 seconds to prepare. Then you will have 45 seconds to read the text aloud.

이 파트에서 여러분은 스크린의 텍스트를 큰 소리로 읽게 됩니다. 45초의 준비 시간이 주어지고, 그 후 45초 동안 텍스트를 큰 소리로 읽으세요.

TOEIC® Speaking

Question 1 of 11

Welcome to this historic ceremony for the new Shamrock Shopping Center. This new mall is the biggest on the eastern seaboard and will have more than 120 stores and shops to choose from. Furthermore, the Shamrock Shopping Center will feature a spacious food court, a fully equipped health center, and a movie theatre megaplex for your entertainment.

새로운 Shamrock 쇼핑 센터의 역사적 행사에 오신 것을 환영합니다. 이 새로운 쇼핑 센터는 동부 해안에서 가장 큰 규모이며 120개가 넘는 상점들이 입주해 있습니다. 이 외에도, Shamrock 쇼핑 센터에는 널찍한 식당가, 완전히 설비된 헬스 센터, 여러분의 여흥을 위한 극장 메가플렉스가 있습니다.

 **Speaking Solution**

Welcome to this **historic ceremony**(중요 의미 강세) for the **new Shamrock Shopping Center**. (고유명사 강세) ＼(문장의 맨 끝) This new **mall** is the **biggest**(최상급 강조) on the **eastern seaboard** / (절 앞에 짧게 끊고) and will have **more** than **one hundred twenty**(시간/날짜/숫자 강세) **stores and shops** to choose from. **Furthermore**(부가 의미 강조), the **Shamrock Shopping Center**(중요 의미 강세) will feature **a spacious food court**↗, **a fully equipped health center**↗, and **a movie theatre megaplex**＼ (A↗, B↗ and C＼) for your **entertainment**.＼(문장의 맨 끝)

 historic 역사적으로 유명한 spacious 널찍한 fully equipped 완전히 장비를 갖춘

All passengers, please listen to the following two announcements. First, departures to Orlando, New Orleans, and Nashville will now begin boarding at Gate 78. Please proceed to Gate 78 for boarding if you already have checked in with security and have your boarding pass. Second, Flight 411 to San Diego is now departing from Gate 19. Thank you.

승객 여러분, 두 가지 안내 말씀을 드리니 주목해 주세요. 첫째, 올랜도, 뉴올리언스, 내슈빌로 향하는 항공편 탑승을 지금 78번 게이트에서 시작할 것입니다. 보안 확인을 마치셨고 탑승권을 지참하셨다면 탑승을 위해 78번 게이트로 이동하세요. 둘째, 샌디에이고로 향하는 항공기 411편이 19번 게이트에서 이제 출발할 것입니다. 감사합니다.

 **Speaking Solution**

All(all/every 강세) **passengers**(중요 의미 강세), ╱(계속 의미/쉼표 뒤 짧게 끊고) **please** listen to the following **two**(시간/날짜/숫자 강세) **announcements**(중요 의미 강세). ╲(문장의 맨 끝) **First**(시간/날짜/숫자 강세), **departures** to **Orlando**╱, **New Orleans**╱, and **Nashville**╲ (A╱, B╱ and C╲) / (긴 주어 뒤에 잠시 끊고) will now begin **boarding** at **Gate 78**(시간/날짜/숫자 강세). **Please** proceed to **Gate 78**(시간/날짜/숫자 강세) for **boarding** / (부사절 앞에 잠시 끊고) if you already have **checked in**(중요 의미 강세) with **security** / and have your **boarding pass**(중요 의미 강세).╲(문장의 맨 끝) **Second**(시간/날짜/숫자 강세), **Flight 411**(시간/날짜/숫자 강세) to **San Diego** is now **departing**(중요 의미 강세) from **Gate 19**(시간/날짜/숫자 강세). Thank you.

 **announcement** 알림, 공지, 방송문   **departure** 출발   **proceed to** ~로 나아가다, 향하다   **boarding pass** 탑승권

Question 3   Describe a Picture

Directions: In this part of the test, you will describe the picture on your screen in as much detail as you can. You will have 30 seconds to prepare your response. Then you will have 45 seconds to speak about the picture.

이 파트에서 여러분은 스크린의 사진을 최대한 자세히 설명하게 됩니다. 대답을 위해 30초의 준비 시간이 주어지고, 그 후 45초 동안 사진에 대해 설명하세요.

 **Possible Answer**

It appears that this picture was taken at a large clothing shop. On the right side of the picture, there is a long clothing rack with men's attire. There is a woman in the middle of the picture who is looking at some of the items on the clothing rack. She is wearing a long black coat and dark pants. Behind the woman, there is a small table with two horizontal handles, which may be for drawers. On the table, there are pieces of merchandise. The floor has light-colored tiles, in a regular square pattern. On the ceiling, there are large bright lights. In the background, you can see a small red-colored seat.

이 사진은 대형 의류 상점에서 촬영된 것으로 보입니다. 사진의 오른쪽에는 남성복이 걸린 긴 옷걸이가 있습니다. 사진의 중간에는 옷걸이에 걸린 몇몇 의류를 살피고 있는 여성이 있습니다. 그녀는 긴 검은색 코트와 어두운 색상의 바지를 입고 있습니다. 여성 뒤에는 두 개의 수평 손잡이가 달린 작은 테이블이 있는데, 서랍을 열고 닫을 수 있는 듯합니다. 테이블 위에는 상품들이 있습니다. 바닥에는 평범한 사각형 패턴의 밝은 색 타일이 깔려 있습니다. 천장에는 크고 밝은 전등들이 있으며, 뒤쪽에는 자그마한 붉은 색 좌석이 보입니다.

 **clothing shop** 옷가게　**clothing rack** 옷걸이　**attire** 의류　**horizontal handle** 수평 손잡이　**drawer** 서랍장　**light-colored tile** 밝은 색으로 된 타일　**regular square** 일반적인 사각형　**ceiling** 천장

Questions 4-6 Respond to Questions

Directions: In this part of the test, you will answer three questions. For each question, begin responding immediately after you hear a beep. No preparation time is provided. You will have 15 seconds to respond to Questions 4 and 5 and 30 seconds to respond to Question 6.

이 파트에서 여러분은 세 가지 질문에 답하게 됩니다. 각 질문에 대해 '삐' 소리가 나면 즉시 대답하세요. 준비 시간은 주어지지 않습니다. 4번과 5번 문제에는 각각 15초, 그리고 6번 문제에는 30초의 응답 시간이 주어집니다.

Imagine that an Australian marketing firm is doing research in your country. You have agreed to participate in a telephone interview about books.

어느 호주 마케팅 회사가 여러분의 나라에서 조사를 하고 있다고 가정해 봅시다. 여러분은 책에 관한 전화 인터뷰 참여를 승낙했습니다.

TOEIC® Speaking

Question 4 of 11

How many novels have you read in the last six months?

지난 6개월간 몇 권의 소설을 읽으셨나요?

 **Possible Answer**

I think I have read only one novel in the past six months.

서는 시난 6개월간 난 한 권의 소설늘 읽었습니다.

Where do you usually get the novels you read?

보통 어디에서 읽을 소설을 구하시나요?

 **Possible Answer**

I usually get the novels I read at the local bookstore. I like to buy the books and not borrow them from the library.

저는 보통 지역 서점에서 읽을 소설을 구합니다. 저는 책을 도서관에서 대여하지 않고 구매하는 것을 좋아합니다.

Would you read the same novel more than once? Why or why not?

같은 소설을 한 번 이상 읽나요? 왜 그렇게, 혹은 왜 그렇게 하지 않나요?

 **Possible Answer**

I occasionally read the same novel more than once if it is very interesting. Also, I would read it again quite some time later — more than a year later. I do this because I don't remember exactly everything about the story.

매우 재미있으면 저는 종종 같은 소설을 한 번 이상 읽습니다. 또한 꽤 시간이 지난 후에도 – 1년 이상 – 그 책을 다시 읽곤 합니다. 이야기를 모두 정확하게 기억할 수가 없어서 다시 읽습니다.

 occasionally 때때로   more than ~이상   exactly 정확히

Questions 7-9   Respond to Questions Using Information Provided

Directions: In this part of the test, you will answer three questions based on the information provided. You will have 30 seconds to read the information before the questions begin. For each question, begin responding immediately after you hear a beep. No additional preparation time is provided. You will have 15 seconds to respond to Questions 7 and 8 and 30 seconds to respond to Question 9.

이 파트에서 여러분은 주어진 정보에 기초하여 세 가지 질문에 대답하게 됩니다. 문제가 시작하기 전에 30초 동안 정보를 읽게 됩니다. 각 질문에 대해 '삐' 소리가 나면 즉시 대답하세요. 준비 시간은 주어지지 않습니다. 7번과 8번 문제에는 각각 15초, 그리고 9번 문제에는 30초의 응답 시간이 주어집니다.

TOEIC® Speaking

Questions 7-9 of 11

Summer Solstice Celebration

Sunny Willows Invites You

Details: June 21, 5:30-10:30 P.M.

Lemonheads Bar and Grille (321) 555-8762

Contact: Chuck Lee - extension 412
       (call for questions)

Responses:

21 Attending

3 Not attending

0 Awaiting reply

Not Attending:	Comments:
Barb Sharky:	Great idea, but already have plans.
Melissa Puentes:	Sorry, friend's wedding that day. Have fun!
Suzy Scott:	Wow, sounds fun... unfortunately, out of town that weekend.

Hi. This is Joanne. I lost my invitation to Sunny's Summer Solstice Celebration. Could you possibly answer a few of my questions since I know you got an invitation as well?

Summer Solstice Celebration
Sunny Willows Invites You

Details: June 21, 5:30-10:30 P.M. Lemonheads Bar and Grille (321) 555-8762 Contact: Chuck Lee-extension 412 (call for questions)	Responses: 21 Attending 3 Not attending 0 Awaiting reply

Not Attending:	Comments:
Barb Sharky:	Great idea, but already have plans.
Melissa Puentes:	Sorry, friend's wedding that day. Have fun!
Suzy Scott:	Wow, sounds fun... unfortunately, out of town that weekend.

Hi. This is Joanne. I lost my invitation to Sunny's Summer Solstice Celebration. Could you possibly answer a few of my questions since I know you got an invitation as well?

하지(夏至) 축제
Sunny Willows가 여러분을 초대합니다.

상세: 6월 21일, 오후 5시 30분 – 10시 30분 Lemonheads Bar and Grille (321) 555-8762 연락처: Chuck Lee – 내선번호 412 (상담 전화)	응답: 21 참석 3 불참 0 답변 대기

불참:	설명:
Barb Sharky:	기발한 생각이네요. 그런데 제가 사전 일정이 있습니다.
Melissa Puentes:	미안합니다. 그날 친구 결혼식이 있습니다. 좋은 시간되세요.
Suzy Scott:	와우, 재미있겠네요. 그런데 제가 주말에 시골에 갑니다.

안녕하세요. Joanne입니다. Sunny의 하지 축제 초대장을 잃어버리고 말았습니다. 귀하 역시 초청받은 것으로 알고 있는데, 제 몇 가지 질문에 답변 좀 해주실 수 있나요?

 **summer solstice** 하지   **extension** 내선번호   **out of town** 도시를 떠나서

Who should I contact for further information?

더 상세한 정보를 알려면 누구에게 연락해야 하나요?

 **Possible Answer**

You can contact the Lemonheads Bar and Grille at (321) 555-8762. Ask for Chuck Lee at extension 412.

(321) 555-8762로 Lemonheads Bar and Grille에 연락하시면 됩니다. 내선번호 412인 Chuck Lee를 찾으세요.

 **contact** 연락하다

TOEIC® Speaking

Question 8 of 11

Do you know how many people were invited? Also, has anyone responded yet?

몇 사람이 초청되었는지 아시나요? 또, 벌써 대답한 사람이 있나요?

 **Possible Answer**

I think twenty-four people have been invited. Of that number, three people have stated that they are not attending.

제가 알기론 24명이 초청되었습니다. 그 중에서 3명은 불참을 알렸습니다.

 **anyone** 누구, 아무도   **respond** 응답하다   **yet** 벌써   **attend** 참석하다

TOEIC® Speaking

Question 9 of 11

Do you know the people who are not attending? I was going to ask Suzy Scott to car pool to the event.

불참하는 사람이 누군인지 아시나요? 저는 축제에 갈 때 Suzy Scott에게 카풀을 부탁할 예정이었습니다.

 **Possible Answer**

The three people who are not attending are Barb Sharky, Melissa Puentes, and Suzy Scott. Barb said she already has plans, Melissa is going to a friend's wedding, and Suzy is out of town that weekend. So I don't think you would be able to car pool with Suzy.

불참하는 3명은 Barb Sharky, Melissa Puentes, Suzy Scott입니다. Barb는 사전 일정이 있다고 합니다. Melissa는 친구 결혼식에 갈 거라는군요. 그리고 Suzy는 주말에 시골에 내려간답니다. 그래서 귀하가 Suzy와 차량 카풀을 할 수 있을 것으로 여겨지지는 않는군요.

 **car pool** 카풀하다

Question 10 Propose a Solution

Directions: In this part of the test, you will be presented with a problem and asked to propose a solution. You will have 30 seconds to prepare. Then you will have 60 seconds to speak.

이 파트에서 여러분에게 한 가지 문제가 주어집니다. 여러분은 그에 대한 해결책을 제시해주세요. 30초 동안 준비한 뒤 60초 동안 응답하세요.

In your response, be sure to
- show that you recognize the problem, and
- propose a way of dealing with the problem.

여러분의 응답에서
- 여러분이 문제를 인식했다는 것을 보여주세요.
- 그 문제를 대처하는 방법을 제안해주세요.

 Hi. It's Mark. I know you're at the hotel, managing the wedding reception but we have a problem with the catering service company. Two of our ovens aren't working properly. It took me and other cooks twice as long as normal to cook those appetizers we sent over. At this rate, we can't have the main course ready in time. I think we would be lucky to get it ready two hours late but not by the time we promised. I called several repair companies, but I'm not sure we can get the ovens fixed today. I know there are going to be many hungry guests at the reception, so I need you to tell me what I should do. Again, it's Mark. Call me at the catering kitchen number.

안녕하세요, 저는 Mark입니다. 전 귀하가 호텔의 결혼식 피로연을 관리하고 있는 것으로 알고 있습니다. 그런데 출장 연회 서비스 회사에 문제가 생겨 말씀드립니다. 우리 오븐 두 대가 제대로 작동하지 않습니다. 저와 다른 조리사들이 먼저 내놓을 애피타이저를 요리하는 데에도 평상시보다 두 배의 시간이 소요되었습니다. 이런 추세라면, 저희는 메인 코스를 제때에 준비할 수 없습니다. 제가 생각하기에, 운이 좋아야 두 시간 더 늦게 메인 코스를 준비할 수 있을 뿐 약속한 시간까지는 어렵습니다. 제가 몇몇 수리 회사에 전화했습니다만 오늘 중으로 오븐을 수리할 수 있을지 확신할 수가 없습니다. 피로연에는 많은 손님들이 허기진 채 오실 것임을 알고 있습니다. 그래서 귀하께서 제가 어떻게 하면 좋을지 말씀해주셨으면 합니다. 저는 Mark입니다. 조리부 전화번호로 연락 부탁드립니다.

 wedding reception 결혼 피로연 catering 출장 연회 work properly 제대로 작동하다 twice as long as normal 평소보다 두 배 더 오래 appetizer 전채 요리, 애피타이저 at this rate 이런 속도로는

 **Possible Answer**

인사	Hi, Mark. This is Sophie, your manager.
문제 상황 인식	I received your message about the two ovens that are not working properly. I understand that without these two ovens, the food for the wedding reception will not be prepared in time. I have also tried calling some repair companies, but it seems that our ovens will not be fixed in time. I have talked to the people at the reception to see if they could delay the dinner as much as possible, but you are right that there are a lot of hungry guests here.
해결책	I have spoken to the manager at the restaurant on the second floor on our hotel. Fortunately, he has agreed to help us out in this situation. He has informed me that his cooks will share their kitchen and ovens with our cooks. Hopefully, this can alleviate the problem. Please send some of our staff members to their kitchen to begin preparing the main course so that we are not too late serving the meals.
마무리	If there are any other problems, please contact me A.S.A.P.

안녕하세요. Mark. 저는 당신의 상관인 Sophie입니다. 제대로 작동하지 않는 오븐 두 개에 관한 메시지를 받았습니다. 이 오븐 두 개 없이는 결혼 피로연 음식이 제시간에 준비되지 않는다는 점을 이해합니다. 저 역시 몇몇 수리 회사에 연락을 했습니다만, 오븐을 제시간에 수리할 수 있을 것 같지는 않습니다. 피로연에 오실 분들께 말씀드려서 가능한 한 그들이 저녁 식사 시간을 연기할 수 있는지 알아보았습니다. 그러나 여기에 많은 손님들이 허기진 채 오실 것이라는 당신의 지적이 옳았습니다. 그래서 저는 우리 호텔의 2층에 있는 레스토랑의 관리자와 이야기했습니다. 운 좋게도, 그분은 우리를 도와주시겠다고 하네요. 조리실과 오븐을 우리 측 조리사들과 함께 쓸 수 있도록 해주겠다고 제게 말씀하셨습니다. 이것이 문제를 해결해 줄 수 있다면 좋겠습니다. 음식 준비에 늦지 않도록 우리 측 직원 일부를 그분들의 조리실로 보내서 메인 코스를 준비하는 것을 시작하도록 하세요. 다른 문제가 있다면 제게 즉시 연락하세요.

fix in time 제시간에 고치다 **see if** ~인지 아닌지 알아보다 **fortunately** 다행스럽게도 **inform** 알려주다 **cook** 요리사 **hopefully** 바라건대 **alleviate** 완화하다

Question 11 Express an Opinion

Directions: In this part of the test, you will give your opinion about a specific topic. Be sure to say as much as you can in the time allowed. You will have 15 seconds to prepare. Then you will have 60 seconds to speak.

이 파트에서 여러분은 특정한 주제에 대한 의견을 말하게 됩니다. 주어진 시간 동안 최대한 많이 말할 수 있도록 하세요. 15초 동안 준비한 뒤 60초 동안 응답하세요.

Do you agree or disagree with the following statement?

> *It is easier for an employee to earn a promotion at a small company than at a large company.*

Give reasons and examples to support your opinion.

다음 진술에 동의하시나요, 동의하지 않으시나요?

대기업보다 소기업에서 직원이 승진하기가 쉽다.

의견을 뒷받침하는 이유와 예시를 들어주십시오.

 Possible Answer 1 (agree)

의견 제시 — I agree with the statement that it is easier for an employee to earn a promotion at a small company than at a large company.

근거 제시 1 — First, there are not that many people in a small company. Thus, he or she is more likely to get a promotion than at a large company.

예시 — To illustrate, imagine if a small company had only ten workers, compared to a large company with fifty workers. If both companies had to give promotions to only one person, the chances that it would be you are greater in a smaller company because there is less competition for the promotion.

근거 제시 2 — Second, it is easier to show off your talents and hard work when you are employed at a small company. People in higher positions will notice your tremendous effort and see that you deserve a promotion. On the other hand, people in higher positions are less likely to notice your hard work if you work at a large company.

마무리 — Therefore, I believe it is easier for an employee to earn a promotion at a small company than at a large company.

저는 대기업보다 소기업에서 직원이 승진하기가 쉽다는 진술에 동의합니다. 첫째로, 소기업에는 사람이 많지 않습니다. 따라서 대기업에 비해 승진하기가 쉽다고 생각합니다. 예를 들어, 10명의 근로자만 있는 소기업과 50명의 근로자가 있는 대기업을 비교해 봅시다. 두 회사 모두 오직 한 사람만 승진시켜야 한다면 소기업 쪽이 당신이 선택될 가능성이 더 높습니다. 승진의 경쟁이 덜 하기 때문입니다. 둘째로, 소기업 쪽이 당신의 능력과 근면을 보여주기가 쉽습니다. 상사들은 당신의 부단한 노력을 인식할 것이며 승진할 자격이 있음을 볼 것입니다. 반면, 대기업의 상사들은 당신의 근면을 인식할 가능성이 더 적습니다. 따라서 저는 대기업보다 소기업에서 직원이 승진하기가 쉽다고 생각합니다.

statement 진술 **thus** 따라서 **be likely to** ~하는 경향이 있다 **illustrate** 설명하다, 예증하다 **less competition** 경쟁이 덜한 **show off** 드러내다, 자랑하다 **talent** 재주, 재능 **tremendous** 굉장한, 거대한 **effort** 노력, 수고 **deserve** ~할 만하다, ~할 가치가 있다 **on the other hand** 반면에

Possible Answer 2 (disagree)

의견 제시 I disagree with the statement that it is easier for an employee to earn a promotion at a small company than at a large company.

근거 제시 1 First, large companies tend to grow and expand at a faster rate compared to smaller companies. Due to faster growth and expansion, there are likely more opportunities for promotions.

근거 제시 2 Another reason, promotions would be easier for an employee at a large company is that the employee is motivated to stand out from the rest. Supervisors and managers have to handle a lot of workers. Thus it is difficult to see how productive each employee is. If employees give a little more effort in showing their supervisors their hard work and effort, they are sure to be noticed. As a result, they will seem like better employees than the rest and are more likely to get promoted.

마무리 For these reasons, I believe it is easier for an employee to earn a promotion at a large company than at a small company.

저는 대기업보다 소기업에서 직원이 승진하기가 쉽다는 진술에 동의하지 않습니다. 첫째로, 대기업은 소기업보다 빠른 속도로 성장하고 확장하는 경향이 있습니다. 빠른 성장과 확장 때문에 더 많은 승진 기회가 있을 것입니다. 대기업에서 승진이 더 쉬울 것이라는 또 다른 이유는 직원이 다른 사람들보다 한층 두드러지려는 동기를 부여 받는다는 것입니다. 감독자와 관리자는 많은 근로자를 관리해야 합니다. 따라서 근로자 각각이 얼마나 생산적인가를 알아차리는 것은 어려운 일입니다. 근로자가 감독자에게 근면과 성실을 보여줌에 있어서 조금 더 노력을 한다면 그들의 상관은 틀림없이 알아차립니다. 그 결과, 그들은 다른 사람들보다 우월한 지원으로 보일 것입니다. 그리고 승진할 가능성이 더 높아질 것입니다. 이러한 이유로 저는 소기업보다 대기업에서 직원이 승진하기가 쉽다고 생각합니다.

tend to ~하는 경향이 있다 **grow** 성장하다 **expand** 넓히다, 확장하다 **opportunity** 기회 **motivate** ~에게 동기를 주다, 사극을 주나 **supervisor** 관리사 **handle** ~를 나루나 **productive** 생산석인 **as a result** 결과석으로

Questions 1-2 Read a Text Aloud

Directions: In this part of the test, you will read aloud the text on the screen. You will have 45 seconds to prepare. Then you will have 45 seconds to read the text aloud.

이 파트에서 여러분은 스크린의 텍스트를 큰 소리로 읽게 됩니다. 45초의 준비 시간이 주어지고, 그 후 45초 동안 텍스트를 큰 소리로 읽으세요.

TOEIC® Speaking

Question 1 of 11

Welcome to the Muskoka Museum of Cultural Arts. Our collection features more than 700 artifacts, including Native American relics, totem poles, and prints. In addition, our musical studio highlights independent music from local musicians. After we finish the tour today, you are encouraged to visit our gift shop beside the front entrance.

Muskoka 문화 예술 박물관에 오신 것을 환영합니다. 저희 전시품은 북미 원주민의 유물, 토템폴, 날염포를 포함하여 700개가 넘는 공예품을 특징으로 합니다. 더불어 지역 음악가들의 인디 음악이 저희 음악 연주실에서 부각되고 선보여집니다. 금일 견학을 마친 후, 정문 옆에 있는 기념품 상점을 방문해 보세요.

 **Speaking Solution**

Welcome to the **Muskoka Museum** of **Cultural Arts**(고유명사 강세).＼(문장의 맨 끝) Our **collection** features more than **seven hundred**(시간/날짜/숫자 강세) **artifacts**, ／(계속 의미/쉼표 뒤 짧게 끊고) including **Native American relics**／, **totem poles**／, and **prints**.＼ (A／, B／ and C＼) **In addition**(부가 의미 / 강조).／ our **musical studio** highlights **independent music**(중요 의미 강세) from **local musicians**(중요 의미 강세).＼(문장의 맨 끝) After we finish the **tour** today, ／(계속 의미/쉼표 뒤 짧게 끊고) you are encouraged to **visit** our **gift shop**(중요 의미 강세) /(전명구 앞 짧게 끊고) beside the **front entrance**.＼(문장의 맨 끝)

 feature 주로 다루다 relic 유물, 유적 totem pole 우리나라의 천하대장군 같은 민간 조각상 highlight 돋보이게 하다, 강조하다 gift shop 기념품 상점 beside 옆에 front entrance 정문

Hello and thank you for calling the Buffalo Bed and Breakfast. Regrettably, we are currently closed for repairs. This means that our rooms, gift shops and tour service centers will be closed until next Thursday. If you have any questions, stay on the line and an operator will be with you shortly. Thank you, and have a wonderful day.

안녕하세요, Buffalo Bed and Breakfast에 전화 주셔서 감사합니다. 안타깝게도 현재 저희는 수리를 위해 영업을 하지 않고 있습니다. 이것은 저희 객실, 선물 상점과 관람 서비스 센터가 다음 주 목요일까지 휴무임을 의미합니다. 질문이 있으시면 전화를 끊지 마시고 기다려 주세요. 그러면 저희 상담원과 곧 연결이 될 것입니다. 감사드리며 멋진 하루 보내세요.

 **Speaking Solution**

Hello and **thank** you for calling the **Buffalo Bed and Breakfast**(고유명사 강세). ＼(문장의 맨 끝) **Regrettably**(부가 의미 강조), we are currently **closed** for **repairs**(중요 의미 강세). ＼(문장의 맨 끝) This means that our **rooms**／, **gift shops**／ and **tour service centers**＼ (A／, B／ and C＼) will be **closed** until **next Thursday**(시간/날짜/숫자 강세). If you have any **questions**, ／(계속 의미/쉼표 뒤 짧게 끊고) **stay on**(이어동사) the line and an **operator** will be **with you** shortly. ＼(문장의 맨 끝) Thank you, and have a **wonderful day**. ＼(문장의 맨 끝)

 regrettably 안타깝게도　repair 수리　mean 의미하다　operator 상담원

Question 3   Describe a Picture

Directions: In this part of the test, you will describe the picture on your screen in as much detail as you can. You will have 30 seconds to prepare your response. Then you will have 45 seconds to speak about the picture.

이 파트에서 여러분은 스크린의 사진을 최대한 자세히 설명하게 됩니다. 대답을 위해 30초의 준비 시간이 주어지고, 그 후 45초 동안 사진에 대해 설명하세요.

 **Possible Answer**

This picture was taken at a produce store or grocery store. You can see a row of fruit on display for customers, such as plums and oranges. There are two people in the picture. One female customer is on the left, and a tall man is on the right. He appears to be an employee of the grocery store. The woman looks like she just bought some produce and is receiving her change or a receipt. In front of the man, there is a digital scale. Behind the man, there looks to be some vegetables, such as lettuce and cauliflower. In the background, there is a display of jars, perhaps pickled items, jams, or jellies.

이 사진은 농산품점 혹은 식료품점에서 촬영된 것입니다. 자두, 오렌지 같은 과일들이 줄지어 진열되어 있는 것을 볼 수 있습니다. 사진 속에는 두 사람이 있습니다. 왼편에 한 여성 고객이 있고 오른편에 한 키 큰 남성이 있습니다. 이 남성은 식료품점의 직원으로 보입니다. 여성은 물품 구매 후 거스름돈이나 영수증을 받고 있는 것 같습니다. 남성의 앞쪽에 디지털 저울이 있습니다. 남성의 뒤쪽에는 양상추와 꽃양배추 같은 야채가 있는 것으로 보입니다. 뒤쪽에는 식초에 절인 물건, 잼, 젤리가 담긴 병들이 진열되어 있습니다.

 produce store 농산품점 grocery store 식료품점 a row of 한 줄의 plum 자두 change 거스름돈 scale 저울 lettuce 상추 cauliflower 꽃양배추 pickled 식초에 절인

Questions 4-6 Respond to Questions

Directions: In this part of the test, you will answer three questions. For each question, begin responding immediately after you hear a beep. No preparation time is provided. You will have 15 seconds to respond to Questions 4 and 5 and 30 seconds to respond to Question 6.

이 파트에서 여러분은 세 가지 질문에 답하게 됩니다. 각 질문에 대해 '삐' 소리가 나면 즉시 대답하세요. 준비 시간은 주어지지 않습니다. 4번과 5번 문제에는 각각 15초, 그리고 6번 문제에는 30초의 응답 시간이 주어집니다.

Imagine that a U.S. marketing firm is doing research in your country. You have agreed to participate in a telephone interview about cooking.

어느 미국 마케팅 회사가 여러분의 나라에서 조사를 하고 있다고 가정해 봅시다. 여러분은 요리에 관한 전화 인터뷰 참여를 승낙했습니다.

TOEIC® Speaking

Question 4 of 11

When was the last time you invited guests to your home for dinner?

마지막으로 집에 손님을 초대해 저녁식사를 함께 한 것이 언제였습니까?

 **Possible Answer**

The last time I asked people to visit my home for dinner was a couple of months ago. It was my birthday.

마지막으로 저희 집에 사람들을 초대해 저녁식사를 함께 했던 때는 두어 달 전이었습니다. 그 때는 제 생일이었습니다.

How long does it usually take you to prepare dinner for visitors, and why?

손님 대접을 위해 저녁식사를 준비하는데 보통 얼마나 걸리며 그 이유는 무엇입니까?

 **Possible Answer**

It actually takes me a few days to prepare dinner for visitors. First, I have to decide on a menu and then I have to buy the groceries. On the day of the dinner, I cook the meal for the visitors.

저는 사실 손님 대접을 위해 저녁식사를 준비하는데 며칠이 걸립니다. 우선 메뉴를 정해야 하고 그 다음 식료품을 구입해야 합니다. 저녁식사 날에는 손님을 위해 음식을 요리합니다.

Do you think it is important to prepare a healthy and nutritious meal for your guests? Why, or why not?

손님을 위해 건강하고 영양가 있는 음식을 준비하는 것이 중요하다고 생각합니까? 왜 그러한가요, 혹은 왜 그렇지 않은가요?

 **Possible Answer**

I certainly believe that it is important to prepare a healthy and nutritious meal for my guests. I agree that you are what you eat. I want my guests to be healthy by eating a nutritious meal, since my guests tend to be people I care for.

저는 제 손님을 위해 건강하고 영양가 있는 음식을 준비하는 것이 당연히 중요하다고 생각합니다. 저는 "당신이 먹는 것이 곧 당신의 몸이 된다"라는 말에 공감합니다. 저는 제 손님이 영양가 있는 음식을 섭취함으로써 건강해지길 바랍니다. 제 손님은 제가 좋아하는 사람이기 때문입니다.

 healthy 건강한 nutritious 영양가 있는 certainly 확실히 you are what you eat 당신이 먹는 것이 바로 곧 당신 자신이다 care for 좋아하다

Questions 7-9   Respond to Questions Using Information Provided

Directions: In this part of the test, you will answer three questions based on the information provided. You will have 30 seconds to read the information before the questions begin. For each question, begin responding immediately after you hear a beep. No additional preparation time is provided. You will have 15 seconds to respond to Questions 7 and 8 and 30 seconds to respond to Question 9.

이 파트에서 여러분은 주어진 정보에 기초하여 세 가지 질문에 대답하게 됩니다. 문제가 시작하기 전에 30초 동안 정보를 읽게 됩니다. 각 질문에 대해 '삐' 소리가 나면 즉시 대답하세요. 준비 시간은 주어지지 않습니다. 7번과 8번 문제에는 각각 15초, 그리고 9번 문제에는 30초의 응답 시간이 주어집니다.

TOEIC® Speaking

Questions 7-9 of 11

Itinerary Dante Shells

Monday, April 24

8:30 A.M.	Depart Tacoma (Seattle-Tacoma International Airport, Sharp Jet flight #S28)
12:45 P.M.	Arrive San Antonio (Hotel accommodations, Drake Hotel)

Tuesday, April 25

10:00 A.M. - 4:30 P.M.	Psychiatric Association Conference (Day 1)
5:00 P.M. - 7:00 P.M.	Give a lecture at Palo Alto College

Wednesday, April 26

10:00 A.M. - 3:30 P.M.	Psychiatric Association Conference (Day 2)

Thursday, April 27

11:10 A.M.	Depart San Antonio (San Antonio International Airport, Sharp Jet flight #S49)
2:25 P.M.	Arrive Tacoma (Tony's Limousine Services, 2:45 P.M. pickup)

Hi. This is Dante Shells. I left my schedule for the business trip I am going to be taking next week in my office. I was hoping you could look at it for me and give me some of the details.

Itinerary Dante Shells		Dante Shells의 일정	
Monday, April 24		**4월 24일, 월요일**	
8:30 A.M.	Depart Tacoma (Seattle-Tacoma International Airport, Sharp Jet flight #S28)	오전 8시 30분	타코마 출발(시애틀—타코마 국제 공항, 샤프 제트 항공편 #S28)
12:45 P.M.	Arrive San Antonio (Hotel Accommodations, Drake Hotel)	오후 12시 45분	샌 안토니오 도착(호텔 숙박, 드레이크 호텔)
Tuesday, April 25		**4월 25일, 화요일**	
10:00 A.M. - 4:30 P.M.	Psychiatric Association Conference (Day 1)	오전 10시 ~ 오후 4시 30분	정신과 협회 컨퍼런스(1일)
5:00 P.M. - 7:00 P.M.	Give a lecture at Palo Alto College	오후 5시 ~ 오후 7시	팔로 알토 대학에서 강연
Wednesday, April 26		**4월 26일, 수요일**	
10:00 A.M. - 3:30 P.M.	Psychiatric Association Conference (Day 2)	오전 10시 ~ 오후 3시 30분	정신과 협회 컨퍼런스(2일)
Thursday, April 27		**4월 27일, 목요일**	
11:10 A.M.	Depart San Antonio (San Antonio International Airport, Sharp Jet flight #S49)	오전 11시 10분	샌 안토니오 출발(샌 안토니오 호텔 국제 공항, 샤프 제트 항공편 #S49)
2:25 P.M.	Arrive Tacoma (Tony's Limousine Services, 2:45 P.M. pickup)	오후 2시 25분	타코마 도착(Tony's 리무진 서비스, 오후 2시 45분 승차)

Hi. This is Dante Shells. I left my schedule for the business trip I am going to be taking next week in my office. I was hoping you could look at it for me and give me some of the details.

안녕하세요, Dante Shells입니다. 다음 주 예정인 출장 일정표를 사무실에 두고 나왔습니다. 그것을 보시고 세부 사항을 제게 말씀해 주시길 부탁드립니다.

 itinerary 일정   psychiatric 정신 의학의   give a lecture 강의하다

What time do I leave Tacoma, and from which airport?

타코마로부터 몇 시에, 어느 공항에서 떠나나요?

 **Possible Answer**

You are scheduled to depart Tacoma at eight-thirty in the morning from Seattle-Tacoma International Airport.

귀하는 아침 8시 30분에 시애틀—타코마 국제 공항에서 떠날 예정입니다.

I'm planning to have dinner with business friends on Tuesday at six o'clock. That should work, right?

저는 동업자와 화요일 6시에 저녁식사를 함께 할 계획입니다. 가능하죠, 그렇죠?

 **Possible Answer**

On Tuesday, you are scheduled to give a lecture at Palo Alto College from five to seven P.M. Thus, you shouldn't plan your dinner for six o'clock.

화요일에 귀하는 오후 5시부터 7시까지 팔로 알토 대학에서 강연 일정이 잡혀 있습니다. 따라서 6시에 저녁식사를 계획해서는 안 됩니다.

 **be scheduled to** ~할 예정이다

Can you give me the details of my return trip?

저의 돌아오는 일정을 상세히 말씀해 주실 수 있나요?

 **Possible Answer**

You depart San Antonio on Thursday, April the twenty-seventh at eleven-ten in the morning from San Antonio International Airport. Your flight number is S49. You arrive in Tacoma at two-twenty-five in the afternoon. Also, you will be picked-up twenty minutes later by Tony's Limousine Services.

귀하는 4월 27일, 목요일, 오전 11시 10분에 샌안토니오 국제 공항에서 샌안토니오를 떠납니다. 항공편은 S49입니다. 오후 2시 25분에 타코마에 도착합니다. 그런 다음 20분 후 Tony's 리무진 서비스가 귀하를 태우고 갈 것입니다

 **depart** 출발하다   **arrive** 도착하다   **pick somebody up** ~를 차에 태우다, ~를 데리러 가다

Question 10   Propose a Solution

Directions: In this part of the test, you will be presented with a problem and asked to propose a solution. You will have 30 seconds to prepare. Then you will have 60 seconds to speak.

이 파트에서 여러분에게 한 가지 문제가 주어집니다. 여러분은 그에 대한 해결책을 제시해주세요. 30초 동안 준비한 뒤 60초 동안 응답하세요.

In your response, be sure to
- show that you recognize the problem, and
- propose a way of dealing with the problem.

여러분의 응답에서
- 여러분이 문제를 인식했다는 것을 보여주세요.
- 그 문제를 대처하는 방법을 제안해주세요.

 Hello. This is Ms. Yoko, your manager. I've seen the schedule for the new staff orientation event next month, and the plan looks like it is coming along very nicely. But I see that there are some blanks on the Saturday afternoon schedule. It says, "Social Time." I know we talked about setting aside some informal time for current employees and new employees to get to know each other, but I want to know your plan for specific activities during that time. I think it's important for there to be some structure to it. Please give me a call and let me know your plan by the end of this weekend. Thanks. It's Ms. Yoko at extension 599.

안녕하세요, 저는 당신의 상관인 Yoko입니다. 다음 달 신입 사원 오리엔테이션 일정을 살펴보았습니다. 계획은 매우 잘된 것 같습니다. 그런데 토요일 오후 일정에 공란이 있더군요. 거기엔 "사교 시간"이라고 쓰여 있습니다. 우리는 기존 사원과 신입 사원이 서로를 알기 위한 격식 없는 시간을 별도로 마련하자고 이야기를 했었죠. 그러나 그 시간에 할 특별한 활동이 있는지 당신의 계획을 알고 싶습니다. 제 생각에 이것은 그 시간의 구조 계획 짜는 데 있어서 중요한 것입니다. 금주 이내로 전화 주셔서 계획을 알려주세요. 고맙습니다. 저는 Yoko이고 내선번호는 599입니다.

 **new staff orientation event** 신입 사원 교육 행사   **come along** 잘 진행하다   **blank** 빈칸   **set aside** 따로 마련하다
get to know each other 서로 알게 되다   **specific** 특정한   **structure** 구조

 **Possible Answer**

인사	Hello, Ms. Yoko.
문제 상황 인식	I'm returning your call regarding the preliminary schedule for the new employee orientation next month.
해결책 제시	The few hours dedicated for "Social Time" will be spent doing team-building activities. I think this could be a good opportunity for current and new employees to get to know one another and build cooperative relationships, which are important in any setting.
세부사항	These activities will stimulate problem-solving skills designed to help employees develop their capacity to work effectively together. I will have various activities listed during that time, and there will be a sign-up sheet posted so that everyone can participate. I have already picked several activities that I think the employees will find challenging and fun.
마무리	Call me back if you want more details, Ms. Yoko.

안녕하세요. Yoko 씨. 다음 달 신입 사원 오리엔테이션 일정의 사전 계획에 관한 답신 드립니다. "사교 시간"으로 할당된 시간은 소속감 다지기 활동을 수행하는데 소요될 것입니다. 제 생각으로는 이것이 기존 사원과 신입 사원이 서로를 알게 되고 협동 간게를 다지는 좋은 게기가 될 수 있을 것이며 이것은 어떠한 환경에서나 중요합니다. 이러한 활동은 사원들이 서로 효율적으로 일하는 역량을 계발하도록 고안된 문제 해결 능력을 촉진할 것입니다. 저는 그 시간 동안 할 다양한 활동을 목록으로 정리할 것이며 모두가 참석할 수 있도록 등록 용지를 게시할 것입니다. 저는 이미 사원들이 도전적이고 재미를 발견할 다양한 활동을 찾아냈습니다. Yoko 씨, 더 상세한 사항을 원하신다면 연락 주세요.

 preliminary schedule 사전 계획   dedicated 할당된, 마련된   team-building activity 소속감 다지기 활동

cooperative 협력적인   setting 환경   stimulate 자극하다, 촉진하다   problem-solving skill 문제 해결 능력

designed to ~하기 위해 만들어진   develop capacity 역량을 개발하다   effectively 효과적으로   various 다양한

sign-up sheet 등록 용지   posted 게시된   challenging 도전적인

Question 11 Express an Opinion

Directions: In this part of the test, you will give your opinion about a specific topic. Be sure to say as much as you can in the time allowed. You will have 15 seconds to prepare. Then you will have 60 seconds to speak.

이 파트에서 여러분은 특정한 주제에 대한 의견을 말하게 됩니다. 주어진 시간 동안 최대한 많이 말할 수 있도록 하세요. 15초 동안 준비한 뒤 60초 동안 응답하세요.

Do you agree or disagree with the following statement?

Memorizing facts and information is the most important part of a high school student's education.

Use specific reasons and examples to support your opinion.

여러분은 다음 진술에 동의하시나요, 동의하지 않으시나요?

사실과 정보를 암기하는 것은 고등학생의 학업에서 가장 중요한 부분입니다.

여러분의 의견을 뒷받침하는 이유와 예시를 들어주십시오.

 **Possible Answer 1 (agree)**

의견 제시
I certainly agree with the statement that memorizing facts and information is the most important part of a high school student's education.

근거 제시
To begin, high school is the stepping stone to college or university. Most educational institutions, if not all of them, use grades achieved to determine admission. Thus, memorizing facts and information would ensure that students obtain high scores on tests and examinations, guaranteeing acceptance offers from their school of choice. Although universities and colleges do take into account other factors besides good grades, less weight is given to these factors.

예시
For instance, high grades obtained through memorization would be more favored than participation in extracurricular activities, such as ballet or basketball.

마무리
Hence, memorizing facts and information is the most important part of a high school student's education.

저는 사실과 정보를 암기하는 것은 고등학생의 학업에서 가장 중요한 부분이라는 진술에 확실히 동의합니다. 우선, 고등학교는 단과 대학이나 종합 대학으로 향하는 디딤돌입니다. 모두 다는 아니지만, 대부분의 교육 기관은 합격 여부를 정하는데 학업 성적을 사용합니다. 따라서 사실과 정보를 암기하는 것은 시험 및 평가에서 그들이 지원한 학교에 합격을 보증하는 높은 점수를 획득하도록 합니다. 비록 단과나 종합 대학이 좋은 등급 이외에 다른 요소를 고려하기는 하지만, 이 요소에 비해서 비중이 낮습니다. 예를 들어, 암기로 획득한 높은 등급은 발레나 농구와 같은 특별 활동의 참여보다 더 선호됩니다. 따라서 사실과 정보를 암기하는 것은 고등학생의 학업에서 가장 중요한 부분입니다.

memorize 암기하다　**stepping stone** 디딤돌　**educational institution** 교육 기관　**grade** 성적, 등급　**admission** 입학
obtain 얻다, 구하다　**thereby** 그래서　**guarantee** 보증하다　**acceptance offer** 합격　**take into account** 고려하다
factor 요소　**less weight** 좀 더 낮은 비중　**for instance** 예를 들어　**favored** 선호되는　**extracurricular activity** 과외
활동

Possible Answer 2 (disagree)

의견 제시　I do not agree with the statement that memorizing facts and information is the most important part of a high school student's education because it is not a very useful skill in a person's life.

근거 제시　High school is an important time for students to discover their identity and their purpose in life. The best way to do this is by experiencing and trying different things to discover what they like and what they are good at. It is true that tests and examinations require memorizing facts and information to obtain good scores. These tests are used to measure what a person is capable of. However, there are other and better ways to determine what a person can do. As I have said, actually trying something and seeing if one is capable of doing it well is a true measure, and perhaps more accurate.

예시　To illustrate, instead of memorizing math equations, a student could work part-time as a bank teller or do volunteer work to gain first-hand experience.

마무리　For these reasons, memorizing facts and information is not really important for high school students.

저는 사실과 정보를 암기하는 것은 고등학생의 학업에서 가장 중요한 부분이라는 진술에 동의하지 않습니다. 암기하는 것은 삶에 있어서 그리 유용한 능력이 아니기 때문입니다. 고등학교 시절은 학생이 자아와 삶의 목적을 탐색하는 중요한 시기입니다. 이 탐색을 위한 가장 좋은 방법은 상이한 것들을 경험하고 시도하여 그들이 무엇을 좋아하고 무엇에 소질이 있는지를 파악하는 것입니다. 시험 및 평가에서 좋은 점수를 획득하기 위해 사실과 정보의 암기가 요구되는 것은 사실입니다. 이러한 시험은 학생이 무엇에 소질이 있는지를 측정하는데 사용됩니다. 그러나 학생이 무엇을 할 수 있는지를 파악하고 정하는데 다른 더 나은 방법들이 있습니다. 말씀드렸다시피, 실제 어떤 것을 시도하여 그것에 소질이 있는지를 알아보는 것이 진짜 측정입니다. 그리고 아마 더욱 정확할 것입니다. 예를 들어, 수학 공식의 암기 대신에 은행 출납원으로서 시간제 아르바이트를 하거나 자원봉사를 하여 직접적인 경험을 해볼 수 있습니다. 이러한 이유로 사실과 정보를 암기하는 것은 고등학교 학생들에게 중요하지 않습니다.

useful 유용한　**skill** 능력　**identity** 자아　**determine** 결정하다, 알아내다　**actually** 실제로　**Illustrate** 예를 들어 설명하다
math equations 수학 방정식　**first-hand experience** 직접적인 경험

Questions 1-2 Read a Text Aloud

Directions: In this part of the test, you will read aloud the text on the screen. You will have 45 seconds to prepare. Then you will have 45 seconds to read the text aloud.

이 파트에서 여러분은 스크린의 텍스트를 큰 소리로 읽게 됩니다. 45초의 준비 시간이 주어지고, 그 후 45초 동안 텍스트를 큰 소리로 읽으세요.

TOEIC® Speaking

Question 1 of 11

Do you need office supplies for your office? Midland Depot offers photocopy machines, scanners, color printers, and paper. Furthermore, we can design a paper plan for you that will meet the specific needs of your office. So call Midland Depot, where office supplies are our business.

사무용품이 필요하십니까? Midland Depot은 복사기, 스캐너, 컬러 프린터, 종이 등을 제공해 드립니다. 나아가, 저희는 귀하의 사무실의 특별한 요구에 맞게 종이 사용 계획을 설정해 드립니다. 그럼, 사무용품을 전문으로 하는 저희 Midland Depot에 연락 바랍니다.

 **Speaking Solution**

Do you need **office supplies**(중요 의미 강세) for your **office?**↗(Do 의문문 맨 끝) **Midland Depot**(고유명사 강세) offers **photocopy machines**↗, **scanners**↗, **color printers**↗, and **paper**↘ (A↗, B↗ and C↘). **Furthermore**(부가 의미 강조)↗ we can design a **paper plan**(중요 의미 강세) for you / (절 앞에 잠시 쉬고) that will meet the **specific needs**(중요 의미 강세) of your **office.**↘(문장의 맨 끝) So call **Midland Depot**(고유명사 강세), (절 앞에 잠시 쉬고) where **office supplies** are our **business.**↘(문장의 맨 끝)

 office supplies 사무용품   furthermore 게다가   specific need 특정한 요구

In business news, automotive sales increased between September and November, which is usually not a very active time for car buying. Industry experts say that more people have been purchasing smaller, compact vehicles instead of larger, utility vehicles. Sales have been mostly from car manufacturers that provide affordable vehicles rather than luxury or high-end car manufacturers. Next, we'll speak to a local car salesman.

비즈니스 뉴스에 따르면, 자동차 판매가 9월과 11월 사이에 증가했는데 이 기간은 대개 차량 구입이 아주 활발한 시기가 아닙니다. 업계 전문가는 더 많은 사람들이 큰 다용도 차 대신 작은 소형차를 구입한다고 합니다. 비싸거나 고급의 자동차보다는 저렴한 자동차가 주로 판매되고 있습니다. 이어서 지역 자동차 판매자와 이야기를 해 보겠습니다.

Speaking Solution

In **business news, automotive sales increased**(중요 의미 강세) / (전명구 앞 짧게 끊고) between **September and November**(시간/날짜/숫자 강세), (절 앞에 잠시 쉬고) which is usually **not**(부정어 강세) a very **active time** for **car buying**(중요 의미 강세). \(문장의 맨 끝) **Industry experts** say that **more people**(중요 의미 강세) have been purchasing **smaller**, **compact vehicles**(비교대상 상호 강조-A)/ instead of **larger**, **utility vehicles**(비교대상 상호 강조-B). **Sales** have been mostly from **car manufacturers**(중요 의미 강세)/ (절 앞에 잠시 쉬고) that provide **affordable vehicles**(비교대상 상호 강조-A) / rather than **luxury or high-end car manufacturers**(비교대상 상호 강조-B). **Next**, we'll speak to a **local car salesman**(중요 의미 강세). \(문장의 맨 끝)

automotive sales 자동차 판매   active time 활발한 시기   expert 전문가   utility vehicle 다용도 차량   mostly 주로, 대개   affordable 저렴한   rather than ~라기 보다   high-end 고급의

Question 3   Describe a Picture

Directions: In this part of the test, you will describe the picture on your screen in as much detail as you can. You will have 30 seconds to prepare your response. Then you will have 45 seconds to speak about the picture.

이 파트에서 여러분은 스크린의 사진을 최대한 자세히 설명하게 됩니다. 대답을 위해 30초의 준비 시간이 주어지고, 그 후 45초 동안 사진에 대해 설명하세요.

 **Possible Answer**

There are two men in a blue-colored room, looking at one another in this picture. They are both wearing light-colored khakis and standing in front of a photocopier. The man on the left is bald and is wearing a short-sleeved collared shirt. The man on the right is wearing a T-shirt and is holding a cup in his left hand. Both men are smiling at each other.

사진에서 청색으로 칠해진 방에 두 남자가 서로 마주보고 있습니다. 이들은 둘 다 밝은 카키색 계열의 옷차림으로 복사기 앞에 서 있습니다. 왼쪽에 있는 남성은 대머리이고 칼라가 달린 반팔 셔츠를 입었습니다. 오른쪽에 있는 남성은 티셔츠를 입고 왼손에 컵을 들고 있습니다. 둘 다 서로를 보며 미소 짓고 있습니다.

 **one another** 서로서로   **khaki** 카키색 천, 카키색의   **photocopier** 복사기   **hold** ~을 잡다   **smile at** ~을 보고 미소 짓다

Questions 4-6 Respond to Questions

Directions: In this part of the test, you will answer three questions. For each question, begin responding immediately after you hear a beep. No preparation time is provided. You will have 15 seconds to respond to Questions 4 and 5 and 30 seconds to respond to Question 6.

이 파트에서 여러분은 세 가지 질문에 답하게 됩니다. 각 질문에 대해 '삐' 소리가 나면 즉시 대답하세요. 준비 시간은 주어지지 않습니다. 4번과 5번 문제에는 각각 15초, 그리고 6번 문제에는 30초의 응답 시간이 주어집니다.

Imagine that a U.S. marketing firm is doing research in your country. You have agreed to participate in a telephone interview about handwritten letters.

어느 미국 마케팅 회사가 여러분의 나라에서 조사를 하고 있다고 가정해 봅시다. 여러분은 손으로 쓴 편지에 관한 전화 인터뷰 참여를 승낙했습니다.

TOEIC® Speaking

Question 4 of 11

For what special occasions do you send cards or handwritten letters to family and friends?

어떤 특별한 때에 가족과 친구에게 카드나 손으로 쓴 편지를 보내시나요?

 **Possible Answer**

I send cards or write letters to family and friends on birthdays, anniversaries, and holidays.

저는 생일, 기념일, 연말연시에 가족과 친구에게 카드나 편지를 보냅니다.

 **anniversary** 기념일   **holiday** 연말연시

Other than cards or letters, how else do you congratulate family and friends for special occasions?

특별한 때에 카드나 편지 대신 다른 어떤 것으로 가족과 친구를 축하해 주나요?

 **Possible Answer**

Other than cards or letters, I congratulate family and friends by buying a small gift such as a cake or a bouquet of flowers.

카드나 편지 대신, 저는 케이크나 꽃다발 같은 작은 선물을 사주어 가족과 친구를 축하해 줍니다.

 a bouquet of flowers 꽃 한 다발

Would you be interested in a service to send online greeting cards? Why, or why not?

온라인 연하장 발송 서비스에 관심이 있으신가요? 왜 그러한가요, 혹은 왜 그렇지 않나요?

 **Possible Answer**

I would definitely be interested in a service to send online greeting cards. The most important reason is that it would be easy and convenient to send them to family and friends. Also, e-cards would not waste paper, thus helping the environment.

물론 저는 온라인 연하장 발송 서비스에 관심이 있습니다. 가장 큰 이유는 가족이나 친구에게 연하장을 보낼 때 쉽고 편리하기 때문입니다. 또한 이메일 카드는 종이를 낭비하지 않으므로 환경에 도움이 될 것입니다.

 greeting card 연하장   definitely 물론, 확실히   e-card 이메일 카드   waste 낭비하다

Questions 7-9 Respond to Questions Using Information Provided

Directions: In this part of the test, you will answer three questions based on the information provided. You will have 30 seconds to read the information before the questions begin. For each question, begin responding immediately after you hear a beep. No additional preparation time is provided. You will have 15 seconds to respond to Questions 7 and 8 and 30 seconds to respond to Question 9.

이 파트에서 여러분은 주어진 정보에 기초하여 세 가지 질문에 대답하게 됩니다. 문제가 시작하기 전에 30초 동안 정보를 읽게 됩니다. 각 질문에 대해 '삐' 소리가 나면 즉시 대답하세요. 준비 시간은 주어지지 않습니다. 7번과 8번 문제에는 각각 15초, 그리고 9번 문제에는 30초의 응답 시간이 주어집니다.

Questions 7-9 of 11

Cooking Meals from Coast to Coast

Fall Course List

- Classes: Two times per week for four weeks
- Price: $75
- Size limit: 12 students per class

SEPTEMBER

| Mon./Wed. | 6:00 - 8:30 P.M. | Vegan and Vegetarian Meals (Class filled) |
| Tue./Thurs. | 5:30 - 8:00 P.M. | Breakfast Beginnings |

OCTOBER

| Mon./Wed. | 7:30 - 9:30 P.M. | Barbeque Techniques (Class filled) |
| Tue./Thurs. | 5:30 - 7:00 P.M. | Diverse Dinner Delights |

NOVEMBER

| Mon./Wed. | 6:30 - 8:00 P.M. | Dessert Design and Decorations (Materials - $35) |
| Tue./Thurs. | 4:30 - 6:00 P.M. | Easy-to-Prepare Meals |

Hi. I was talking to a friend about your cooking classes, and she told me that you came out with your new course list. I was wondering if I could ask you a few questions.

Cooking Meals from Coast to Coast

Fall Course List

- Classes: Two times per week for four weeks
- Price: $75
- Size limit: 12 students per class

SEPTEMBER

| Mon./Wed. | 6:00 - 8:30 P.M. | Vegan and Vegetarian Meals (Class filled) |
| Tue./Thurs. | 5:30 - 8:00 P.M. | Breakfast Beginnings |

OCTOBER

| Mon./Wed. | 7:30 - 9:30 P.M. | Barbeque Techniques (Class filled) |
| Tue./Thurs. | 5:30 - 7:00 P.M. | Diverse Dinner Delights |

NOVEMBER

| Mon./Wed. | 6:30 - 8:00 P.M. | Dessert Design and Decorations (Materials - $35) |
| Tue./Thurs. | 4:30 - 6:00 P.M. | Easy-to-Prepare Meals |

Hi. I was talking to a friend about your cooking classes, and she told me that you came out with your new course list. I was wondering if I could ask you a few questions.

전역을 아우르는 요리

가을 수업 목록

- 수업: 4주 동안 주 2회
- 가격: 75달러
- 정원 제한: 수업 당 12명

9월

| 월/수요일 | 오후 6시~8시 30분 | 엄격한 채식주의자와 채식주의자 음식 (정원 마감) |
| 화/목요일 | 오후 5시 30분~8시 | 조식 시작 |

10월

| 월/수요일 | 오후 7시 30분~9시 30분 | 바비큐 요리법 (정원 마감) |
| 화/목요일 | 오후 5시 30분~7시 | 다양한 저녁식사의 즐거움 |

11월

| 월/수요일 | 오후 6시 30분~8시 | 디저트 디자인 및 꾸미기 (재료비— 35달러) |
| 화/목요일 | 오후 4시 30분~6시 | 쉽게 준비하는 음식 |

안녕하세요. 저는 친구와 선생님의 요리 수업에 대해 이야기하고 있었습니다. 그리고 친구 말로는 선생님께서 새로운 수업 목록으로 수업을 진행하실 것이라고 하더군요. 몇 가지 여쭤볼까 합니다.

 **vegan** 엄격한 채식주의자   **vegetarian** 채식주의자   **diverse** 다양한

Which months does the course list cover?

수업 목록은 몇 개월에 걸쳐 진행되나요?

 **Possible Answer**

The course list covers the fall months, from September to November.

수업 목록은 9월에서 11월까지의 가을 동안 진행됩니다.

 **course list** 수업 목록   **cover** 다루다

I know you usually offer a class on barbecue techniques, so I'd like to register for that class right now.

저는 선생님께서 통상 바비큐 요리법 수업을 하신다고 들었습니다. 그래서 당장 그 수업에 등록하고 싶습니다.

 **Possible Answer**

I am sorry to inform you that the barbecue techniques class for this fall is already filled.

미안한 말씀을 드려야겠군요. 올 가을 바비큐 요리법 수업은 이미 정원이 다 찼습니다.

 filled 가득 찬

I think I'll have a lot of time to take classes toward the end of fall. Could you give me information about the classes in November?

저는 올 가을 말까지 수업을 들을 충분한 시간이 있습니다. 11월 수업 계획을 말씀해 주시겠어요?

 **Possible Answer**

During the month of November, two classes will be offered — Dessert Design and Decorations which is offered on Mondays and Wednesdays from six-thirty to eight P.M. Also, this course has a thirty-five dollar materials surcharge. The second class is offered on Tuesdays and Thursdays. This class teaches Easy-to-Prepare Meals and takes place from four-thirty to six P.M.

11월에는 두 가지 수업이 진행될 것입니다. 월요일과 수요일, 오후 6시 30분에서 8시 사이에 디저트 디자인 및 꾸미기 수업이며 35달러의 재료비가 듭니다. 두 번째 수업은 화요일과 목요일에 진행됩니다. 이 수업은 쉽게 준비하는 음식을 가르쳐 드리며 오후 4시 30분에서 6시까지입니다.

 material 재료   surcharge 추가 요금   take place 일어나다, 발생하다

Question 10 Propose a Solution

Directions: In this part of the test, you will be presented with a problem and asked to propose a solution. You will have 30 seconds to prepare. Then you will have 60 seconds to speak.

이 파트에서 여러분에게 한 가지 문제가 주어집니다. 여러분은 그에 대한 해결책을 제시해주세요. 30초 동안 준비한 뒤 60초 동안 응답하세요.

In your response, be sure to
- show that you recognize the problem, and
- propose a way of dealing with the problem.

여러분의 응답에서
- 여러분이 문제를 인식했다는 것을 보여주세요.
- 그 문제를 대처하는 방법을 제안해주세요.

 Hello. It's Jina, the regional manager of Magnolia clothing stores. I'm calling all of the local store managers to hear your thoughts on how best to implement a change of your company's dress code which we hope will have a positive impact on our sales. As you know, we want to encourage all members of the sales staff when they are working to wear the clothes that our stores are selling. You know, like a live advertisement for our merchandise. We're hoping to implement this next month as an important part of our new marketing strategy. I think you, the local store manager, would best know your employees and also the most effective strategy to get them excited about wearing our company's clothes. Again, it's Jina.

안녕하세요. 저는 Magnolia 의류점의 지역 상점 관리자인 Jina입니다. 저는 각 지점장 모두에게 연락을 하여 우리의 판매에 긍정적 영향을 끼칠 것으로 기대되는 복장 규정의 변화를 실행하는 최상의 방법에 대한 귀하의 생각을 듣고자 합니다. 아시다시피, 모든 판매 직원이 근무시간에 우리 상점이 판매하고 있는 옷을 입도록 장려하고자 합니다. 우리 상품의 생생한 광고와 같은 것입니다. 새로운 마케팅 전략의 중요한 부분으로서 다음 달에 실행하려고 합니다. 귀하는 지점장이시기에 귀 상점의 직원에 대해 가장 잘 아실 것이며, 우리 회사 상품을 입는 것에 판매 직원이 흥미를 느끼게 할 가장 효율적인 방법을 알고 계시리라 여깁니다. 부탁드립니다. 저는 Jina입니다.

 **implement** 시행하다 **dress code** 복장 규정 **impact** 영향 **merchandise** 상품 **strategy** 전략

 **Possible Answer**

인사	Hi, Jina. This is Jason, the store manager at the downtown location.
문제 상황 인식	I got your message about the dress code and new marketing strategy. I don't think it would be a big problem to get our sales staff members to wear the clothes that they are trying to sell.
해결책 제시	I think the best way to get them to wear the clothes is to offer them a large discount on the clothing — a discount that is significantly higher than we offer to our customers. Since this dress code is going to be enforced next month, I think it is only fair to allow employees to buy the clothes inexpensively. This way, they won't feel bad about having to wear the store merchandise as they work. I think we could also give bonuses the first month to sales staff members who sell a lot of clothing while wearing their new clothes. I think that they would be motivated to show off their new clothes and encourage customers to buy the clothing, too.
마무리	Please let me know what you think.

안녕하세요, Jina. 상업 지구의 지점장인 Jason입니다. 복장 규정과 새로운 미케팅 전략에 관한 귀하의 메시지를 받았습니다. 우리 판매 직원에게 그들이 판매할 옷을 입게 하는 것은 그리 어려운 일이 아닐 것입니다. 제 생각으로는 직원이 옷을 입게 할 최선책은 그들에게 옷을 고객 할인보다 훨씬 더 큰 폭의 할인을 해 주는 것입니다. 복장 규정이 다음 달에 실행될 것이므로 제 생각에는 직원이 옷을 저렴하게 살 수 있도록 배려하는 것이 유일한 수단입니다. 이렇게 하면 직원은 근무 시간에 상점의 상품을 입는 것에 대해서 불만을 가지지 않을 것입니다. 우리는 또한 첫 달에 새로운 옷을 입고 많은 옷을 판매한 직원에게 보너스를 지급할 수 있습니다. 판매 직원은 자신의 새로운 옷을 보여주고 그 옷을 고객에게 팔고 싶은 동기를 부여받을 것입니다. 어떻게 생각하는지 알려주세요.

 **best way** 최선의 방법　**offer** 제공하다　**significantly** 상당히　**enforce** 강행하다　**fair** 공정한　**allow** 허락하다, 고려하다
inexpensively 값싸게, 많은 비용을 들이지 않고　**encourage** 권장하다, 격려하다, 부추기다

Question 11 Express an Opinion

Directions: In this part of the test, you will give your opinion about a specific topic. Be sure to say as much as you can in the time allowed. You will have 15 seconds to prepare. Then you will have 60 seconds to speak.

이 파트에서 여러분은 특정한 주제에 대한 의견을 말하게 됩니다. 주어진 시간 동안 최대한 많이 말할 수 있도록 하세요. 15초 동안 준비한 뒤 60초 동안 응답하세요.

Some people think success is mainly the result of intelligence. Other people think success is mainly the result of hard work. Which do you think is more important to success?

Intelligence or hard work?

Give reasons or examples to support your opinion.

어떤 사람들은 성공이 주로 지능의 결과라고 생각합니다. 다른 사람들은 성공이 주로 근면의 결과라고 생각합니다. 지능과 근면 중 성공에 있어 어느 것이 더 중요하다고 생각하십니까?

당신의 의견을 뒷받침하는 이유와 예시를 들어주십시오.

💬 Possible Answer 1 (hard work)

의견 제시	I think that success is mainly the result of hard work and not intelligence.
근거 제시	To begin with, it is true that all people have the capability to work hard; however, not all people have the willingness to work hard. The people who become successful are those who have the willingness and motivation to work hard. No doubt others would recognize the tremendous effort that these types of people put forth. As a result, hard workers tend to get rewarded for their efforts by receiving bonuses or promotions.
마무리	By continually working hard, these people will repeatedly be rewarded and continue their pattern of success.

저는 성공이 지능의 결과가 아니라 주로 근면의 결과라고 생각합니다. 우선, 모든 사람들은 열심히 일할 능력이 있는 게 사실입니다. 하지만 모든 사람들이 열심히 일하려고 하지는 않습니다. 성공하는 사람들은 열심히 일하려고 하는 의지와 동기가 있는 사람들입니다. 다른 사람들은 이런 사람들이 쏟은 엄청난 노력을 틀림없이 인정할 겁니다. 결과적으로 열심히 일하는 사람들이 보너스를 받거나 승진을 함으로써 노력에 대한 보상을 얻게 됩니다. 계속 열심히 일함으로써 이런 사람들이 여러 차례 보상을 받고 계속해서 성공을 하게 됩니다.

to begin with 먼저 capability 능력 willingness 의지 motivation 동기 no doubt 의심할 바 없이, 틀림없이 recognize 인정하다 tremendous 상당한 tend to ~하는 경향이 있다 get rewarded 보상받다 promotion 승진

 **Possible Answer 2 (intelligence)**

의견 제시	I think that success is mainly the result of intelligence and not hard work.
근거 제시 1	First, intelligence allows people to solve problems easily and quickly. By doing so, smart people can be more productive and efficient. Other people will notice how intelligent people work and reward them, such as giving them a pay raise or promotion.
근거 제시 2	Next, intelligence comes in many different forms so it can be more useful in a variety of situations.
예시	For instance, psychologist Howard Gardner has identified seven types of intelligence in his Multiple Intelligences Theory.
마무리	Because intelligence can be categorized in many ways, success is also likely to be achieved in a variety of ways.

저는 성공이 근면의 결과가 아니라 주로 지능의 결과라고 생각합니다. 우선, 지능은 사람들이 문제를 쉽고 빠르게 해결하도록 합니다. 그렇게 함으로써, 지적인 사람들은 조금 더 생산적이고 효율적일 겁니다. 다른 사람들은 지적인 사람들이 어떻게 일하는지에 주목할 것이고 봉급 인상과 승진과 같은 보상을 해줍니다. 다음으로 지능은 형태가 매우 다양하므로 여러 상황에 더 유용할 수 있습니다. 예를 들어, 심리학자 Howard Gardner는 다중 지능 이론에서 지능의 7가지 형태를 밝혀냈습니다. 지능은 여러 방식으로 분류될 수 있기 때문에 성공은 또한 다양한 방법으로 성취될 것 같습니다.

 intelligent 지적인 productive 성취적인, 생산적인 efficient 효율적인 notice 알아채다 pay raise 월급 인상 come in different forms 다양한 형태로 다가오다 useful 유용한 a variety of 다양한 psychologist 심리학자 identify 확인하다, 발견하다 categorize 분류하다

Questions 1-2 Read a Text Aloud

Directions: In this part of the test, you will read aloud the text on the screen. You will have 45 seconds to prepare. Then you will have 45 seconds to read the text aloud.

이 파트에서 여러분은 스크린의 텍스트를 큰 소리로 읽게 됩니다. 45초의 준비 시간이 주어지고, 그 후 45초 동안 텍스트를 큰 소리로 읽으세요.

TOEIC® Speaking

Question 1 of 11

Welcome to Shakespeare's Theatre Company. This is a reminder to deactivate your cellular phones, pagers, or other electronic devices. If you would like to purchase snacks or drinks, they are available at the refreshment booth on the main floor. Finally, please be considerate of other audience members by refraining from talking during the performance.

Shakespeare's 극단을 찾아 주셔서 감사합니다. 휴대폰, 호출기, 다른 전자 기기의 전원을 꺼 주시길 바랍니다. 간식이나 음료를 구매하시려면 1층에 위치한 매점을 이용하시면 됩니다. 마지막으로 공연 중에는 다른 관객에게 방해가 되지 않도록 대화를 삼가주시길 바랍니다.

 **Speaking Solution**

Welcome to **Shakespeare's Theatre Company**(고유명사 강세).＼(문장의 맨 끝) This is a **reminder** to **deactivate**(중요 의미 강세) your **cellular phones**↗, **pagers**↗, or other **electronic devices**＼. (A↗, B↗ or C＼). If you would like to purchase **snacks or drinks**(중요 의미 강세), ↗(계속 의미/쉼표 뒤 짧게 끊고) they are **available** at the **refreshment booth**(중요 의미 강세) on the **main floor**.＼(문장의 맨 끝) **Finally**(마지막 강조), please be **considerate** of other **audience members** (부사구 앞 잠시 끊고) / by **refraining** from **talking**(중요 의미 강세) during the **performance**. ＼(문장의 맨 끝)

 This is a reminder ~ ~을 알려주고자 합니다   deactivate 정지시키다   electronic device 전자 장비   refreshment booth 매점   considerate 배려하는   refrain from 삼가다

Thank you for calling Lakeheed Waterworks. Regrettably, all our operators are currently busy. Please be advised that emergency crews are working to restore water to the downtown, midtown, and uptown neighborhoods. If you are calling to inform us of another emergency, please stay on the line. Someone will be with you shortly.

Lakeheed 상수도에 전화 주셔서 감사합니다. 안타깝게도, 저희 상담원 모두가 현재 통화 중입니다. 비상 근무조가 상업지구, 중앙지구, 주택지구의 상수도 복원 작업 중임을 알려드립니다. 저희에게 또 다른 비상사태를 통지하시려는 것이라면, 전화를 끊지 마시고 기다려 주세요. 저희 직원이 곧 귀하를 도와드릴 것입니다.

Speaking Solution

Thank you for calling **Lakeheed Waterworks**.(고유명사 강세) **Regrettably**, ╱(계속 의미/쉼표 뒤 짧게 끊고) all our **operators** are currently **busy**(중요 의미 강세).╲(문장의 맨 끝) Please be **advised** that **emergency crews**(중요 의미 강세) are working to **restore water**(중요 의미 강세) ╱ (부사구 앞 잠시 끊고) to the **downtown** ╱, **midtown** ╱, and **uptown neighborhoods**. ╲ (A ╱, B ╱ and C ╲) If you are calling to **inform** us of another **emergency** ╱(계속 의미/쉼표 뒤 짧게 끊고) please **stay on**(이어동사) the line. **Someone** will be **with you** shortly. ╲(문장의 맨 끝)

waterworks 상수도   **regrettably** 안타깝게도   **operator** 상담원   **Please be advised that ~** ~을 알려드립니다
emergency crew 비상 근무원   **restore** 복원하다   **stay on the line** 전화를 끊지 않고 있다   **shortly** 곧

Question 3 Describe a Picture

Directions: In this part of the test, you will describe the picture on your screen in as much detail as you can. You will have 30 seconds to prepare your response. Then you will have 45 seconds to speak about the picture.

이 파트에서 여러분은 스크린의 사진을 최대한 자세히 설명하게 됩니다. 대답을 위해 30초의 준비 시간이 주어지고, 그 후 45초 동안 사진에 대해 설명하세요.

 **Possible Answer**

There are two women in this picture. The woman on the left has long blonde hair, and the woman on the right has long brown hair. They appear to be in a women's clothing shop. Behind the blonde woman and in the background, there are clothing racks. The blonde woman is wearing a shiny silver overcoat that is tied around her waist. She appears to be helping the other woman shop. The brunette is holding up a light blue blouse to her chest to check how it would look on her.

이 사진 속에는 두 여성이 있습니다. 왼쪽에 있는 여성은 긴 짙은 금발 머리고, 오른쪽에 있는 여성은 긴 갈색 머리입니다. 두 사람은 여성용 의류 상점에 있는 것 같습니다. 금발 머리 여성의 뒤쪽 배경으로 옷걸이가 있습니다. 금발 머리 여성은 허리를 묶은 반짝거리는 은색 외투를 입고 있습니다. 금발 머리 여성은 다른 여성의 쇼핑을 도와주는 것 같습니다. 갈색 머리 여성은 옷이 어울리는지 확인하고자 가슴에 밝은 청색 블라우스를 대보고 있습니다.

 blonde hair 금발 머리   clothing rack 옷걸이   shiny 반짝거리는   brunette 갈색 머리의 여성   hold up 잡다

Questions 4-6 Respond to Questions

Directions: In this part of the test, you will answer three questions. For each question, begin responding immediately after you hear a beep. No preparation time is provided. You will have 15 seconds to respond to Questions 4 and 5 and 30 seconds to respond to Question 6.

이 파트에서 여러분은 세 가지 질문에 답하게 됩니다. 각 질문에 대해 '삐' 소리가 나면 즉시 대답하세요. 준비 시간은 주어지지 않습니다. 4번과 5번 문제에는 각각 15초, 그리고 6번 문제에는 30초의 응답 시간이 주어집니다.

Imagine that a British marketing firm is doing research in your country. You have agreed to participate in a telephone interview about giving gifts to coworkers.

어느 영국 마케팅 회사가 여러분의 나라에서 조사를 하고 있다고 가정해 봅시다. 여러분은 동료들에게 선물을 주는 것에 관한 전화 인터뷰 참여를 승낙했습니다.

TOEIC® Speaking

Question 4 of 11

Why do you give gifts to your coworkers?

당신은 왜 동료에게 선물을 주나요?

 **Possible Answer**

I give gifts to my coworkers to show support and appreciation when they get a promotion or are rewarded for hard work.

저는 제 동료가 승진하거나 근면의 대가로 포상을 받을 때 지지와 감사를 표현하기 위해 선물을 줍니다.

 promotion 승진　reward 보상하다　hard work 근면

How much time do you tend to spend deciding on gifts for coworkers?

동료에게 줄 선물을 고르는데 시간을 얼마나 쓰시나요?

 **Possible Answer**

I don't spend too much time deciding on gifts for coworkers. Perhaps I spend an hour or so considering what to buy them.

저는 동료에게 줄 선물을 고르는데 지나치게 많은 시간을 쓰지 않습니다. 아마도 저는 무엇을 살지 고르는데 한 시간 정도 쓸 것입니다.

 tend to ~하는 경향이 있다

What do you take into account when you are choosing gifts for coworkers, and why?

동료에게 줄 선물을 고를 때 고려하는 점은 무엇이며 왜 그러한가요?

 **Possible Answer**

One factor I would take into account when I am choosing gifts for coworkers is their gender. It might be easier to pick something masculine for a man and feminine for a woman.

동료에게 줄 선물을 고를 때 고려하는 한 요소는 성별입니다. 남성이라면 남성에게 어울리는 물건을, 여성이라면 여성에게 어울리는 물건을 고르는 것이 무난합니다.

 take into account 고려하다   gender 성별   masculine 남성적인   feminine 여성적인

Questions 7-9   Respond to Questions Using Information Provided

Directions: In this part of the test, you will answer three questions based on the information provided. You will have 30 seconds to read the information before the questions begin. For each question, begin responding immediately after you hear a beep. No additional preparation time is provided. You will have 15 seconds to respond to Questions 7 and 8 and 30 seconds to respond to Question 9.

이 파트에서 여러분은 주어진 정보에 기초하여 세 가지 질문에 대답하게 됩니다. 문제가 시작하기 전에 30초 동안 정보를 읽게 됩니다. 각 질문에 대해 '삐' 소리가 나면 즉시 대답하세요. 준비 시간은 주어지지 않습니다. 7번과 8번 문제에는 각각 15초, 그리고 9번 문제에는 30초의 응답 시간이 주어집니다.

TOEIC® Speaking

Questions 7-9 of 11

Moonwalker Savings & Loans

Yearly Convention: Friday, May 11
Center of Operations, Philadelphia, Pennsylvania

8:30 A.M.	Welcome Address	Bobby Mack, President
9:00 A.M.	Customer Satisfaction Evaluations	Gordon Light, Market Research
10:30 A.M.	Restructuring of the Loans Division	Tonto Reynolds, Regional Manager
11:45 A.M.	Paris & Hong Kong Branch Openings	Lauren Reed, Branch Officer
12:30 P.M.	Lunch Buffet	
1:30 P.M.	New International Policies	Walter Williams, Legal Division
2:15 P.M.	New Products: Online Investing	Michael Meyers, Information Technology
3:00 P.M.	General Inquiries	All members
4:30 P.M.	Closing Notes	Bobby Mack, President

Hello. I work at Moonwalker Savings and Loans in the Washington, D.C. office, and I'll be going to the yearly convention in Philadelphia next week. I haven't received a schedule, so I hope you can give me some information over the phone.

Moonwalker Savings & Loans	Moonwalker 저축 대부
Yearly Convention: Friday, May 11 *Center of Operations, Philadelphia, Pennsylvania*	*연례 회의: 5월 11일, 금요일* *펜실베니아 주, 필라델피아 시, 운영 센터*

8:30 A.M.	Welcome Address	Bobby Mack, President
9:00 A.M.	Customer Satisfaction Evaluations	Gordon Light, Market Research
10:30 A.M.	Restructuring of the Loans Division	Tonto Reynolds, Regional Manager
11:45 A.M.	Paris & Hong Kong Branch Openings	Lauren Reed, Branch Officer
12:30 P.M.	Lunch Buffet	
1:30 P.M.	New International Policies	Walter Williams, Legal Division
2:15 P.M.	New Products: Online Investing	Michael Meyers, Information Technology
3:00 P.M.	General Inquiries	All members
4:30 P.M.	Closing Notes	Bobby Mack, President

오전 8:30	환영사	Bobby Mack, 사장님
오전 9:00	고객 만족 평가	Gordon Light, 시장 조사팀
오전 10:30	대부 부서 구조조정	Tonto Reynolds, 지역 관리자
오전 11:45	파리 및 홍콩 지점 개장	Lauren Reed, 지점장
오후 12:30	뷔페식 점심 식사	
오후 1:30	신 국제 정책	Walter Williams, 법률 부서
오후 2:15	신제품: 온라인 투자	Michael Meyers, 정보 통신 기술부
오후 3:00	일반 문의	모든 회원
오후 4:30	폐회사	Bobby Mack, 사장님

Hello. I work at Moonwalker Savings and Loans in the Washington, D.C. office, and I'll be going to the yearly convention in Philadelphia next week. I haven't received a schedule, so I hope you can give me some information over the phone.

안녕하세요. 저는 워싱턴 D.C.에 위치한 Moonwalker 저축 대부에서 근무하며 다음 주 필라델피아에서 열리는 연례 회의에 참석하려고 합니다. 제가 일정표를 받지 못해서 그러는데 전화상으로 몇 가지 정보를 말씀해 주시면 좋겠습니다.

 welcome address 환영사　evaluation 평가　restructuring 구조조정　branch 지점　closing note 폐회사　over the phone 전화로

What time does the convention start, and who is speaking?

회의 시작은 언제이고 누가 연설을 합니까?

 **Possible Answer**

The meeting starts at eight-thirty in the morning, and the first speaker is the president, Bobby Mack.

회의는 오전 8시 30분에 시작하고 첫 번째 연설자는 Bobby Mack 사장님이십니다.

I would like to know more about our strategy for expansion outside of the United States. Who will be talking about that?

미국 밖으로 확장을 위한 전략에 대해 조금 더 자세히 알고 싶습니다. 이것에 대해 어느 분께서 이야기합니까?

 **Possible Answer**

The strategy for expansion outside of the United States will be in Paris and Hong Kong. Lauren Reed, the branch officer, will begin her talk at eleven-forty-five that morning.

미국 밖으로 확장을 위한 전략은 파리와 홍콩에서 이루어질 겁니다. Lauren Reed 지점장님께서 오전 11시 45분에 연설을 시작할 겁니다.

 strategy 전략　expansion 확장

I'm afraid I'll have to depart the convention at two o'clock. Can you let me know what I will miss?

아쉽지만 저는 2시에 회의장을 떠나야 합니다. 제가 놓치는 부분이 무엇인지 알려 주시겠습니까?

 **Possible Answer**

You will miss three scheduled events. At two-fifteen, online investing will be discussed by Michael Meyers, from the IT department. Then at three P.M., all members will be given an opportunity to make general inquiries. Finally, closing notes will be given by the president, Bobby Mack.

일정 중 3개의 행사를 놓치게 됩니다. 2시 15분에는 정보 통신 기술부의 Michael Meyers가 온라인 투자에 대해 논의를 할 것입니다. 이어서 3시에는 회의 참석자 모두가 일반적인 질문을 할 수 있는 시간이 마련되어 있습니다. 마지막으로는 Bobby Mack 사장님께서 폐회사를 하십니다.

 depart 출발하다　miss 놓치다　give the opportunity 기회를 주다

Question 10   Propose a Solution

Directions: In this part of the test, you will be presented with a problem and asked to propose a solution. You will have 30 seconds to prepare. Then you will have 60 seconds to speak.

이 파트에서 여러분에게 한 가지 문제가 주어집니다. 여러분은 그에 대한 해결책을 제시해주세요. 30초 동안 준비한 뒤 60초 동안 응답하세요.

In your response, be sure to
- show that you recognize the problem, and
- propose a way of dealing with the problem.

여러분의 응답에서
- 여러분이 문제를 인식했다는 것을 보여주세요.
- 그 문제를 대처하는 방법을 제안해주세요.

 Hi. This is Monica calling from the Tech Support Department. I want to reach the manager at the Advertising Department. We just finished setting up the new color printer on your floor, and it works very well! But learning how to use it is actually not easy. Members of your staff will surely need to be given training on how to operate it. I'd like to train your staff about using the color printer. However, it's hard to find the time when everyone is free, especially in a division as large as yours. As the manager, what arrangement do you think should be made? Please call me back and let me know what you would like to do. Again, it's Monica and my extension is 218.

안녕하세요. 저는 기술 지원 부서의 Monica입니다. 홍보 부서 부장님께 연락을 취하고 싶습니다. 저희가 귀 부서의 층에 새 컬러 프린터를 설치했는데 작동이 잘 됩니다! 그런데 사용법을 익히기가 사실 쉬운 일이 아닙니다. 귀 부서의 사원들은 사용법에 대한 교육을 받을 필요가 있습니다. 저는 컬러 프린터의 사용법을 귀 부서의 사원들에게 가르쳐 드리고 싶습니다. 하지만 모두가 교육 받을 수 있는 여유 시간을 찾기가 힘듭니다. 귀 부서처럼 규모가 큰 부서에서는 특히 그렇습니다. 부장님께서는 어떻게 조치를 취해야 한다고 생각하십니까? 저에게 다시 전화주셔서 어떻게 하고 싶으신지 말씀해 주세요. 저는 Monica이며 내선번호는 218입니다.

 **reach** 연락하다   **set up** 설치하다   **work** 작동하다   **training** 교육   **division** 부서   **arrangement** 조치, 처리 방식

 **Possible Answer**

인사	Hi, Monica. This is Brandon, the manager of the Advertising Department.
문제 상황 인식	First, I would like to thank you and the Tech Department for setting up the new color printer on our floor. However, I have yet to use it because you are right in that it is quite complicated. My staff members and I would appreciate training on how to use the color printer.
해결책 제시	Let's schedule a training session for next Monday, when all employees and myself will be at work. If anyone misses the training session, then I will train him or her personally at another time. I think this would be the best solution since our department is very large.
마무리	Please let me know if Monday works for you. My extension is 611.

안녕하세요, Monica. 홍보 부서 부장인 Brandon입니다. 우선 당신과 기술 지원 부서가 저희 부서의 층에 새 컬러 프린터를 설치해 주셔서 감사드립니다. 하지만 저는 아직 그것을 사용해 보지 못했습니다. 당신의 말씀처럼 매우 복잡하기 때문입니다. 컬러 프린터 사용법의 교육을 해준다니 저와 저희 부서 사원들은 감사를 표합니다. 교육 일정을 저와 사원 모두가 내근하는 다음 주 월요일로 잡아봅시다. 만일 누군가가 교육에 참여하지 못한다면, 제가 개인적으로 시간을 내어 그들에게 가르쳐 주겠습니다. 저희 부서의 규모가 매우 크므로 이것이 최선의 해결책이라고 봅니다. 월요일에 교육이 가능한지 알려 주세요. 제 내선번호는 611입니다.

 **have yet to** 아직 ~하지 않았다 **quite complicated** 상당히 복잡한 **appreciate** 고마워하다 **miss** 놓치다 **personally** 직접, 개인적으로 **at another time** 다른 시간에 **solution** 해결(책)

Question 11 Express an Opinion

Directions: In this part of the test, you will give your opinion about a specific topic. Be sure to say as much as you can in the time allowed. You will have 15 seconds to prepare. Then you will have 60 seconds to speak.

이 파트에서 여러분은 특정한 주제에 대한 의견을 말하게 됩니다. 주어진 시간 동안 최대한 많이 말할 수 있도록 하세요. 15초 동안 준비한 뒤 60초 동안 응답하세요.

Do you agree or disagree with the following statement?

Eating home-cooked meals is the best way to maintain a healthy diet.

Give reasons and examples to support your answer.

여러분은 다음 진술에 동의하시나요, 동의하지 않으시나요?

집에서 요리한 음식을 먹는 것이 건강한 식생활을 유지하는 최선의 길입니다.

여러분의 의견을 뒷받침하는 이유와 예시를 들어주십시오.

 **Possible Answer 1 (agree)**

의견 제시	I absolutely agree with the statement that eating home-cooked meals is the best way to maintain a healthy diet.
근거 제시 1	First, it is likely that a loved one or yourself is preparing the meal. Thus, much care is likely to be put into preparing the meal so that it is nutritious, as well as tasty.
예시	For instance, when I prepare a home-cooked meal, I make sure to buy the freshest produce available. Furthermore, I try to search for healthy meals that are not high in saturated fats, or lacking in vitamins or minerals.
근거 제시 2	Another reason why eating home-cooked meals is the best way to maintain a healthy diet is that the meals available outside are usually high in calories.
예시	For example, a lot of fast food restaurants rely on the cooking method of deep frying as a way to provide quick, inexpensive food.
마무리	Thus, a home-cooked meal is the best option.

저는 집에서 요리한 음식을 먹는 것이 건강한 식생활을 유지하는 최선의 길이라는 진술에 절대적으로 동의합니다. 우선, 음식을 준비하는 사람이 바로 당신 자신이거나 사랑하는 사람일 것입니다. 따라서 음식을 준비할 때 더 정성을 다할 것이므로 영양이 풍부하고 맛이 있습니다. 예를 들어, 저는 집에서 음식을 요리할 때, 가급적 신선한 재료를 사려고 합니다. 나아가, 포

화 지방 함량이 낮고, 비타민이나 미네랄 함량이 높은 건강식을 찾으려고 합니다. 집에서 요리한 음식을 먹는 것이 건강한 식생활을 유지하는 최선의 길인 또 다른 이유는 바깥 음식은 대체로 칼로리가 높다는 것입니다. 예를 들어, 패스트푸드점 대부분은 빠르고 저렴한 음식을 내놓고자 기름을 듬뿍 넣어 튀기는 요리법에 의존합니다. 그러므로 집에서 요리한 음식이 최선의 선택입니다.

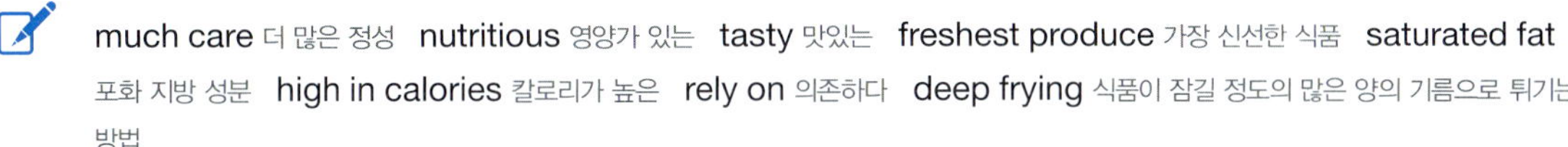

much care 더 많은 정성　**nutritious** 영양가 있는　**tasty** 맛있는　**freshest produce** 가장 신선한 식품　**saturated fat** 포화 지방 성분　**high in calories** 칼로리가 높은　**rely on** 의존하다　**deep frying** 식품이 잠길 정도의 많은 양의 기름으로 튀기는 방법

Possible Answer 2 (disagree)

의견 제시　I disagree with the statement that eating home-cooked meals is the best way to maintain a healthy diet.

근거 제시 1　First of all, organic food restaurant chains are located in many convenient areas. These restaurants provide healthy food cooked with fresh produce that is low in saturated fat but high in vitamins and minerals. Moreover, these restaurants are known to cook by not adding any chemical seasonings. People can simply walk in there and get a variety of healthy food.

근거 제시 2　Another reason is that due to their busy life style, a majority of people don't cook these days. As a result, they don't know how to cook. For that matter, relying on home-cooked meals as a way of maintaining a healthy diet for oneself would be risky.

근거 제시 3　Plus, people don't have enough time to do grocery shopping and cook. If they have to rely on home-cooked meals, they might get malnutrition.

마무리　However, if they eat heathy meals from organic food restaurants, for sure they will get to consume healthy food and be able to maintain a healthy diet.

서는 집에서 요리한 음식을 먹는 것이 건강한 식생활을 유지하는 최선의 길이라는 진술에 동의하지 않습니다. 우선, 여러 편리한 장소에 유기농 음식을 다루는 레스토랑 체인이 있습니다. 이런 음식점은 포화 지방이 낮고 비타민과 미네랄 함량이 높은 신선한 농산물로 요리한 건강식을 제공합니다. 또한 이런 음식점은 화학조미료를 넣지 않은 것으로 알려져 있습니다. 사람들은 이러한 음식점에 가서 건강에 좋은 음식을 사서 먹기만 하면 됩니다. 다른 이유는 바쁘게 돌아가는 삶 때문에 요리를 하지 않습니다. 그 결과 어떻게 음식을 요리하는지 모릅니다. 그렇기 때문에 음식을 요리해서 건강한 식생활을 한다는 것은 아마도 큰 위험이 따를지도 모릅니다. 그리고 건강식을 만드는 것을 비롯하여 신선하고 영양가 있는 재료를 살 시간이 없습니다. 그럼에도 집에서 요리한 음식에 의존한다면 영양실조에 걸릴 수도 있습니다. 그러니 만약 사람들이 유기농 음식을 다루는 레스토랑에서 식사를 한다면 틀림없이 건강한 식생활로 그들의 건강을 유지할 수 있을 것입니다.

minerals 무기질　**chemical seasoning** 화학조미료　**a variety of** 다양한　**a majority of** 대다수의　**risky** 위험한, 모험적인　**grocery shopping** 장보기　**rely on** 의지하다　**malnutrition** 영양실조　**for sure** 확실히, 틀림없이

Questions 1-2 Read a Text Aloud

Directions: In this part of the test, you will read aloud the text on the screen. You will have 45 seconds to prepare. Then you will have 45 seconds to read the text aloud.

이 파트에서 여러분은 스크린의 텍스트를 큰 소리로 읽게 됩니다. 45초의 준비 시간이 주어지고, 그 후 45초 동안 텍스트를 큰 소리로 읽으세요.

TOEIC® Speaking

Question 1 of 11

Thank you for joining us on Fashion Forward. Today, our guest is Giovanni Carlo who is the owner of Milan Mode. He'll tell us about the latest styles in suits, ties, and dress shoes. After that, one of the lucky audience members will get a free style over. You will want to stay tuned!

Fashion Forward 행사에 참석해 주셔서 감사합니다. 금일 저희 초대연사는 Milan Mode의 소유주이신 Giovanni Carlo입니다. Carlo 씨는 정장, 넥타이, 정장 구두의 최신 스타일에 대해서 말씀하실 것입니다. 이후에 운 좋은 관객 중 한 명의 스타일을 무료로 변신시켜드릴 것입니다. 채널을 고정하세요.

 **Speaking Solution**

Thank you for **joining** us on **Fashion Forward**(고유명사 강세). ↘(문장의 맨 끝) **Today**(시간/날짜/숫자 강세), our **guest** is **Giovanni Carlo**(고유명사 강세) /(절 앞에 짧게 끊고) who is the **owner** of **Milan Mode**(고유명사 강세). ↘(문장의 맨 끝) He'll **tell** us about the **latest styles**(최상급 강세) in **suits**↗, **ties**↗, and **dress shoes**↘ (A↗, B↗ and C↘). After that, **one** of the lucky **audience** members(중요 의미 강세) will get a **free style over**(중요 의미 강세). You will want to **stay tuned!**

 suit 정장   dress shoes 정장 구두   stay tuned 채널을 고정하다

Your attention please, Toronto Transit commuters. Because of a major construction project, the Bathurst Subway Station will be closed during the months of September, October, and November. During these months, there will be a temporary shuttle-bus service available for commuters who wish to go to Bathurst Street. We apologize for the inconvenience.

토론토 철도 이용 승객님 주목해 주시기 바랍니다. 대규모 공사 때문에 Bathurst 지하철역이 9월, 10월, 11월 동안 폐쇄될 것입니다. 이 기간 동안 Bathurst 거리로 가시려는 승객을 위해 근거리 왕복 버스를 임시로 운행할 것입니다. 불편을 드려서 대단히 죄송합니다.

Speaking Solution

Your **attention**(주목! 강세) **please**, **Toronto Transit commuters**(고유명사 강세). ↘(문장의 맨 끝) **Because of a major construction project**(중요 의미 강세), ↗(계속 의미/쉼표 뒤 짧게 끊고) the **Bathurst Subway Station**(고유명사 강세) will be **closed**(중요 의미 강세) / (전명구 앞에 잠시 쉬고) during the months of **September**↗, **October**↗, and **November**↘(A↗, B↗ and C↘). ↘(문장의 맨 끝) During these months, ↗(계속 의미/쉼표 뒤 짧게 끊고) there will be a **temporary shuttle-bus service**(중요 의미 강세) available for **commuters**(중요 의미 강세) / (절 앞에 잠시 쉬고) who wish to go to **Bathurst Street**(고유명사 강세). We **apologize** for the **inconvenience**. ↘(문장의 맨 끝)

major construction project 대규모 공사 작업   temporary 임시의   commuter 통근자   apologize for ~에 대해 사과하다

Question 3   Describe a Picture

Directions: In this part of the test, you will describe the picture on your screen in as much detail as you can. You will have 30 seconds to prepare your response. Then you will have 45 seconds to speak about the picture.

이 파트에서 여러분은 스크린의 사진을 최대한 자세히 설명하게 됩니다. 대답을 위해 30초의 준비 시간이 주어지고, 그 후 45초 동안 사진에 대해 설명하세요.

💬 Possible Answer

There are four people in this picture. In the forefront, there are two women. The blonde-haired woman on the left is wearing a white button-up shirt and a black jacket on top. The woman with a black ponytail is wearing a green-colored shirt underneath a brown check-pattern jacket. Both are holding some papers in their hands and looking at them. They seem very pleased. In the background, there are two men wearing nice shirts and ties. Both men are also looking at some papers. I think this picture was taken in an office.

사진 속에는 네 사람이 있습니다. 앞쪽에는 두 여성이 있습니다. 사진 왼쪽에 있는 여성은 금발 머리에 흰 셔츠를 그리고 그 위에 검정색 재킷을 입고 있습니다. 검은색 머리를 길게 묶은 여성이 초록색의 셔츠와 체크 무늬로 된 갈색 재킷을 입고 있습니다. 두 여성 모두 종이를 손에 들고 그것을 보고 있습니다. 그들은 만족스러워 하는 듯 보입니다. 사진 뒤쪽으로는 두 남성이 셔츠와 넥타이를 착용하고 있습니다. 마찬가지로, 두 남성 모두 종이를 보고 있습니다. 제가 볼 때 이 사진은 사무실에서 찍힌 것 같습니다.

 in the forefront 앞쪽에   in the background 뒤쪽에   suit 정장   hold 쥐다   underneath ~의 아래에
check- pattern jacket 체크무늬의 재킷   pleased 기뻐하는, 만족하는

Questions 4-6 Respond to Questions

Directions: In this part of the test, you will answer three questions. For each question, begin responding immediately after you hear a beep. No preparation time is provided. You will have 15 seconds to respond to Questions 4 and 5 and 30 seconds to respond to Question 6.

이 파트에서 여러분은 세 가지 질문에 답하게 됩니다. 각 질문에 대해 '삐' 소리가 나면 즉시 대답하세요. 준비 시간은 주어지지 않습니다. 4번과 5번 문제에는 각각 15초, 그리고 6번 문제에는 30초의 응답 시간이 주어집니다.

Imagine that an Australian marketing firm is doing research in your country. You have agreed to participate in a telephone interview about alarm clocks.

어느 호주 마케팅 회사가 여러분의 나라에서 조사를 하고 있다고 가정해봅시다. 여러분은 알람시계에 관한 전화 인터뷰 참여를 승낙했습니다.

When was the last time you bought an alarm clock, and where did you buy it?

마지막으로 알람시계를 구입한 게 언제이고 어디서 구입했습니까?

 **Possible Answer**

The last time I bought an alarm clock was about seven years ago. I bought it at a dollar shop in the strip mall that is near my home.

마지막으로 알람시계를 구입한 것은 약 7년 전이었습니다. 저희 집 근처의 스트립 몰 내에 있는 달러 숍에서 구입했습니다.

 **a dollar shop** 1달러로 물건을 살 수 있는 가게   **strip mall** 번화가에 상점과 식당들이 일렬로 늘어서 있는 곳

When do you usually use the alarm clock?

보통 언제 알람시계를 사용합니까?

 **Possible Answer**

I usually use my alarm clock when I have to wake up early. For example, I would use it if I have to go to work early in the morning.

저는 보통 일찍 일어나야 할 때 알람시계를 사용합니다. 예를 들어, 아침 일찍 일하러 나가야 한다면 알람시계를 사용할 겁니다.

 **go to work** 출근하다

What are the most important features that you look for in an alarm clock, and why?

알람시계 선택 시 최우선으로 고려하는 점은 무엇이며 그 이유는 무엇인가요?

 **Possible Answer**

The most important feature that I look for in an alarm clock is that it provides accurate time because I do not want to be late for work or a meeting. Another feature that is important is the sound when the alarm goes off. It shouldn't be too loud or annoying, or so soft that I won't wake up.

알람시계 선택 시 최우선으로 고려하는 점은 시각의 정확성입니다. 직장이나 회의에 늦고 싶지 않으니까요. 또 중요하게 고려하는 점은 알람 소리입니다. 너무 요란하거나 거슬리는 소리는 안 되며, 깨우지 못할 정도로 너무 작은 소리도 안 됩니다.

 **feature** 특징, 기능 **go off** (알람 등이) 울리다 **loud** 시끄러운 **annoying** 성가신, 괴롭히는

Questions 7-9 Respond to Questions Using Information Provided

Directions: In this part of the test, you will answer three questions based on the information provided. You will have 30 seconds to read the information before the questions begin. For each question, begin responding immediately after you hear a beep. No additional preparation time is provided. You will have 15 seconds to respond to Questions 7 and 8 and 30 seconds to respond to Question 9.

이 파트에서 여러분은 주어진 정보에 기초하여 세 가지 질문에 대답하게 됩니다. 문제가 시작하기 전에 30초 동안 정보를 읽게 됩니다. 각 질문에 대해 '삐' 소리가 나면 즉시 대답하세요. 준비 시간은 주어지지 않습니다. 7번과 8번 문제에는 각각 15초, 그리고 9번 문제에는 30초의 응답 시간이 주어집니다.

TOEIC® Speaking

Questions 7-9 of 11

Maple Recreation Center
Children's Story Book Celebration

Title	Date	Time	Location
Around the World	February 14	10:30 A.M.	Rec. Room 7
Surfer's Paradise	February 28	6:30 P.M.	Rec. Room 8
The Banana Boat	March 4	1:30 P.M.	Rec. Room 7
A Secret Agent	March 12	10:30 A.M.	Rec. Room 8
Barbarella's Ball	April 6	3:00 P.M.	Rec. Room 7
Samurai Versus Santa	April 21	9:30 A.M.	Rec. Room 8
One Thousand Pianos	May 7	6:30 P.M.	Rec. Room 7

Hi. My name is Ken Muira. A coworker told me the recreation center reads children's story books, and I'd like to get some more information.

Maple Recreation Center
Children's Story Book Celebration

Title	Date	Time	Location
Around the World	February 14	10:30 A.M.	Rec. Room 7
Surfer's Paradise	February 28	6:30 P.M.	Rec. Room 8
The Banana Boat	March 4	1:30 P.M.	Rec. Room 7
A Secret Agent	March 12	10:30 A.M.	Rec. Room 8
Barbarella's Ball	April 6	3:00 P.M.	Rec. Room 7
Samurai Versus Santa	April 21	9:30 A.M.	Rec. Room 8
One Thousand Pianos	May 7	6:30 P.M.	Rec. Room 7

Maple 레크리에이션 센터
어린이 동화책 축하회

제목	날짜	시간	장소
세계 일주	2월 14일	오전 10:30	레크리에이션 룸 7
서퍼의 파라다이스	2월 28일	오후 6:30	레크리에이션 룸 8
바나나 보트	3월 4일	오후 1:30	레크리에이션 룸 7
비밀 요원	3월 12일	오전 10:30	레크리에이션 룸 8
바브렐라의 공	4월 6일	오후 3:00	레크리에이션 룸 7
사무라이 대 산타	4월 21일	오전 9:30	레크리에이션 룸 8
천 대의 피아노	5월 7일	오후 6:30	레크리에이션 룸 7

Hi. My name is Ken Muira. A coworker told me the recreation center reads children's story books, and I'd like to get some more information.

안녕하세요. 저는 Ken Muira입니다. 제 동료에게 들은 바로는 레크리에이션 센터에서 동화책을 낭독해준다고 하더군요. 그래서 더 자세히 알고 싶어 문의 드립니다.

 coworker 직장동료

My coworker was telling me about "The Banana Boat," and I think I'd really like to bring my children to hear it. When and where will that story be told?

제 동료가 "바나나 보트"에 대해서 이야기해 주었습니다. 그리고 전 정말로 제 아이들에게 그것을 들려주고 싶습니다. 언제 어디에서 그 이야기를 낭독해 주시나요?

 **Possible Answer**

"The Banana Boat" will be read on March fourth at one-thirty P.M. It will be read in recreational room number seven.

"바나나 보트"는 3월 4일 오후 1시 30분에 낭독이 있습니다. 레크리에이션 룸 7에서 낭독합니다.

I heard that "One Thousand Pianos" will be read sometime in February. Is that correct?

제가 들은 바로는 "천 대의 피아노"의 낭독이 2월에 있다고 하던데요. 맞나요?

 **Possible Answer**

"One Thousand Pianos" will not be read in February. Instead, it will be read in the month of May.

"천 대의 피아노"는 2월에 낭독이 없습니다. 대신, 5월에 낭독이 있습니다.

I tend to be busy in the afternoons and evenings. Are there any books being read in the morning?

저는 보통 오후와 밤 시간에 바쁩니다. 오전 시간에 낭독하는 책이 있나요?

 **Possible Answer**

Yes, there are three books that will be read in the morning. First, "Around the World" will be read on February fourteenth at ten-thirty. Next, "A Secret Agent" will be read on March twelfth, also at ten-thirty. Finally, "Samurai Versus Santa" will be read on April twenty-first at nine-thirty.

예, 3권의 책이 오전 시간에 낭독이 있습니다. 먼저, "세계 일주"가 2월 14일 10시 30분에 낭독이 있습니다. 다음으로, "비밀 요원"이 3월 12일 10시 30분에 낭독이 있습니다. 마지막으로, "사무라이 대 산타"가 4월 21일 9시 30분에 낭독이 있습니다.

Question 10   Propose a Solution

Directions: In this part of the test, you will be presented with a problem and asked to propose a solution. You will have 30 seconds to prepare. Then you will have 60 seconds to speak.

이 파트에서 여러분에게 한 가지 문제가 주어집니다. 여러분은 그에 대한 해결책을 제시해주세요. 30초 동안 준비한 뒤 60초 동안 응답하세요.

In your response, be sure to   여러분의 응답에서
- show that you recognize the problem, and   • 여러분이 문제를 인식했다는 것을 보여주세요.
- propose a way of dealing with the problem.   • 그 문제를 대처하는 방법을 제안해주세요.

 Hi. This is Whitney Tennis. Thanks for volunteering to help me out with the new recycling proposal here at the university. I am really thrilled that the various departments decided that they will be recycling paper, metals, and glass. As the planners of this new proposal, you and I ought to discuss the changes that need to be made around campus. How do you think we should tell the department heads about the new requirements, and how can we convince everyone to follow the new regulations? Please give me a call back when you get a chance and let me know your ideas for how we should handle this. Again, it's Whitney Tennis and you can reach me at extension 519.

안녕하세요. Whitney Tennis입니다. 이 곳 대학의 새로운 재활용 제안에 대해 저를 도와 자원 봉사해 주셔서 감사드립니다. 여러 부서에서 종이, 금속, 유리를 재활용한다는 결정을 내렸다니 정말 기쁩니다. 이 새로운 제안의 계획자로서 귀하와 제가 캠퍼스에 필요한 변화에 대해 논의하는 것이 좋을 듯합니다. 저희가 부서 책임자에게 새로운 요구 사항을 이야기하는 것을 귀하는 어떻게 생각하나요? 그리고 어떻게 하면 저희가 새로운 규정을 따르도록 사람들을 설득할 수 있다고 생각하나요? 시간이 있을 때 전화 부탁드립니다. 그리고 이 문제를 풀 방법에 대한 귀하의 아이디어를 알려 주세요. 저는 Whitney Tennis이며, 내선번호 519로 연락하시면 됩니다.

 volunteer 자원하다, 자원 봉사로 하다   recycling proposal 재활용 제안   thrilled 흥미진진하게 된, 흥분된   department head 부서장   requirement 요구 사항   regulation 규제   handle 다루다, 처리하다   extension 내선번호

Possible Answer

Hi, Whitney.

문제 상황 인식
I'm enthusiastic about helping you organize the new recycling proposal at the university. We should definitely try to set aside some time to talk about the changes.

해결책 제시
As for my ideas on how to handle this, I think we should type a memo explaining the new changes and regulations, and deliver it to all department heads. In addition, we could encourage everyone to start recycling by offering a small incentive if they come by the various recycling stations. The small incentive could be a small prize or food reward. I was thinking of offering either a canned drink, such as a can of coffee, or a bottled drink or juice. We can then remind them to recycle the container of their drink. This action will reinforce the desired recycling behaviors, and people will become familiar with the recycling locations across campus. Let me know what you think of this suggestion.

마무리
You can reach me at extension 416.

안녕하세요. Whitney. 대학의 새로운 재활용 제안을 체계화하는 것을 도울 수 있어서 기쁩니다. 변화에 대해 논의할 시간은 따로 정하도록 합시다. 이 문제를 풀 방법에 대한 제 생각을 말씀드리면, 새로운 변화와 규정을 설명하는 통신문을 작성해서 모든 부서장에게 배포해야 한다고 생각합니다. 더불어, 사람들이 다양한 재활용 활동에 참여한다면 조그마한 보상을 제공함으로써 그들이 재활용을 시작하도록 고무시킬 수 있습니다. 조그마한 보상은 작은 상이나 음식입니다. 저는 캔 커피나 병 음료 혹은 주스를 제공하는 것을 생각하고 있었습니다. 그런 다음 저희는 그들에게 다 마신 음료 용기를 재활용하도록 상기시킬 수 있습니다. 이 행동은 바람직한 재활용 활동을 증대시킬 것이며 사람들은 학교 곳곳에 있는 재활용 위치에 익숙해질 것입니다. 제 아이디어가 어떤가요? 제 내선번호 416으로 연락 가능합니다.

enthusiastic 열심인, 열광적인 **organize** 체계화하다, 구성하다 **definitely** 확실히, 틀림없이 **set aside** 확보하다 **explain** 설명하다 **regulation** 규정 **in addition** 추가적으로 **incentive** 장려금 **prize** 상품 **remind** ~을 상기 시켜주다 **reinforce** 강화하다, 보강시키다 **behavior** 행동 **become familiar with** ~와 친숙해지나, 익숙해시나

Question 11 · Express an Opinion

Directions: In this part of the test, you will give your opinion about a specific topic. Be sure to say as much as you can in the time allowed. You will have 15 seconds to prepare. Then you will have 60 seconds to speak.

이 파트에서 여러분은 특정한 주제에 대한 의견을 말하게 됩니다. 주어진 시간 동안 최대한 많이 말할 수 있도록 하세요. 15초 동안 준비한 뒤 60초 동안 응답하세요.

Some people prefer to do all of their shopping at one large store. Others prefer to go to several smaller specialty stores.

Which do you think is better?

Give specific reasons or examples to support your opinion.

어떤 사람들은 모든 쇼핑을 하나의 커다란 상점에서 하는 것을 선호합니다. 어떤 사람들은 여러 작은 전문 상점으로 찾아가는 것을 선호합니다.

여러분은 어떤 것이 낫다고 생각하시나요?

여러분의 의견을 뒷받침하는 이유와 예시를 들어주십시오.

 **Possible Answer 1 (shopping at one large store)**

의견 제시 I think that doing all the shopping at one large store is better.

근거 제시 This is because you can get all the necessary items in a single place, which allows you to save a lot of time, money, and energy.

예시 For example, when I go shopping, I prefer to go to a mart or a department store. In these stores, I can find all the necessary items from food, clothes, shoes, utensils, and even entertainment products. By not driving from one store to another, which can be a really time-consuming process due to traffic congestion in most cities these days, I can save a lot of time and energy as well. It also helps me save money on gas while I don't have to drive all over the city to shop at different stores.

마무리 As a result, it is better to shop at one large store.

저는 하나의 커다란 상점에서 모든 쇼핑을 하는 것이 더 좋다고 생각합니다. 우리가 필요로 하는 모든 물건을 한 곳에서 구할 수 있고 이는 많은 시간, 돈, 에너지를 아낄 수 있습니다. 예를 들어, 쇼핑을 갈 때 저는 마트나 백화점에 가는 것을 선호합니다. 이러한 상점에서는 음식, 의복, 신발, 용구 등에서 나아가 오락에 이르기까지 필요한 모든 물건을 구할 수 있습니다. 요즘 어디에서나 겪을 수 있는 교통체증에 막혀버리면 시간을 많이 소비하기에 다른 상점으로 이동하지 않음으로써 많은 시간과 에너지를 절약할 수 있습니다. 물건을 사기 위해 이곳저곳을 가지 않는다면 유류비 또한 아낄 수 있습니다. 그 결과, 하나의 커다란 상점에서 모든 쇼핑을 하는 것이 낫다고 생각합니다.

 **in a single place** 한 곳에서 **save** 아끼다 **department store** 백화점 **utensils** 주방도구 **entertainment** 오락
by doing so 그렇게 함으로써 **traffic congestion** 교통 체증 **as a result** 그 결과

 Possible Answer 2 (shopping at several specialty stores)

의견 제시	I think that shopping at several specialty stores is better.
근거 제시	This is because in a specialty store, you get the best quality and a variety of items that you are looking for. Also, if you are aware of certain brands, you would always prefer to go to the specialty stores.
예시	For example, one time I wanted to buy a pair of Adidas sneakers, so I went to a large mart. But I was disappointed as the store did not have that specific model that I was looking for. So I decided to go to an Adidas showroom instead, and there to my surprise, I found the model as well as many other newly launched products. I also got some discounts on the sneakers due to some of the special offers in that store.
마무리	For these reasons, I think shopping at several specialty stores is better than shopping at one large store.

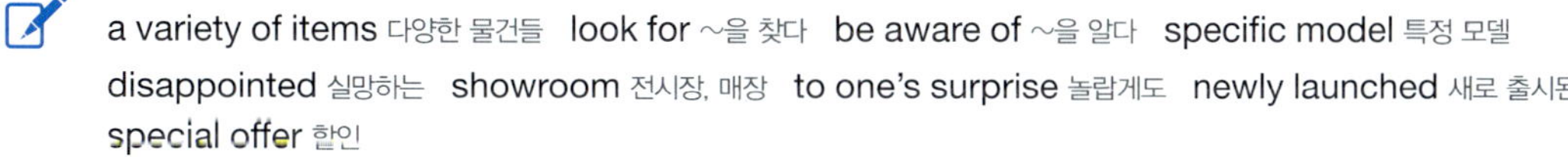

저는 여러 전문 상점에서 쇼핑을 하는 것이 더 좋다고 생각합니다. 전문 상점에서는 최고의 품질과 다양한 상품을 구할 수 있기 때문입니다. 또한 브랜드를 안다면 늘 전문 상점에 가는 것을 선호할 것입니다. 예를 들어, 저는 아디다스 스니커즈를 구매하고 싶어 대형 상점에 갔습니다. 그러나 그 곳에는 이 특정 모델이 없었기에 전 실망했습니다. 그래서 전 아디다스 매장으로 가기로 결정했습니다. 그리고 놀랍게도 전 찾고 있는 모델뿐만 아니라 새로 출시된 모델들을 발견했습니다. 또한 전문 상점의 특별 판매 행사 덕분에 스니커즈를 어느 정도 할인 받았습니다. 이러한 이유 때문에 전 하나의 커다란 상점보다는 여러 전문 상점에서 쇼핑하는 것이 낫다고 생각합니다.

a variety of items 다양한 물건들 **look for** ~을 찾다 **be aware of** ~을 알다 **specific model** 특정 모델
disappointed 실망하는 **showroom** 전시장, 매장 **to one's surprise** 놀랍게도 **newly launched** 새로 출시된
special offer 할인

Questions 1-2 Read a Text Aloud

Directions: In this part of the test, you will read aloud the text on the screen. You will have 45 seconds to prepare. Then you will have 45 seconds to read the text aloud.

이 파트에서 여러분은 스크린의 텍스트를 큰 소리로 읽게 됩니다. 45초의 준비 시간이 주어지고, 그 후 45초 동안 텍스트를 큰 소리로 읽으세요.

TOEIC® Speaking

Question 1 of 11

Thank you for selecting the new Traveling Global Positioning System from Kent Technologies. Once you've charged and installed the battery, getting started is very simple. First, input the address of your destination. Then merely follow the step-by-step directions to get you there. You can also use the "search" menu to locate rest stops, restaurants, and tourist attractions along the way.

Kent Technologies의 새로운 위성 위치 확인 시스템(GPS)을 선택해 주셔서 감사합니다. 배터리를 충전하고 장착하고 나면 시작은 아주 쉽습니다. 먼저, 여러분의 목적지 주소를 입력하세요. 그런 다음 단계별 지침을 따라 하면 그곳에 다다르게 됩니다. 또한 가는 길에 있는 휴게소, 레스토랑, 관광 명소를 찾아내는 "검색" 메뉴를 사용할 수 있습니다.

 **Speaking Solution**

Thank you for **selecting** the **new Traveling Global Positioning System**(고유명사 강세) / from **Kent Technologies**(고유명사 강세). ＼(문장의 맨 끝) Once you've **charged and installed**(중요 의미 강세) the **battery**, ／(계속 의미/쉼표 뒤 짧게 끊고) getting **started** is very simple. **First**(시간/날짜/숫자 강세), **input**(명령문 동사 강조) the **address** of your **destination.** Then merely **follow**(명령문 동사 강조) the **step-by-step directions**(중요 의미 강세) to get you there. You can also use the **"search"**(중요 의미 강세) menu to locate **rest stops**／, **restaurants**／, and **tourist attractions**＼ (A／, B／ and C＼) along the way.＼(문장의 맨 끝)

 select 선택하다　Global Positioning System(=GPS) 위성 위치 확인 시스템　charge 충전하다　input 입력하다
merely 단지　follow 따라가다　rest stop 휴게소

This is Ernie's Diner. Today, our visitor is Ray Kwon, the chef from Macao. His new cookbook is full of organic recipes that add variety to your meals. It will help you cook food that is healthy, easy to prepare, and most important, delectable. Now, let's welcome Ray to the program.

Ernie's Dine입니다. 오늘 저희 손님은 마카오 출신 요리사이신 Ray Kwon입니다. 그의 새 요리책은 귀하의 식사에 다양성을 추가할 유기농 요리법으로 가득합니다. 건강에 좋고 쉽게 준비하며 가장 중요한 요소인 맛있는 음식을 요리하는 데 도움을 줄 것입니다. 프로그램에 오신 Ray 씨를 환영합니다.

 **Speaking Solution**

This is **Ernie's Diner**(고유명사 강세). **Today**, our visitor is **Ray Kwon**(고유명사 강세), ↗(계속 의미/쉼표 뒤 짧게 끊고) the **chef** from **Macao**(고유명사 강세). His **new cookbook**(중요 의미 강세) is full of **organic recipes** (중요 의미 강세) / (절 앞에 잠시 쉬고) that add **variety to your meals**. It will help you **cook** food / (절 앞에 잠시 쉬고) that is **healthy**↗, **easy to prepare**↗, and **most important**, **delectable**. ↘(A↗, B↗ and C↘) Now, let's **welcome Ray** to the program.↘(문장의 맨 끝)

 chef 요리사   recipe 조리법   variety of 다양한   delectable 아주 맛있는, 매력 있는

Question 3 Describe a Picture

Directions: In this part of the test, you will describe the picture on your screen in as much detail as you can. You will have 30 seconds to prepare your response. Then you will have 45 seconds to speak about the picture.

이 파트에서 여러분은 스크린의 사진을 최대한 자세히 설명하게 됩니다. 대답을 위해 30초의 준비 시간이 주어지고, 그 후 45초 동안 사진에 대해 설명하세요.

 **Possible Answer**

This picture seems to be taken at an art gallery. There are framed black and white pictures on the white walls. There are five people visible in this picture. All of the people are looking at the pictures on the walls. One man on the left is closest to the forefront of the picture. He is wearing a dark suit with his hands in his pockets and facing left looking at a picture. On the right side of the picture, there are four men. One man is wearing a light beige jacket and has his arms crossed. This gallery has wooden floors, and there are bright lights hanging above.

이 사진은 화랑에서 촬영된 장면으로 보입니다. 흰 벽에 검고 하얀 액자에 끼워진 그림들이 걸려 있습니다. 이 사진 속에는 다섯 사람이 보입니다. 모두들 벽에 걸린 그림들을 보고 있습니다. 좌측의 한 남성이 사진의 구도에서 가장 두드러져 보이는 위치에 있습니다. 그는 그림을 보면서 좌측을 향하여 있으며, 주머니에 손을 넣은 채 어두운 색상의 정장 차림입니다. 사진 우측에는 네 남성이 있습니다. 한 사람은 팔짱을 낀 채 밝은 베이지 색상의 재킷 차림입니다. 이 화랑의 바닥에는 나무 재질이 깔려 있고 천장에는 밝은 전등들이 있습니다.

 **art gallery** 미술관, 화랑 **visible** 눈에 보이는 **forefront** 최전방에 **suit** 정장 **arms crossed** 팔짱을 끼고 있는 **wooden floor** 목재 바닥

Questions 4-6 Respond to Questions

Directions: In this part of the test, you will answer three questions. For each question, begin responding immediately after you hear a beep. No preparation time is provided. You will have 15 seconds to respond to Questions 4 and 5 and 30 seconds to respond to Question 6.

이 파트에서 여러분은 세 가지 질문에 답하게 됩니다. 각 질문에 대해 '삐' 소리가 나면 즉시 대답하세요. 준비 시간은 주어지지 않습니다. 4번과 5번 문제에는 각각 15초, 그리고 6번 문제에는 30초의 응답 시간이 주어집니다.

Imagine that an American marketing firm is doing research in your country. You have agreed to participate in a telephone interview about cellular phones.

어느 미국 마케팅 회사가 여러분의 나라에서 조사를 하고 있다고 가정해 봅시다. 여러분은 휴대전화에 관한 전화 인터뷰 참여를 승낙했습니다.

TOEIC® Speaking

Question 4 of 11

What kind of cellular phone do you use, and where did you get it?

어떤 종류의 휴대전화를 사용하며 어디에서 그것을 구매하셨나요?

 **Possible Answer**

My cell phone is a new smart phone from Samsung. I bought it at an electronics shop in the mall near my apartment.

제 휴대전화는 삼성의 신형 스마트 폰입니다. 제 아파트 근처 몰에 있는 전자제품 매장에서 구매했습니다.

 cellular phone 휴대폰   electronics shop 전자제품 매장

What do you normally use your cellular phone for, and what did you do with your cellular phone most recently?

평소에 무엇을 하는데 휴대전화를 사용하시나요? 그리고 가장 최근에 휴대전화로 무엇을 하셨나요?

 **Possible Answer**

In addition to calling and texting people, I normally use my smart phone to play games and surf the Internet. The last thing I did with my phone was sending an e-mail to my mother.

통화와 문자 메시지 발송 외에도 전 보통 게임을 하고 인터넷을 하려고 스마트 폰을 사용합니다. 최근에 스마트 폰으로 어머니에게 이메일을 보냈습니다.

 normally 평소에   text 문자를 보내다   surf the Internet 인터넷을 하다

What is the most important feature you consider when buying a cellular phone?

휴대전화 구매 시 가장 중요하게 고려하는 기능은 무엇인가요?

 **Possible Answer**

The most important feature I consider when buying a cell phone is its memory capacity. I download a lot of things, such as music, television shows, movies, and applications. My cell phone is very versatile so I need a lot of space so I can do many different things on it. So if there is a lot of space, I can just keep downloading stuff without worry.

휴대전화 구매 시 제가 가장 중요하게 고려하는 점은 메모리 용량입니다. 전 음악, 텔레비전 영상, 영화, 응용 프로그램 등 많은 것을 다운로드합니다. 제 휴대전화는 용도가 다양해서 여러 가지를 하려면 많은 메모리 공간을 필요로 합니다. 그러므로 많은 공간이 있다면 걱정 없이 자료를 계속 다운받을 수 있습니다.

 feature 기능   memory capacity 메모리 용량   download 자료를 받다   application 응용 프로그램   versatile 다용도의
space 공간   stuff 자료

Questions 7-9 Respond to Questions Using Information Provided

Directions: In this part of the test, you will answer three questions based on the information provided. You will have 30 seconds to read the information before the questions begin. For each question, begin responding immediately after you hear a beep. No additional preparation time is provided. You will have 15 seconds to respond to Questions 7 and 8 and 30 seconds to respond to Question 9.

이 파트에서 여러분은 주어진 정보에 기초하여 세 가지 질문에 대답하게 됩니다. 문제가 시작하기 전에 30초 동안 정보를 읽게 됩니다. 각 질문에 대해 '삐' 소리가 나면 즉시 대답하세요. 준비 시간은 주어지지 않습니다. 7번과 8번 문제에는 각각 15초, 그리고 9번 문제에는 30초의 응답 시간이 주어집니다.

TOEIC Speaking

Questions 7-9 of 11

The Catsup Chalet
Lakeridge, North York, Ontario
555-3321

Availability: June 1-7

X: reserved

	Rate	June 1	June 2	June 3	June 4	June 5	June 6	June 7
Basil (2 rooms)	$95	X			X	X	X	X
Moonrise (2 rooms)	$109		X			X	X	X
Tulip (3 rooms)	$159			X		X	X	
Oak (4 rooms)	$179			X		X	X	

Hi. This is Jim Norlen. I am going on a vacation with my family the first week of June. So I'd like to get some information.

The Catsup Chalet
Lakeridge, North York, Ontario
555-3321

Availability: June 1-7   X: reserved

	Rate	June 1	June 2	June 3	June 4	June 5	June 6	June 7
Basil (2 rooms)	$95	X			X	X	X	X
Moonrise (2 rooms)	$109		X			X	X	X
Tulip (3 rooms)	$159			X		X	X	
Oak (4 rooms)	$179			X		X	X	

The Catsup Chalet
온타리오 주, 노스요크 시, 레이크리지
555-3321

이용 날짜: 6월 1일–7일   X: 예약됨

	요금	6월 1일	6월 2일	6월 3일	6월 4일	6월 5일	6월 6일	6월 7일
바질 (2 객실)	$95	X			X	X	X	X
문라이즈 (2 객실)	$109		X			X	X	X
튤립 (3 객실)	$159			X		X	X	
오크 (4 객실)	$179			X		X	X	

Hi. This is Jim Norlen. I am going on a vacation with my family the first week of June. So I'd like to get some information.

안녕하세요, 저는 Jim Norlen이라고 합니다. 저는 6월 첫째 주에 제 가족과 함께 휴가를 가려고 합니다. 그래서 문의를 드립니다.

Where are you located?

어디에 위치해 있습니까?

 **Possible Answer**

The Catsup Chalet is located in Lakeridge, North York, Ontario.

The Catsup Chalet는 온타리오 주 노스요크 시 레이크리지에 있습니다.

I want to rent a room. Can I rent your cottage by the week?

객실 하나를 빌리고 싶습니다. 일주일간 객실(코티지)을 빌릴 수 있을까요?

 **Possible Answer**

Yes, our cottages are available to be rented by the week. Unfortunately, none of our cottages are currently available for a full-week rental because some are already reserved on certain days.

네, 저희 객실은 일주일간 예약이 가능합니다만, 안타깝게도 현재 일주일간 대여가 가능한 객실은 남아 있지 않습니다. 객실 일부가 특정 일자에 이미 예약이 되었기 때문에 그렇습니다.

 cottage 객실　by the week 일주일 단위로　currently available 현재 구할 수 있는　reserved 예약된

I have a final question. Could you tell me about renting on the 6th?

마지막으로 문의가 있습니다. 6일에는 가능한지 말씀해 주시겠습니까?

 **Possible Answer**

I am afraid to inform you that the rooms on the 6th are all reserved, so it's not possible to rent any room on that day.

죄송하지만 6일은 방이 모두 예약된 상태여서 그날 방을 빌리는 것은 불가능할 것 같습니다.

Question 10   Propose a Solution

Directions: In this part of the test, you will be presented with a problem and asked to propose a solution. You will have 30 seconds to prepare. Then you will have 60 seconds to speak.

이 파트에서 여러분에게 한 가지 문제가 주어집니다. 여러분은 그에 대한 해결책을 제시해주세요. 30초 동안 준비한 뒤 60초 동안 응답하세요.

In your response, be sure to
- show that you recognize the problem, and
- propose a way of dealing with the problem.

여러분의 응답에서
- 여러분이 문제를 인식했다는 것을 보여주세요.
- 그 문제를 대처하는 방법을 제안해주세요.

 Hi. This is Tanya calling. We have a problem and because you're the owner of Century Home Restaurant I want you to help me out. As the manager of your restaurant, I've noticed that sales have gone way down lately ever since another fast-food place opened up nearby. We used to be full every day around lunch and dinner time but not anymore. We're well known for making healthy food and serving it in a comfortable home-style setting. But it seems like a lot of people would rather get their meals fast and cheap at the place down the block. I want to figure out a way to get our sales back up. Please call me back as soon as you can with your ideas. Again, it's Tanya, the manager at Century Home Restaurant.

안녕하세요. Tanya입니다. 문제가 있습니다. 귀하가 "Century Home 레스토랑"의 소유주이시므로 도움을 청합니다. 귀하의 레스토랑의 관리자로서, 최근 근처에 다른 패스트푸드 매장이 개업한 이후로 우리의 판매 매출이 하락하고 있음을 말씀드립니다. 우리 레스토랑은 점심과 저녁 식사 때면 날마다 만원이었습니다만 더 이상은 그렇지가 않습니다. 우리는 몸에 좋은 건강식을 요리하고 집처럼 편안한 분위기에서 서비스하는 것으로 잘 알려져 있습니다. 그러나 많은 사람들이 한 블록 아래의 그 매장에서 음식을 빠르고 저렴하게 구매하는 것 같습니다. 우리의 판매 매출을 회복할 수 있는 방도를 구상하고 싶습니다. 최대한 빨리 전화 주셔서 의견을 말씀해 주시길 부탁드립니다. "Century Home 레스토랑"의 관리자 Tanya입니다.

 go way down 상당히 아래로 내려가다   ever since 그 이후로   fast-food place 패스트푸드점   nearby 근처에   used to (과거에) 하곤 했다   full 가득 찬   would rather ~하기를 원하다   figure out 해결하다   get sales back up 판매를 다시 회복하다

 **Possible Answer**

인사	Hi, Tanya. This is Shawn returning your call.
문제 상황 인식	I have also noticed that sales have certainly dropped since the fast-food joint opened up near my restaurant. I have visited the restaurant a few times in the past weeks and there are definitely fewer customers for lunch than in the past.
해결책 제시 1	I have thought of some ways to boost business, so I am glad that you called. Starting next Monday, we will have daily lunch specials. These specials will be offered at a lower-than-usual price so that we may compete with the cheaper prices of the fast-food place.
해결책 제시 2	In addition, I have already hired more wait staff and kitchen help. This way I hope our service will become faster. We will continue to serve healthy food in a comfortable home-style atmosphere, which I think no fast-food chain can beat. In the end, I am sure this line of action will entice our customers to return and stay.
마무리	As the manager, Tanya, I hope I can count on you as always. I will talk to you soon.

안녕하세요, Tanya. 저 Shawn이예요. 당신의 전화에 답신을 드립니다. 패스트푸드 매장이 우리 레스토랑 근처에 영업을 시작한 이후 우리의 판매 매출이 하락하고 있음을 저 역시 감지하고 있습니다. 지난주에 레스토랑을 몇 번 방문했었는데 예전에 비해 확연하게 점심 시간대의 손님 수가 줄어들었더군요. 제가 매출을 올릴 방법을 생각했는데 마침 전화를 주셔서 기쁘네요. 다음 주 월요일부터 시작해서, 우리는 점심 특선을 내놓을 것입니다. 이 특선은 통상 가격보다 저렴하게 제공될 것입니다. 그리하면 우리는 패스트푸드 매장의 저렴한 가격과 경쟁할 수 있을 것입니다. 또한 저는 이미 서빙하는 사람과 주방 보조를 추가로 고용했습니다. 이 방법이 우리의 서비스를 더욱 빠르게 하길 바랍니다. 계속해서 우리는 몸에 좋은 건강식을 요리하고 집처럼 편안한 분위기에서 서비스를 할 것입니다. 이것은 어떠한 패스트푸드 체인점도 넘볼 수 없는 점입니다. 결국 이러한 활동이 우리 고객의 발걸음을 되돌리고 늘 찾아오게 하리라 확신합니다. Tanya, 저는 늘 관리자인 당신에게 맡겨 두고 싶습니다. 곧 당신과 이야기하겠습니다.

notice 알아채다   certainly 확실히   drop 떨어지다   fast-food joint 패스트푸드 체인점   in the past weeks 지난 몇 주 동안에   definitely 확실히   boost 올리다   daily lunch specials 점심 특선   wait staff 서빙하는 사람   kitchen help 주방 보조   comfortable 편안한   atmosphere 분위기   this line of action 이러한 일련의 조치   entice 끌어모으다   return and stay 계속 찾아주다   count on 믿다   as always 항상 그러하듯이

Question 11 Express an Opinion

Directions: In this part of the test, you will give your opinion about a specific topic. Be sure to say as much as you can in the time allowed. You will have 15 seconds to prepare. Then you will have 60 seconds to speak.

이 파트에서 여러분은 특정한 주제에 대한 의견을 말하게 됩니다. 주어진 시간 동안 최대한 많이 말할 수 있도록 하세요. 15초 동안 준비한 뒤 60초 동안 응답하세요.

Do you think it is better to grow up in a city than to grow up in the country?

Why or why not?

Give specific reasons and details to support your answer.

시골에서 성장하는 것보다 도시에서 성장하는 것이 낫다고 생각하십니까?

이유가 무엇인가요?

여러분의 의견을 뒷받침하는 이유와 예시를 들어주십시오.

 Possible Answer 1 (grow up in a city)

의견 제시	I think it is better to grow up in a city than to grow up in the country for several reasons.
근거 제시 1	First, cities have many more entertainment options compared to the country.
예시	For instance, I can go watch professional sports being played live, or go to the theater, concerts, or museums. The country is quite limited in its entertainment options.
근거 제시 2	Also, I can meet many more people from diverse backgrounds in a city. It has a larger population, and it is likely that some of these people have come from other parts of the country or world.
예시	For instance, New York is said to be the most culturally diverse city in the world. I can learn about other cultures all in one location and without leaving the city.
근거 제시 3	Finally, cities have more job opportunities than the country. I will have a larger selection of what career I would like to have and probably be more satisfied with my work.
마무리	Therefore, I would not prefer to grow up in the country and rather grow up in a city for these reasons.

저는 시골보다 도시에서 성장하는 것이 여러 가지 이유로 인해 더 낫다고 생각합니다. 우선, 도시에는 시골에 비해 더욱 넓은 문화 활동 선택의 폭이 있습니다. 예를 들어, 저는 실제로 행해지는 프로 스포츠, 영화, 콘서트, 박물과 전시를 보러 갈 수 있습니다. 시골은 이러한 문화 활동 선택의 폭이 매우 제한적입니다. 또한, 도시에서는 다양한 배경의 사람들을 더욱 많이 만날 수 있습니다. 도시에는 인구가 더 많으며 이들 중 일부는 다른 지역이나 다른 나라에서 도시로 온 사람들일 것입니다. 예를 들어, 뉴욕은 세계에서 문화적으로 가장 다양한 도시로 불립니다. 저는 도시를 벗어나지 않고 한 곳에서 다른 문화를 익힐 수 있습니다. 마지막으로 도시에는 시골보다 더 많은 취업 자리가 있습니다. 일에 있어서 제가 선호하고 만족할 업종을 선택할 수 있는 폭이 넓습니다. 따라서 이러한 이유로 저는 시골보다 도시에서 성장하는 것이 더 낫다고 생각합니다.

grow up 성장하다   entertainment option 즐길 거리   diverse backgrounds 다양한 배경   the most culturally diverse city 가장 문화적으로 다양한 도시   job opportunity 취업 기회   therefore 그래서

Possible Answer 2 (grow up in the country)

의견 제시 There are a few reasons why I believe it is better to grow up in the country than in a city.

근거 제시 1 Most importantly, growing up in the country allows me to develop in an environment that is not very polluted.

예시 For instance, because there are fewer automobiles, the air quality is better. In addition, there will be less, maybe even no noise pollution since there are not that many people or things creating unwanted noise. These types of pollution can cause stress to an individual that can adversely affect his or her health.

근거 제시 2 Another reason is that with today's technology, living in the country is more comfortable than it was in the past. For example, entertainment and educational information can be easily accessed through the Internet. I do not have to travel all the way to the city or even live there when I can access this information on the Internet in the comfort of my home.

근거 제시 3 Finally, the county is more appealing to the eye than a city. In the country you can witness all of nature's beauty first hand and benefit from its calming effect. However, in a city, the natural world is replaced with mostly concrete— a dull gray color.

마무리 Hence, I feel that it is better to grow up in the country than in a city.

제가 도시보다 시골에서 성장하는 것이 더 낫다고 생각하는 데에는 몇 가지 이유가 있습니다. 우선, 시골에서 성장하는 것은 오염되지 않은 환경에서 자랄 수 있게 합니다. 예를 들어, 자동차가 적기 때문에 공기의 질이 좋습니다. 또한 달갑지 않은 소음을 야기하는 시설이나 많은 사람들이 없기 때문에 소음 역시 덜 하거나 전혀 없을 것입니다. 이러한 유형의 공해는 건강에 나쁜 해를 끼치는 스트레스를 개인에게 안겨줄 수 있습니다. 다른 이유는 현대의 기술을 갖춘, 시골에서의 생활은 과거보다 훨씬 편리합니다. 예를 들어 인터넷을 통해 오락 및 교육 정보에 쉽게 접속할 수 있습니다. 집에서 편리하게 인터넷을 통해 이러한 정보에 접속할 수 있다면, 멀리 도시로 갈 필요가 없으며 도시에서 생활할 필요도 없습니다. 마지막으로 시골은 도시보다 겉보기에 더 매력적입니다. 시골에서는 자연의 모든 아름다움을 직접 체험하면서 볼 수 있고 진정 효과의 혜택을 받을 수 있습니다. 그러나 도시에서는 자연이 거의 다 콘크리트로 대체되어 있습니다. — 우중충한 회색으로 뒤덮여 있죠. 그래서 저는 도시보다 시골에서 성장하는 것이 더 낫다고 생각합니다.

noise pollution 소음 공해   adversely affect 나쁘게 영향을 미치다   comfortable 편안한   easily accessed 쉽게 접근하는   travel all the way to a city 도시까지 쭉 가다   in the comfort of my home 내 집 같은 편안함 속에서   more appealing 좀 더 매력적인   witness 목격하다   nature's beauty 자연의 아름다움   first hand 직접   benefit from ~로부터 혜택을 얻다   calming effect 진정 효과   be replaced with ~와 교체되다   dull 칙칙한, 지루한   hence 그래서

Questions 1-2 Read a Text Aloud

Directions: In this part of the test, you will read aloud the text on the screen. You will have 45 seconds to prepare. Then you will have 45 seconds to read the text aloud.

이 파트에서 여러분은 스크린의 텍스트를 큰 소리로 읽게 됩니다. 45초의 준비 시간이 주어지고, 그 후 45초 동안 텍스트를 큰 소리로 읽으세요.

TOEIC® Speaking

Question 1 of 11

Hello. You've reached the St. Luis Society Information Line. Because of predictions of heavy precipitation, the folk fiesta has been delayed at Rainbow Courtyard until next Friday. On Friday, the features are a singing quartet, a comical performance, and games. On Saturday, the town rock band will perform at High Park at 7 P.M. The entrance cost is $4.

안녕하세요, St. Luis 학술 정보입니다. 폭우 예보로 인해 민속 축제가 연기되어 다음 주 금요일 Rainbow Courtyard에서 하기로 하였습니다. 금요일에는 4중주 합창, 개그 공연, 게임이 마련되어 있습니다. 토요일에는 지역 록 밴드가 오후 7시 High Park에서 공연을 하며, 입장료는 4달러입니다.

Speaking Solution

Hello. You've reached the **St. Luis Society Information Line**(고유명사 강세). ＼(문장의 맨 끝) Because of **predictions** of heavy **precipitation**, ／(계속 의미/쉼표 뒤 짧게 끊고) the **folk fiesta** has been **delayed** / (전명구 앞 짧게 끊고) at **Rainbow Courtyard**(고유명사 강세) until **next Friday**(시간/날짜/숫자 강세). On **Friday**(시간/날짜/숫자 강세), ／(계속 의미/쉼표 뒤 짧게 끊고) the **features** are **a singing quartet**／, **a comical performance**／, and **games**＼(A／, B／ and C＼) On **Saturday**(시간/날짜/숫자 강세), (계속 의미/쉼표 뒤 짧게 끊고) the **town rock band** will perform / (전명구 앞 짧게 끊고) at **High Park**(고유명사 강세) at **7 P.M.** The **entrance cost** is **four dollars**(시간/날짜/숫자 강세).

You have reached ~ ~에 전화 연결 되었습니다   prediction 예상   heavy precipitation 폭우   feature 공연   singing quartet 4중주 합창   entrance cost 입장료

If your children need extra help with reading, writing, mathematics or the sciences, consider Goheen Education Institution. Our personnel of passionate and qualified educators will construct personalized lesson plans to meet your children's precise needs. What's more, improvements in academic performance are guaranteed. So what are you waiting for? Phone us today at 555-5981!

여러분의 자녀가 독해, 작문, 수학 혹은 과학을 배우는데 특별한 도움을 필요로 한다면, Goheen 교육 기관을 고려해 보세요. 저희의 열정적이고 우수한 자질을 갖춘 교육자들은 여러분의 자녀의 필요에 맞는 맞춤식 수업 계획을 고안해낼 것입니다. 게다가, 학업 능력 향상을 보증합니다. 무엇을 기다리시나요? 555–5981로 오늘 전화주세요.

Speaking Solution

If your children need **extra help** with **reading**↗, **writing**↗, **mathematics**↗ or the **sciences**↘ (A↗, B↗ or C↘), ↗(계속 의미/쉼표 뒤 짧게 끊고) consider **Goheen Education Institution**(고유명사 강세). ↘(문장의 맨 끝) Our **personnel** of passionate and qualified **educators** will construct personalized **lesson plans**(중요 의미 강세) / (부사구 앞 잠시 끊고) / to meet your children's **precise needs**(중요 의미 강세). ↘(문장의 맨 끝) **What's more**(부가 의미 강조), **improvements** in academic **performance** are **guaranteed**. So what are you **waiting for**?↘(wh의문문 내림) **Phone** us today at **555-5981**!(시간/날짜/숫자 강세)

loved ones 가족, 친척 **consider** 고려하다 **passionate** 열정을 품은 **qualified** 자격이 있는 **personalized** 개인이 원하는 대로 할 수 있는 **lesson plan** 학습 계획안 **meet** 충족시키다 **precise** 정확한 **needs** 요구 **improvement** 개선 **guarantee** 장담하다, 보장하다

Question 3 Describe a Picture

Directions: In this part of the test, you will describe the picture on your screen in as much detail as you can. You will have 30 seconds to prepare your response. Then you will have 45 seconds to speak about the picture.

이 파트에서 여러분은 스크린의 사진을 최대한 자세히 설명하게 됩니다. 대답을 위해 30초의 준비 시간이 주어지고, 그 후 45초 동안 사진에 대해 설명하세요.

 **Possible Answer**

This picture appears to be taken at the boarding gate of an airport. There are many people with backpacks and carry-on bags. Some people are standing in line to board. Some people are waiting around, and some are sitting on a row of black seats. It appears to have been taken during the daytime. There are large glass windows on the left side of the picture, and it is sunny outside. There are two counters with airport personnel checking people in line before they enter. The smaller counter on the left has one airport employee and the larger counter on the right has two.

이 사진은 공항의 탑승구에서 촬영된 것으로 보입니다. 배낭과 휴대용 가방을 지닌 많은 사람들이 있습니다. 몇몇 사람들은 탑승을 위해 줄을 서 있고 몇몇 사람들은 서성이며 기다리고 있으며 다른 몇몇 사람들은 한 줄로 늘어선 검은 좌석에 앉아 있습니다. 낮에 찍은 사진으로 보여집니다. 사진 속의 왼편에 커다란 창문이 있고 햇살이 비칩니다. 두 카운터에 공항 직원이 있는데 줄을 선 사람들을 들어가기 전에 확인하고 있습니다. 인원이 더 적은 왼쪽 카운터에는 한 사람의 공항 직원이 있고 그리고 인원이 더 많은 오른쪽 카운터에는 두 명의 공항 직원이 있습니다.

 **boarding gate** 탑승구 **backpack** 배낭 **carry-on bag** 기내에 갖고 들어갈 수 있는 휴대 가방 **people in line** 줄 서 있는 사람들

Questions 4-6 Respond to Questions

Directions: In this part of the test, you will answer three questions. For each question, begin responding immediately after you hear a beep. No preparation time is provided. You will have 15 seconds to respond to Questions 4 and 5 and 30 seconds to respond to Question 6.

이 파트에서 여러분은 세 가지 질문에 답하게 됩니다. 각 질문에 대해 '삐' 소리가 나면 즉시 대답하세요. 준비 시간은 주어지지 않습니다. 4번과 5번 문제에는 각각 15초, 그리고 6번 문제에는 30초의 응답 시간이 주어집니다.

Imagine that an Australian marketing firm is doing research in your country. You have agreed to participate in a telephone interview about drinks.

어느 호주 마케팅 회사가 여러분의 나라에서 조사를 하고 있다고 가정해 봅시다. 여러분은 음료에 관한 전화 인터뷰 참여를 승낙했습니다.

How often do you drink coffee or tea during the day, and when do you usually drink it?

하루에 얼마나 자주 커피나 차를 드시나요? 그리고 보통 언제 드시나요?

 **Possible Answer**

I usually drink coffee twice a day. I have a cup of coffee in the morning to get the day started and one in the afternoon to keep me going.

저는 보통 하루 두 번 커피를 마십니다. 하루를 시작하는 아침에 한 번, 그리고 저를 북돋기 위해 오후에 한 번 마십니다.

 **twice a day** 하루에 두 번   **get the day started** 하루를 시작하다   **keep going** 계속 견디다

Where can you usually buy coffee or tea in your country?

당신의 나라에서는 보통 어디에서 커피나 차를 구매할 수 있나요?

 **Possible Answer**

In my country, I can buy coffee or tea almost anywhere. For instance, I buy coffee at Starbucks. It is a nationwide coffee shop that sells good coffee. And I can buy it at gas stations and supermarkets.

우리나라에서는 거의 모든 곳에서 커피나 차를 구매할 수 있습니다. 예를 들어, 저는 Starbucks에서 커피를 구매하는데 그 곳은 전국적으로 있는 커피 상점으로 질 좋은 커피를 판매합니다. 그리고 편의점, 주유소, 및 슈퍼마켓에서도 커피를 구매하기도 합니다.

 convenience store 편의점

Do you prefer to drink coffee or tea at home? Why or why not?

커피나 차를 집에서 드시는 것을 좋아하시나요? 그렇거나 그렇지 않다면 그 이유는 무엇입니까?

 **Possible Answer**

I prefer to drink tea at home because I have an assortment of teas that I like to enjoy. Most coffee or tea shops do not have a good selection to choose from. However, I can drink whatever I desire at home.

저는 집에서 차를 마시는 것을 좋아합니다. 왜냐하면 즐겨 찾는 각종 차가 있기 때문입니다. 대부분의 커피숍이나 찻집은 고를 수 있는 선택의 범위가 좁지만 집에서는 내가 마시고 싶은 것을 마실 수 있습니다.

 an assortment of 각종의   selection 선택 가능한 것들   desire 바라다, 원하다

Questions 7-9 Respond to Questions Using Information Provided

Directions: In this part of the test, you will answer three questions based on the information provided. You will have 30 seconds to read the information before the questions begin. For each question, begin responding immediately after you hear a beep. No additional preparation time is provided. You will have 15 seconds to respond to Questions 7 and 8 and 30 seconds to respond to Question 9.

이 파트에서 여러분은 주어진 정보에 기초하여 세 가지 질문에 대답하게 됩니다. 문제가 시작하기 전에 30초 동안 정보를 읽게 됩니다. 각 질문에 대해 '삐' 소리가 나면 즉시 대답하세요. 준비 시간은 주어지지 않습니다. 7번과 8번 문제에는 각각 15초, 그리고 9번 문제에는 30초의 응답 시간이 주어집니다.

TOEIC® Speaking

Questions 7-9 of 11

Revival Game Corporation
Conference Call
Local Starting Times (Friday, August 30)

Call Access Information

Portland: 9:00 A.M. (Pacific time) Call-in number: (800) 555-1982

Memphis: 11:00 A.M. (Central time) Conference code: 3864

Schedule

1. Sales for May to July: Kent Payne (Memphis)

2. Customer complaints: Yo-Yo Min Koo Ahn (Portland)

3. New merchandise: Explaining remote boomerang, Sera Stevens (Memphis)

4. Future campaigns: Winter sports, Wanda Fish (Memphis)

5. Market research: Leonard Bradley (Portland)

Hi. This is Leonard Bradley. I'm on my way to work now, but I'm going to be a little late. Seeing as you organized this morning's conference call, I trust you can answer a few questions about it.

<table>
<tr><td>

Revival Game Corporation
Conference Call

Local Starting Times (Friday, August 30)

Call Access Information

Portland: 9:00 A.M. (Pacific time) Call-in number: (800) 555-1982

Memphis: 11:00 A.M. (Central time) Conference code: 3864

Schedule

1. Sales for May to July: Kent Payne (Memphis)
2. Customer complaints: Yo-Yo Min Koo Ahn (Portland)
3. New merchandise: Explaining remote boomerang, Sera Stevens (Memphis)
4. Future campaigns: Winter sports, Wanda Fish (Memphis)
5. Market research: Leonard Bradley (Portland)

Hi. This is Leonard Bradley. I'm on my way to work now, but I'm going to be a little late. Seeing as you organized this morning's conference call, I trust you can answer a few questions about it.

</td><td>

Revival 게임 회사
전화 회의(컨퍼런스 콜)

현지 시작 시각 (8월 30일 금요일)

전화 연결 정보

포틀랜드: 오전 9시(태평양 표준시) 전화번호: (800) 555-1982

멤피스: 오전 11시(중부 표준시) 회의 코드: 3864

일정

1. 5월에서 7월까지의 판매: Kent Payne(멤피스)
2. 고객 불만 사항: Yo-Yo Min Koo Ahn(포틀랜드)
3. 신상품: 원격 부메랑 설명, Sera Stevens(멤피스)
4. 향후 캠페인: 겨울 스포츠, Wanda Fish(멤피스)
5. 시장 조사: Leonard Bradley(포틀랜드)

안녕하세요, 저는 Leonard Bradley라고 합니다. 지금 출근하는 길입니다만 약간 늦을 것 같습니다. 귀하가 오늘 아침 전화 회의를 편성하셨으므로, 그에 대한 질문에 답변해 주실 거라 믿습니다.

</td></tr>
</table>

 remote 원격의

What time does the call begin here in Portland?

이 곳 포틀랜드에서는 전화 회의 시작 시각이 언제인가요?

 **Possible Answer**

According to the agenda, the call begins at 9 A.M. in Portland.

일정표에 의하면 포틀랜드에서는 회의가 오전 9시에 시작합니다.

 agenda 회의 일정표

I'm going to be talking about "Market research" and I think I am the first speaker. Could you reschedule my presentation for late in the call?

저는 "시장 조사"에 대해서 발표할 예정입니다. 그리고 제가 첫 번째 발표자인 것으로 알고 있습니다. 저의 발표 스케줄을 뒤로 조정해 주실 수 있습니까?

 **Possible Answer**

You are correct that you are going to be talking about "Market research." However, you are not the first speaker. Actually, you are the last speaker in the call, so there will be no need to reschedule your presentation.

말씀처럼 당신이 "시장 조사"에 대해서 발표할 것입니다. 그러나 당신이 첫 번째 발표자가 아닙니다. 사실, 회의의 가장 마지막 발표자입니다. 따라서 일정을 조정할 필요가 없을 것입니다.

 **reschedule** 일정을 다시 조정하다

Who will be calling from Memphis, and what will they be talking about?

멤피스에서 누가 회의 발표를 하나요? 또 그들은 무엇에 대해 논의하나요?

 **Possible Answer**

There will be three calls from Memphis. The first caller is Kent Payne, and he will be discussing sales from May to July. The next caller from Memphis is Sera Stevens, who will be discussing new merchandise; specifically she will be explaining the remote boomerang. Finally, Wanda Fish will discuss future campaigns regarding winter sports

멤피스에서 세 가지 회의 발표가 있을 것입니다. 첫 회의 발표는 Kent Payne이며 5월에서 7월까지의 판매에 대해 논의할 것입니다. 다음 순서의 회의 발표자는 Sera Stevens이며 신상품을 논의할 것입니다. 특히 그녀는 원격 부메랑을 설명할 것입니다. 마지막으로 Wanda Fish가 겨울 스포츠에 관련한 향후 캠페인을 논의할 것입니다.

 **merchandise** 상품 **specifically** 구체적으로

Question 10   Propose a Solution

Directions: In this part of the test, you will be presented with a problem and asked to propose a solution. You will have 30 seconds to prepare. Then you will have 60 seconds to speak.

이 파트에서 여러분에게 한 가지 문제가 주어집니다. 여러분은 그에 대한 해결책을 제시해주세요. 30초 동안 준비한 뒤 60초 동안 응답하세요.

In your response, be sure to
- show that you recognize the problem, and
- propose a way of dealing with the problem.

여러분의 응답에서
- 여러분이 문제를 인식했다는 것을 보여주세요.
- 그 문제를 대처하는 방법을 제안해주세요.

 Hello. This is Trevor from Public Relations. As you know from the meeting earlier this week, we have decided to hold an event for our work colleagues and their families next month. I have been chosen to arrange all matters related to this event. But as this is the first time for me, I am calling to ask for some advice since you had a similar experience last year. There are many things to decide such as the place, games and food for the event. Do you think you can give some detailed advice on this issue? Once again this is Trevor, and you can reach me at extension 34. Thanks.

안녕하세요. 저는 홍보부의 Trevor입니다. 알다시피 이번 주 초에 있었던 회의에서 저희는 다음 달에 회사 동료와 가족을 위한 행사를 하기로 정했습니다. 제가 이번 행사와 관련한 모든 사항을 처리하도록 뽑혔습니다. 하지만 저는 이번이 처음이기 때문에 귀하가 지난해에 비슷한 경험이 있으므로 조언을 구하고자 전화를 드렸습니다. 행사를 위해 장소, 게임, 음식과 같은 많은 것들을 결정해야 합니다. 이 문제에 관해 상세한 조언을 해주실 수 있으십니까? 저는 Trevor이고 내선 34번으로 연락하실 수 있습니다. 감사합니다.

 Public Relations 홍보부   hold 개최하다   related to ~과 연관된   since ~이기 때문에   such as 예를 들어

 **Possible Answer**

인사	Hello, Trevor.
문제 상황 인식	I received your message about hosting an event for our colleagues and their family members next month. Although you may not have organized a large event like this before, I am confident that you will have a rewarding experience as I did last year.
해결책 제시	I recommend that you arrange an outdoor barbecue for the colleagues and their family members. There is a large park not far from the office which has facilities you can use, like barbecue pits, tables, and benches. Furthermore, this park has numerous recreational activities such as basketball, football, and a small pond which young children really enjoy exploring. There are also many quiet locations where people can just sit or lay down, and relax in the shade. Regardless of what you decide, I am sure the people will be happy to enjoy quality time with their friends and family.
마무리	Please let me know if you want to discuss this further. Bye.

안녕하세요, Trevor 씨. 다음 달 저희 동료와 가족을 위한 행사 주최에 관련한 귀하의 메시지를 받았습니다. Trevor 씨께서 이전에 이와 같은 대형 행사를 담당한 적은 없지만 작년의 저처럼 보람된 경험을 하게 되시리라 확신합니다. 저는 동료와 가족들을 위해 야외 바비큐 파티 준비를 추천합니다. 사무실에서 그다지 멀지 않은 곳에 바비큐 화덕, 탁자, 의자와 같은 시설이 구비된 커다란 공원이 하나 있습니다. 더욱이 공원에는 농구, 축구와 같은 많은 여가활동 시설과 어린 아이들이 탐험을 즐기는 작은 연못이 구비되어 있습니다. 또한 사람들이 그늘 밑에서 편히 앉거나 누워서 쉴 수 있는 조용한 곳이 많이 있습니다. Trevor 씨가 어떤 것을 선택하든지 저는 사람들이 친구와 가족과 함께 귀중한 시간을 보내면서 만족할 것이라고 확신합니다. 더 상세하게 의논하고 싶으시다면 연락 주세요. 수고하세요.

organize 준비하다   confident 확신하는   rewarding 보람 있는   recommend 제안하다   arrange ~을 준비하다
facilities 시설물   barbecue pit 바비큐 화덕   pond 연못   lay down 눕다   shade 그늘   regardless of ~에 상관없이

Question 11   Express an Opinion

Directions: In this part of the test, you will give your opinion about a specific topic. Be sure to say as much as you can in the time allowed. You will have 15 seconds to prepare. Then you will have 60 seconds to speak.

이 파트에서 여러분은 특정한 주제에 대한 의견을 말하게 됩니다. 주어진 시간 동안 최대한 많이 말할 수 있도록 하세요. 15초 동안 준비한 뒤 60초 동안 응답하세요.

Question 11 of 11

Do you agree or disagree with the following statement?

> *The best way to reward hard-working employees is to give them extra vacation time.*

Use specific reasons or examples to support your answer.

여러분은 다음 진술에 동의하시나요, 동의하지 않으시나요?

열심히 일하는 직원에 대한 최선의 포상은 특별 휴가 시간을 주는 것입니다.

여러분의 의견을 뒷받침하는 이유와 예시를 들어주십시오.

 Possible Answer 1 (agree)

의견 제시   I certainly agree with the statement that the best way to reward hard-working employees is to give them extra vacation time.

근거 제시   To begin with, hard-working employees will consistently meet and surpass expectations. To do this, these types of employees give much more effort mentally and physically than do others. Thus, it is only right to reward them by giving them extra vacation time. They can spend their extra time recharging and alleviating their stress.

예시   For example, these employees could spend quality time with their loved ones and family members. In addition, the extra time could be used to travel to a tropical destination.

마무리   Regardless of how the time is spent, employees can return to work refreshed, rejuvenated, and ready to continue to work hard.

저는 열심히 일하는 직원에 대한 최선의 포상은 특별 휴가 시간을 주는 것이라는 진술에 확신을 가지고 동의합니다. 우선, 열심히 일하는 직원은 끊임없이 기대에 부응하고 기대를 넘어설 것입니다. 이렇게 하고자, 이 유형의 직원은 다른 사람들보다 정신적으로나 육체적으로 더 분발합니다. 따라서 특별 휴가를 마련해주어 그들을 포상하는 것이 옳습니다. 그들은 그 여가 시간에 에너지를 다시 모으고 스트레스를 해소하는데 쓸 것입니다. 예를 들어, 이 직원은 연인이나 가족과 알찬 시간을 보낼 수 있습니다. 또한 여가 시간에 열대 지역으로 여행을 갈 수도 있습니다. 어떻게 시간을 보내든지 직원은 활력과 원기를 회복하고 계속 열심히 일할 준비가 되어 일터로 돌아올 것입니다.

 to begin with 먼저   consistently 꾸준히   meet and surpass expectations 기대치를 충족 및 초과달성하다

mentally 정신적으로   physically 육체적으로   recharge 재충전하다   alleviate 줄이다   quality time 알찬 시간   loved ones 사랑하는 사람들   tropical 열대의   regardless of ~에 상관없이   refreshed 재충전된   rejuvenated 다시 활기를 가진

Possible Answer 2 (disagree)

의견 제시 I do not agree with the statement that the best way to reward hard-working employees is to give them extra vacation time.

근거 제시 1 First of all, not all people like to be rewarded in the same way.

예시 For instance, one employee might be motivated to work hard to earn more money. Another employee might work hard for personal recognition. Thus, I think it is important to ascertain what kind of rewards employees desire because I do not believe that all workers want to be rewarded with extra vacation time.

근거 제시 2 Another important reason why more time off is not the best reward is that these types of people get satisfaction by working hard and getting their jobs well done, and even surpassing others' expectations.

마무리 Therefore, more vacation time would mean more time away from the tasks that they love doing.

저는 열심히 일하는 직원에 대한 최선의 포상은 특별 휴가 시간을 주는 것이라는 진술에 동의하지 않습니다. 우선, 모두가 다 같은 방법으로 포상받기를 바라는 것은 아닙니다. 예를 들어, 어떤 직원은 돈을 더 버는 데에서 열심히 일하고픈 동기를 부여 받을 수 있습니다. 다른 어떤 직원은 스스로가 인정을 받는 데에서 근로 의욕이 고취될 수 있습니다. 따라서 저는 각자가 바라는 포상의 유형을 확인하는 것이 중요하다고 봅니다. 왜냐하면 근로자 모두가 다 특별 휴가 시간으로 포상받기를 바라는 것은 아니라고 여기기 때문입니다. 더 많은 근로 시간 면제가 최선의 포상이 아닌 또 다른 이유는, 이러한 유형의 사람들은 열심히 일하여 업무를 잘 수행하거나 다른 사람들의 기대치를 넘어설 때 만족을 느끼기 때문입니다. 따라서 그들에게 더 많은 휴가 시간이란 그들이 좋아하는 일로부디 멀어지는 더 많은 시간을 의미힐 깃입니다.

 first of all 무엇보다도 먼저   for instance 예를 들어   motivated 동기 부여된   personal recognition 개인적인 (공로) 인정

ascertain 확인하다   job well done 잘 마무리된 일   surpass 능가하다

Questions 1-2 Read a Text Aloud

Directions: In this part of the test, you will read aloud the text on the screen. You will have 45 seconds to prepare. Then you will have 45 seconds to read the text aloud.

이 파트에서 여러분은 스크린의 텍스트를 큰 소리로 읽게 됩니다. 45초의 준비 시간이 주어지고, 그 후 45초 동안 텍스트를 큰 소리로 읽으세요.

TOEIC® Speaking

Question 1 of 11

The Furniture Corporation is having a closing sale this Thursday and Friday. Assorted dining sets, desks, and all oil paintings must be sold. Because it is forty to seventy percent off, you'll be sure to get awesome discounts. Everything is the lowest price in our store's history for these two days only. You can reach us at 555-6578.

Furniture 사에서 이번 주 목요일과 금요일에 점포 정리 세일을 합니다. 다양한 식탁 세트, 책상, 그리고 온갖 유화를 판매합니다. 40에서 70퍼센트까지 가격 할인을 하기 때문에 여러분은 대폭 할인을 받으실 거라 확실합니다. 기간은 이틀이며 상점이 생긴 이래로 모든 제품은 최저가입니다. 555–6578로 전화 주세요.

Speaking Solution

The **Furniture Corporation**(고유명사 강세) is having a **closing sale**(주요 내용 강세) this **Thursday and Friday**(시간/날짜/숫자 강세). ＼(문장의 맨 끝) **Assorted dining sets**↗, **desks**↗, and **all**(all/every 강세) **oil paintings**＼(A↗, B↗ and C＼) **must be sold**(주요 내용 강세). ＼(문장의 맨 끝) Because it is **forty to seventy percent off**(시간/날짜/숫자 강세), you'll be **sure** / (부사구 앞에 잠시 쉬고) to get **awesome discounts**.＼(문장의 맨 끝) **Everything**(all/every 강세) is the **lowest price**(최상급 강조) in our store's **history** for these **two days only**(시간/날짜/숫자 강세). You can reach us at **555-6578**(시간/날짜/숫자 강세).

closing sale 마감 세일, 재고정리 세일　assorted 다채로운　oil painting 유화　awesome 대단한, 엄청난

Today's speaker is Norma Bosk from New Entrepreneurs Incorporated and Sisko Manufacturing. Under her supervision, Sisko factories have been opened in France, Belgium, and Austria. In addition, another branch opening is being planned. Now, her talk is about "Your company and your direction." Please welcome Mrs. Bosk.

오늘의 연사는 새로운 법인 기업인 Sisko 제조사에서 오신 Norma Bosk입니다. 그녀의 지휘 하에 Sisko 공장들이 프랑스, 벨기에, 오스트리아에서 새로 문을 열었습니다. 더하여, 다른 지부의 개설이 계획 중입니다. 자, 그녀의 연설은 "회사와 여러분이 가야할 방향"에 대한 것입니다. Bosk 씨를 환영해주세요.

Speaking Solution

Today's **speaker** is **Norma Bosk**(고유명사 강세) / from **New Entrepreneurs Incorporated** and **Sisko Manufacturing**(고유명사 강세). ↘(문장의 맨 끝) Under her **supervision**↗(계속 의미/쉼표 뒤 짧게 끊고) **Sisko factories** have been **opened**(중요 의미 강세) / in **France**↗, **Belgium**↗, and **Austria**.↘(A↗, B↗ and C↘) **In addition**(부가 강조), **another branch opening** is being **planned**(중요 의미 강세). ↘(문장의 맨 끝) Now, her **talk** is about "Your **company** and your **direction**"(제목-중요 의미 강세). Please **welcome Mrs. Bosk**.↘(문장의 맨 끝)

under one's supervision ~의 감독 아래   in addition 게다가   branch 지점

Question 3 Describe a Picture

Directions: In this part of the test, you will describe the picture on your screen in as much detail as you can. You will have 30 seconds to prepare your response. Then you will have 45 seconds to speak about the picture.

이 파트에서 여러분은 스크린의 사진을 최대한 자세히 설명하게 됩니다. 대답을 위해 30초의 준비 시간이 주어지고, 그 후 45초 동안 사진에 대해 설명하세요.

 **Possible Answer**

Two large brown horses are pulling a blue wagon on the paved street. There is a group of people riding in the back of the blue wagon. Also, there are two people sitting at the front of the wagon who appear to be driving. This picture was taken in the winter time. There is snow on the ground and the people are wearing winter clothes to stay warm. In the background, there are tall evergreen trees and some bare trees. It looks like this scene is from a rural area.

포장도로에서 파란색 마차를 끄는 커다란 갈색 말 두 마리가 있습니다. 한 무리의 사람들이 파란색 마차 뒤에 타고 있습니다. 또한 마차를 모는 걸로 보이는 두 사람이 마차 앞쪽에 앉아 있습니다. 이 사진은 겨울철에 찍혔으며 땅에는 눈이 있고 사람들은 보온을 위해 겨울옷을 입고 있습니다. 배경에는 키가 큰 상록수와 잎이 다 떨어진 나무가 있습니다. 시골에서 볼 수 있는 장면인 듯합니다.

 **pull** 당기다, 끌다 **paved street** 포장도로 **wagon** 마차 **appear** ~처럼 보이다 **evergreen tree** 상록수 **bare tree** 앙상한 나무, 잎이 없는 나무 **rural area** 시골

Questions 4-6 Respond to Questions

Directions: In this part of the test, you will answer three questions. For each question, begin responding immediately after you hear a beep. No preparation time is provided. You will have 15 seconds to respond to Questions 4 and 5 and 30 seconds to respond to Question 6.

이 파트에서 여러분은 세 가지 질문에 답하게 됩니다. 각 질문에 대해 '삐' 소리가 나면 즉시 대답하세요. 준비 시간은 주어지지 않습니다. 4번과 5번 문제에는 각각 15초, 그리고 6번 문제에는 30초의 응답 시간이 주어집니다.

Imagine that a U.S. marketing firm is doing research in your country. You have agreed to participate in a telephone interview about watching news programs on television.

어느 미국 마케팅 회사가 여러분의 나라에서 조사를 하고 있다고 가정해 봅시다. 여러분은 텔레비전 뉴스 프로그램 시청에 관한 전화 인터뷰 참여를 승낙했습니다.

TOEIC® Speaking

Question 4 of 11

In a typical week, how many times do you watch the weather report on television?

한 주에 보통 텔레비전에서 기상 예보를 몇 번 시청하시나요?

 **Possible Answer**

In a typical week, I watch the weather report about three times on television.

저는 한 주에 보통 텔레비전에서 기상 예보를 약 세 번 시청합니다.

Question 5 of 11

When you watch the weather report on television, what kinds of information interest you the most?

텔레비전에서 기상 예보를 시청하실 때, 어떤 정보가 가장 관심을 끄나요?

 **Possible Answer**

I am most interested in seeing information on extreme weather when I watch the weather report on television. I like this the most because I am amazed to see the power that Mother Nature is capable of.

텔레비전에서 기상 예보를 시청할 때, 저는 극심한 기상 정보에 가장 관심이 갑니다. 가장 관심이 가는 이유는 대자연의 힘을 보노라면 경이로움을 느끼기 때문입니다.

 **be interested in** ~하고 싶다   **amazed** 깜짝 놀란   **Mother Nature** 대자연   **be capable of** ~을 할 수 있다

Question 6 of 11

Do you prefer to get your weather report from the television or from another source, such as the Internet, radio, or newspapers? Why?

기상 예보를 알아볼 때 텔레비전을 선호하시나요, 아니면 인터넷, 라디오, 신문과 같은 다른 매체를 선호하시나요? 왜 그러한가요?

 **Possible Answer**

I prefer to get my weather report not from the television but rather the Internet. Of course, television is convenient but I prefer the Internet because it tends to be more up-to-date and thus, more accurate.

저는 텔레비전보다는 인터넷에서 기상 예보를 알아보는 것을 선호합니다. 텔레비전이 편리하긴 합니다만 인터넷을 선호하는 이유는 보다 더 최신이라 보다 더 정확하기 때문입니다.

 **get weather report** 일기 예보 소식을 얻다   **tend to** ~하는 경향이 있다   **up-to-date** 가장 최신의   **accurate** 정확한

Questions 7-9   Respond to Questions Using Information Provided

Directions: In this part of the test, you will answer three questions based on the information provided. You will have 30 seconds to read the information before the questions begin. For each question, begin responding immediately after you hear a beep. No additional preparation time is provided. You will have 15 seconds to respond to Questions 7 and 8 and 30 seconds to respond to Question 9.

이 파트에서 여러분은 주어진 정보에 기초하여 세 가지 질문에 대답하게 됩니다. 문제가 시작하기 전에 30초 동안 정보를 읽게 됩니다. 각 질문에 대해 '삐' 소리가 나면 즉시 대답하세요. 준비 시간은 주어지지 않습니다. 7번과 8번 문제에는 각각 15초, 그리고 9번 문제에는 30초의 응답 시간이 주어집니다.

Questions 7-9 of 11

Speedy Stylish Garments Distributor

Customer Invoice

Ordered: December 12

Ship to: Fashion Outlet, 965 Tobermory Avenue, Detroit, MI

Shipped: January 3

Item #	Amount	Description	Total Price
23-456	40	Checkered cardigans: black/red	782.20
11-909	36	Men's polo's: 18 light, 18 dark	456.00
50-001	16	Women's skirts: 7 purple, 9 pink	375.64
92-411	20	Overcoats: 5 gray, 15 charcoal	915.50
			$2,529.34

For information, please call 888-555-7654.

Hey. This is Jason Crisp, calling from our Fashion Outlet location. Our order tracking system isn't working. So I'd like to confirm some details with you about our recent order.

Speedy Stylish Garments Distributor	**배송 빠르고 우아한 의상 판매자**
Customer Invoice	*세관 송장*

Ordered: December 12

Ship to: Fashion Outlet 965 Tobermory Avenue, Detroit, MI

Shipped: January 3

Item #	Amount	Description	Total Price
23-456	40	Checkered cardigans: black/red	782.20
11-909	36	Men's polo's: 18 light, 18 dark	456.00
56-001	16	Women's skirts: 7 purple, 9 pink	375.64
92-411	20	Overcoats: 5 gray, 15 charcoal	915.50
			$2,529.34

For information, please call 888-555-7654.

Hey. This is Jason Crisp, calling from our Fashion Outlet location. Our order tracking system isn't working. So I'd like to confirm some details with you about our recent order.

주문일: 12월 12일

발송: 미시건 주, 디트로이트 시, 토버머리 가 965 Fashion Outlet

선적일: 1월 3일

품목 No.	수량	기재 사항	총액
23–456	40	체크무늬 카디건: 검정/빨강	782.20
11–909	36	남성용 폴로 셔츠: 밝은 색 18벌, 어두운 색 18벌	456.00
56–001	16	여성용 치마: 보라색 7벌, 분홍색 9벌	375.64
92–411	20	외투: 회색 5벌, 암회색 15벌	915.50
			$2,529.34

문의사항은 888–555–7654로 전화 주세요.

안녕하세요, Fashion Outlet의 Jason Crisp라고 합니다. 주문 조회 시스템을 현재 정상적으로 이용할 수가 없습니다. 그래서 최근 주문품에 대한 상세 사항을 확인하려고 전화 드렸습니다.

 garment 옷   distributor 유통사   invoice 송장

Could you tell me when the order was shipped?

주문한 물품을 언제 발송하셨나요?

 **Possible Answer**

Your clothing order was shipped on January third to 965 Tobermory Avenue, Detroit, Michigan.

1월 3일에 미시건 주, 디트로이트 시, 토버머리 가 965로 손님이 주문하신 의류를 발송해 드렸습니다.

I was going to order some of your jean jackets, but I am not sure whether I included them in this order. Could you check on that?

저는 청재킷을 주문하려고 했습니다만, 이를 주문에 포함했는지 잘 모르겠습니다. 이 사항을 확인해 주실 수 있습니까?

 **Possible Answer**

I have checked on your clothing order dated December twelfth, and there do not appear to be any orders for our jean jackets.

12월 12일자 손님의 의류 주문을 확인해 보았습니다만 저희 청재킷에 관한 주문은 전혀 없습니다.

I'd like to know what I'm getting this time. Could you give me the details about the order?

이번에 배송받을 물품이 무엇인지 알고 싶습니다. 이번 주문의 상세 내역을 알려주시겠습니까?

 **Possible Answer**

Your latest order has four items. The first item you ordered was forty black-and-red checkered cardigans. The second item was thirty-six men's polo's, half being dark, and the other half light. Next, you ordered 16 women's skirts. Of the skirts, seven are purple and nine are pink. Finally, you ordered twenty overcoats. Five of the overcoats are gray, while the remaining ones are charcoal.

손님께서는 이번에 네 가지 품목을 주문하셨습니다. 주문하신 첫 번째 품목은 검은색과 빨강색 체크무늬 카디건 40벌이었습니다. 두 번째 품목은 반은 어두운 색과 나머지는 밝은 색으로 남성용 폴로 셔츠 36벌이었습니다. 또한 여성용 치마 16벌을 주문하셨습니다. 이들 치마 중에서 일곱 벌은 보라색이고 아홉 벌은 분홍색입니다. 마지막으로 외투 20벌을 주문하셨습니다. 외투 중 다섯 벌은 회색인 반면에 나머지는 암회색입니다.

 pleated 주름을 잡은

Question 10   Propose a Solution

Directions: In this part of the test, you will be presented with a problem and asked to propose a solution. You will have 30 seconds to prepare. Then you will have 60 seconds to speak.

이 파트에서 여러분에게 한 가지 문제가 주어집니다. 여러분은 그에 대한 해결책을 제시해주세요. 30초 동안 준비한 뒤 60초 동안 응답하세요.

In your response, be sure to
- show that you recognize the problem, and
- propose a way of dealing with the problem.

여러분의 응답에서
- 여러분이 문제를 인식했다는 것을 보여주세요.
- 그 문제를 대처하는 방법을 제안해주세요.

 Hello. This is Dion, the tour guide. I'm here at the airport to pick up the undergraduates who are going to stay at your hotel, and we will arrive there before long. But I have a problem. Nine students in the group are vegetarians. I know a roast meat is prepared for a meal. But they can't eat meat at all. So, is it possible to prepare another option for vegetarians? We will arrive in less than an hour. If you want to contact me, please call 555-6969.

안녕하세요. 저는 관광 가이드 Dion입니다. 저는 귀 호텔에 투숙할 예정인 대학생들을 데리러 이곳에 와있습니다. 그리고 저희는 곧 호텔에 도착할 것입니다. 그러나 문제점이 있습니다. 일행 중 학생 9명이 채식주의자입니다. 제가 알기로는 식사로 고기 구이가 준비되어 있다고 들었습니다. 그러나 그들은 모두 고기를 먹지 못합니다. 그래서 채식주의자를 위해서 다른 선택을 준비해 주시는 것이 가능할까요? 저희는 한 시간 내에 도착할 것입니다. 555-6969로 연락 부탁드립니다.

 **pick up** 데리러 가다   **undergraduate** 대학생   **vegetarian** 채식주의자   **roast** 구이 요리

Possible Answer

인사 Hello, Dion. This is Britney. I am the concierge at the hotel.

문제 상황 인식 I got your message stating that there are nine vegetarians in the group of undergraduates.

해결책 제시 It will not be a problem to prepare another option for these students. We offer a wide variety of food here at the hotel that can easily meet the needs of our guests. Nevertheless, you may want to hear more details of today's roast. First off, you are correct that a roast will be prepared. Besides the roast pig, meat products will not be the only food item that will be roasted. There will be a lot of other non-meat products such as baked potatoes, corn on the cob, and grilled vegetables. Several side dishes will be served in addition to the roast. Some dishes include a garden salad, a potato salad, a bean salad, and an assortment of breads and non-dairy dips.

마무리 If these options still do not meet the food requirements of the guests, please let me know. As I have said, we can easily prepare an alternative to satisfy everyone.

안녕하세요, Dion 씨. 저는 호텔 관리인 Britney라고 합니다. 대학생 일행에 채식주의자가 9명이 있다는 메시지를 받았습니다. 그 학생들을 위해서 다른 선택을 준비하는 것은 문제가 아닙니다. 저희 호텔에는 고객님의 필요에 알맞은 광범위하고 다양한 음식이 있습니다. 그럼에도 불구하고, 귀하는 금일 고기 구이에 대해 더 자세한 사항을 듣기를 원하실 지도 모릅니다. 우선, 고기 구이가 준비될 것이라는 고객님의 말씀이 맞습니다. 돼지고기 구이와 고기류 음식이 유일한 구이 음식은 아닙니다. 구운 감자, 옥수수, 구운 야채 등 많은 다른 비고기류 음식이 있습니다. 다음으로 여러 가지 곁들임 요리가 고기 구이에 제공됩니다. 곁들임 요리에는 가든 샐러드, 감자 샐러드, 콩 샐러드, 각종 빵과 유제품을 함유하지 않은 소스가 있습니다. 이 음식들이 고객님 기호에 맞지 않는다면 알려주세요. 말씀드린 것처럼 저희는 여러분을 만족시킬 대안을 준비할 수 있습니다.

concierge 안내원 a wide variety of 매우 다양한 meet the needs 요구를 맞추다 nevertheless 그럼에도 불구하고 first off 먼저 non-meat product 고기가 아닌 요리 baked potato 구운 감자 corn on the cob 옥수수 grilled vegetable 구운 야채 side dish 곁들임 요리 an assortment of 갖가지의, 여러 가지의 non-dairy 우유를 넣지 않은 dip (음식을 먹기 전에 살짝 적시는) 소스

Question 11 Express an Opinion

Directions: In this part of the test, you will give your opinion about a specific topic. Be sure to say as much as you can in the time allowed. You will have 15 seconds to prepare. Then you will have 60 seconds to speak.

이 파트에서 여러분은 특정한 주제에 대한 의견을 말하게 됩니다. 주어진 시간 동안 최대한 많이 말할 수 있도록 하세요. 15초 동안 준비한 뒤 60초 동안 응답하세요.

Some people like to work with people who have similar interests and backgrounds.

Others prefer to work with people who have different interests and backgrounds.

Which do you think is better? Why or why not?

어떤 사람들은 비슷한 관심과 배경을 가진 사람들과 일하는 걸 좋아합니다.

어떤 사람들은 상이한 관심과 배경을 가진 사람들과 일하는 걸 좋아합니다.

어느 쪽이 더 낫다고 생각하십니까? 그런 이유와 또는 그렇지 않은 이유를 말해주세요.

 **Possible Answer 1 (work with people who have similar interests and backgrounds)**

의견 제시	In my experience, I prefer to work with people who have similar interests and backgrounds.
근거 제시 1	To begin with, it is easier to work with like-minded individuals.
예시	For example, I don't have to explain myself in great detail because a person who has similar interests would know what I am probably thinking, and can anticipate my thoughts and behavior.
근거 제시 2	Another reason I like to work with people with similar interests and backgrounds is that I spend a good portion of my day with my coworkers, so it would be beneficial if we could become good friends. So, while at work, my time working won't feel like such a chore since I can have a good time with my friends.
근거 제시 3	Last but not least, I can learn new and interesting things from my coworkers. Since we would have similar interests, my coworkers might have some information that I don't know but would be fascinated to learn about.
마무리	For all of these reasons, I think it is better to work with people who have similar interests and backgrounds rather than people who don't.

제 경험을 비춰보면, 저는 비슷한 관심과 배경을 가진 사람과 일하는 걸 좋아합니다. 우선, 비슷한 생각을 가진 사람들과 일하는 게 더 쉽습니다. 예를 들어, 비슷한 관심을 가진 사람이라면 제가 무슨 생각을 하고 있는지 알고 있으며 제 생각과 행동을 예측할 수 있기 때문에 그리 세세하게 제 자신을 설명할 필요가 없습니다. 비슷한 관심과 배경을 가진 사람과 일하는 걸 좋아하는 다른 이유는, 동료와 즐거운 하루를 보낼 수 있다는 점입니다. 그리하여 친한 친구가 될 수 있다면 아주 유익할 것입니다. 그러므로 친구 같은 동료와 즐겁게 보낼 수 있기 때문에 회사에서 하는 일을 하기 싫다고 느끼지 않을 것입니다. 마지막으로 가장 중요한 것은 동료에게 새롭고 재미있는 것을 배울 수 있습니다. 비슷한 관심을 가지고 있으므로, 제가 모르지만 알게 되면 매혹될 어떤 정보를 동료가 알고 있을 수 있습니다. 이런 이유 때문에 저는 상이한 관심과 배경을 가진 사람들보다는 비슷한 관심과 배경을 가진 사람들과 일하는 게 더 낫다고 생각합니다.

interests and backgrounds 관심사와 배경 like-minded 생각이 비슷한 anticipate 예상하다 thought 생각 behavior 행동 a good portion of 많은 부분의 beneficial 유익한 chore 하기 싫은 일 last but not least 마지막으로 가장 중요한 것은 fascinated 흥미를 가지게 되는 rather than ~라기 보다

Possible Answer 2 (work with people who have different interests and backgrounds)

의견 제시
In my experience, I prefer to work with people who have different interests and backgrounds.

근거 제시 1
To begin with, I think it is more interesting working with people who are different from me.

예시
For example, I can meet people from other countries. While at work, I can learn about other cultures. In the same way, I can teach other people from different backgrounds about my cultural heritage. In this way, I can feel like I am travelling the world while working.

근거 제시 2
Another reason why I think it is better to work with coworkers who are different from me is that I can discover new and different ways of accomplishing my job. Because my coworkers will have different interests and backgrounds, they will also be likely to think differently than me. Thus, they will have another perspective on how to carry out the work at hand that might be more efficient than my own. Consequently, we could finish our work more proficiently.

마무리
For all of these reasons, I think it is better to work with people who have different interests and backgrounds, rather than people who are more similar.

제 경험을 비춰보면, 저는 상이한 관심과 배경을 가진 사람과 일하는 걸 좋아합니다. 우선, 저와는 다른 사람들과 일하는 게 더 재미있다고 생각합니다. 예를 들어, 다른 나라 사람들을 만날 수 있습니다. 근무 중에 저는 다른 나라 문화를 배울 수 있습니다. 같은 방법으로 저는 제 문화적 유산을 다른 배경을 가진 사람들에게 알려줄 수 있습니다. 이런 식으로 저는 근무를 하면서도 세계 여행을 하고 있다는 기분을 느낄 수 있습니다. 저와 다른 사람들과 일하는 게 더 낫다고 생각하는 다른 이유는, 제 일을 성취하는 데 있어서 새롭고 다른 방법을 생각해낼 수 있다는 것입니다. 왜냐하면 제 동료는 상이한 관심과 배경을 가지고 있으므로, 저와는 다른 생각을 할 것이기 때문입니다. 즉, 제 동료에게 제 방식보다 더 효율적일 수 있는 다른 시각의 업무처리 방법이 있을 수 있습니다. 그 결과, 저희는 업무를 더욱 능숙하게 마무리할 수 있습니다. 이런 이유 때문에 저는 비슷한 관심과 배경을 가진 사람들보다는 상이한 관심과 배경을 가진 사람들과 일하는 게 더 낫다고 생각합니다.

prefer 선호하다 culture 문화 in the same way 똑같은 방식으로 cultural heritage 문화유산 in this way 이렇게 discover 발견하다 accomplish 성취하다 thus 그러므로 perspective 관점, 시점 carry out 실행하다 at hand 수중에, 가까이에 consequently 따라서 proficiently 능숙하게

Questions 1-2 Read a Text Aloud

Directions: In this part of the test, you will read aloud the text on the screen. You will have 45 seconds to prepare. Then you will have 45 seconds to read the text aloud.

이 파트에서 여러분은 스크린의 텍스트를 큰 소리로 읽게 됩니다. 45초의 준비 시간이 주어지고, 그 후 45초 동안 텍스트를 큰 소리로 읽으세요.

TOEIC® Speaking

Question 1 of 11

Are you looking for a new condominium? This July, Velco Realtors will begin leasing rental units in Tribeca Square, officially recognized as the Tribeca Condominium Square. The central locality, free underground parking, and alluring architecture will fascinate customers. What's more, you'll get free Wi-Fi Internet access and on-site IT support. For more information, call 1-800-555-7734.

새로운 콘도를 찾고 계십니까? 이번 7월 Velco 부동산은 공식적으로 Tribeca Condominium Square로 명명된 Tribeca Square에서 건물을 임대하기 시작합니다. 중심지 소재, 무료 지하 주차장, 그리고 매력적 구조가 여러분을 매혹시킬 것입니다. 게다가 무료 와이파이 인터넷 접속 및 현장 IT 지원 서비스를 제공해 드립니다. 더 자세한 내용은 1-800-555-7734로 전화 주세요.

 **Speaking Solution**

Are you looking for a new **condominium**?↗(be동사 의문문 맨 끝) This **July**(시간/날짜/숫자 강세), ↗(계속 의미/쉼표 뒤 짧게 끊고) **Velco Realtors**(고유명사 강세) will begin leasing **rental units** in **Tribeca Square**(고유명사 강세), ↗(계속 의미/쉼표 뒤 짧게 끊고) officially **recognized** as the **Tribeca Condominium Square**(고유명사 강세). ↘(문장의 맨 끝) **The central locality**↗, **free underground parking**↗, and **alluring architecture**↘(A↗, B↗ and C↘) will **fascinate customers**.↘(문장의 맨 끝) **What's more**(부가 강조), you'll get **free Wi-Fi Internet access**(주요 내용 강세) and **on-site IT support**(주요 내용 강세). For more information, call **1-800-555-7734**(시간/날짜/숫자 강세). ↘(문장의 맨 끝)

 condominium 아파트   realtor 부동산   lease 임대하다   be recognized as ~로서 인정되다   central locality 중앙 지역
underground 지하의   alluring 매력적인   fascinate 매혹시키다

This is Robert Thornson with Daybreak Traffic Watch. Because of last night's severe hailstorms, many areas of the city have no electricity. This situation will make the morning drive especially difficult. At the present time, the traffic lights on Yonge, Bay and St. George streets are not functioning. So you may want to steer clear of these areas.

새벽 교통 정보의 Robert Thornson입니다. 지난밤 우박을 동반한 폭풍 때문에 도시의 많은 지역이 현재 정전 상태입니다. 이 상황은 아침 운전을 어렵게 할 것입니다. 현재 Yonge, Bay 및 St. George 가의 교통 신호등이 작동하지 않습니다. 따라서 여러분께서는 이 지역으로의 통행을 피하시기 바랍니다.

 **Speaking Solution**

This is **Robert Thornson**(고유명사 강세) / (전명구 앞 짧게 끊고) with **Daybreak Traffic Watch**.↘(문장의 맨 끝) Because of last night's severe **hailstorms**.↗(계속 의미/쉼표 뒤 짧게 끊고) many areas of the **city** have **no**(부정어 강세) **electricity**.↘(문장의 맨 끝) This **situation** will make the morning drive **especially difficult**.↘(문장의 맨 끝) At the **present time**.↗(계속 의미/쉼표 뒤 짧게 끊고) the **traffic light** on **Yonge**↗, **Bay**↗ and **St. George streets**↘(A↗, B↗ and C↘) are **not**(부정어 강세) **functioning**.↘(문장의 맨 끝) So you may want to **steer clear**(중요 의미 강세) of these areas.↘(문장의 맨 끝)

 daybreak traffic watch 새벽 교통 정보   hailstorm 폭풍   electricity 전기   morning drive 아침 출근 운전
especially 특히   difficult 어려운   present time 현재   function 작동하다   steer clear of ~을 피하다

Question 3   Describe a Picture

Directions: In this part of the test, you will describe the picture on your screen in as much detail as you can. You will have 30 seconds to prepare your response. Then you will have 45 seconds to speak about the picture.

이 파트에서 여러분은 스크린의 사진을 최대한 자세히 설명하게 됩니다. 대답을 위해 30초의 준비 시간이 주어지고, 그 후 45초 동안 사진에 대해 설명하세요.

 **Possible Answer**

In this picture, there is a large bed that has been made. There are three white pillows by the wooden headboard and a white comforter spread on top of the bed. There are two nightstands lit on each edge side of the headboard. On the left side of the bed is a night table that matches the color of the headboard. On the far right side is a window that has white curtains drawn. I think that this picture is from a hotel room because of the professionally made bed and lack of any personal belongings like pictures.

이 사진 속에는 대형 침대가 정돈되어 있습니다. 침대 위 나무 머리판 가까이 세 개의 하얀 베개들이 있고 하얀 이불이 놓여져 있습니다. 머리판 양쪽 옆에는 침실용 스탠드가 켜져 있습니다. 침대 왼쪽으로 침실용 탁자가 있고 그것은 침대 나무색과 잘 어울립니다. 멀리 오른쪽에는 하얀 커튼이 쳐져 있는 창문이 있습니다. 전문적으로 잘 정돈된 침대와 사진과 같은 개인 용품이 보이지 않기 때문에 이 사진은 호텔방에서 찍힌 것이라고 생각됩니다.

 **make a bed** 침대를 정돈하다   **pillow** 베개   **headboard** 침대 머리판   **comforter** 이불   **white curtains drawn** 쳐져 있는 하얀색의 커튼

Questions 4-6　Respond to Questions

Directions: In this part of the test, you will answer three questions. For each question, begin responding immediately after you hear a beep. No preparation time is provided. You will have 15 seconds to respond to Questions 4 and 5 and 30 seconds to respond to Question 6.

이 파트에서 여러분은 세 가지 질문에 답하게 됩니다. 각 질문에 대해 '삐' 소리가 나면 즉시 대답하세요. 준비 시간은 주어지지 않습니다. 4번과 5번 문제에는 각각 15초, 그리고 6번 문제에는 30초의 응답 시간이 주어집니다.

Imagine that an American marketing firm is doing research in your country. You have agreed to participate in a telephone interview about clothes.

어느 미국 마케팅 회사가 여러분의 나라에서 조사를 하고 있다고 가정해 봅시다. 여러분은 옷에 관한 전화 인터뷰 참여를 승낙했습니다.

TOEIC® Speaking

Question 4 of 11

What kind of attire do people wear at your school or work?

여러분의 학교나 회사에서 사람들은 어떤 종류의 옷을 입습니까?

 **Possible Answer**

At my place of work, most people dress in a business casual fashion. Men and women are encouraged to wear button shirts, dress pants, and dress shoes. On Fridays, however, we are allowed to dress more casually than normal.

제 회사에서 대부분의 사람들은 비즈니스 캐주얼 패션을 취합니다. 남녀는 와이셔츠, 정장 바지와 정장 구두의 착용을 권고받습니다. 하지만 금요일에는 평상시보다 더 캐주얼하게 입을 수 있습니다.

 **attire** 옷　**dress** 옷을 입다　**be encouraged to** ~하도록 권고받다　**dress pants** 정장 바지　**dress shoes** 정장 구두
be allowed to ~가 허락되다

How often do you buy outfits for your school or work?

학교나 회사용 옷을 얼마나 자주 구매하시나요?

 **Possible Answer**

I usually buy outfits for my place of work twice a year. I don't like to spend much time shopping so I buy a few outfits each time.

저는 보통 일 년에 두 번 회사용 옷을 구매합니다. 저는 쇼핑에 많은 시간을 쓰는 걸 좋아하지 않습니다. 그래서 그때마다 두세 벌의 옷을 구매합니다.

 outfit 옷

What kind of features should a good clothing store have?

좋은 의류 상점이 지녀야 할 특징이 무엇입니까?

 **Possible Answer**

In my opinion, a good clothing store should have a variety of clothes. It should be quite big and should have good collections in casuals as well as formals. It should also have clothes of the latest fashion. And most importantly, it should have discounts on the products.

제 의견으로, 좋은 의류 상점은 다양한 옷을 구비해야 합니다. 상점은 꽤 커야 하고 정장뿐만 아니라 캐주얼 옷을 아우르는 괜찮은 물건이 있어야 합니다. 또한 최신 패션 의류를 구비해야 합니다. 그리고 가장 중요한 점은 제품 할인입니다.

 feature 특징   a variety of 다양한   latest 최신의

Questions 7-9 Respond to Questions Using Information Provided

Directions: In this part of the test, you will answer three questions based on the information provided. You will have 30 seconds to read the information before the questions begin. For each question, begin responding immediately after you hear a beep. No additional preparation time is provided. You will have 15 seconds to respond to Questions 7 and 8 and 30 seconds to respond to Question 9.

이 파트에서 여러분은 주어진 정보에 기초하여 세 가지 질문에 대답하게 됩니다. 문제가 시작하기 전에 30초 동안 정보를 읽게 됩니다. 각 질문에 대해 '삐' 소리가 나면 즉시 대답하세요. 준비 시간은 주어지지 않습니다. 7번과 8번 문제에는 각각 15초, 그리고 9번 문제에는 30초의 응답 시간이 주어집니다.

Questions 7-9 of 11

New Music Releases – Sam's Disc Superstore

Title	Date Released	Genre
The Jetsons	June 12	Alternative

*** Monthly Special – 15% discount on all New Releases (Members only!)**

Title	Date Released	Genre
~~Fantastic Seven~~	~~July 21~~	~~Trance~~
American Sweets	July 24	Disco
Samsonites	July 26	Rock and Roll

*** Monthly Special – Buy 3 albums and get 1 free**

Title	Date Released	Genre
Bach's Greatest Hits	August 3	Classical

*** Monthly Special – To be announced in July**

I am a customer at Sam's Disc Superstore. Could you answer some questions for me?

New Music Releases – Sam's Disc Superstore

Title	Date Released	Genre
The Jetsons	June 12	Alternative

* Monthly Special – 15% discount on all New Releases (Members only!)

Title	Date Released	Genre
~~Fantastic Seven~~	~~July 21~~	~~Trance~~
American Sweets	July 24	Disco
Samsonites	July 26	Rock and Roll

* Monthly Special – Buy 3 albums and get 1 free

Title	Date Released	Genre
Bach's Greatest Hits	August 3	Classical

* Monthly Special – To be announced in July

I am a customer at Sam's Disc Superstore. Could you answer some questions for me?

새로운 노래를 발매합니다 – Sam's Disc Superstore

제목	발매일	장르
더 젯손	6월 12일	얼터네이티브

* 월별 특별 행사 – 모든 새로운 노래 15% 할인(회원만 해당!)

제목	발매일	장르
~~판타스틱 세븐~~	~~7월 21일~~	~~트랜스~~
아메리칸 스위트	7월 24일	디스코
샘소니티	7월 26일	록앤 롤

* 월별 특별 행사 – 앨범 3장 구매 시 1장 무료

제목	발매일	장르
바흐의 베스트 앨범	8월 3일	클래식

* 월별 특별 행사 – 7월에 공지 예정

저는 Sam's Disc Superstore의 이용자입니다. 문의를 드려도 될까요?

 **release** 발매하다, 출시하다; 발매 음반

Which album is being released in June?

6월에 어떤 앨범이 발매되나요?

 **Possible Answer**

According to the schedule, the album "The Jetsons" will be released in June.

스케줄에 따르면 6월에 "더 젯손" 앨범이 발매될 것입니다.

I am really looking forward to listening to the album, "Fantastic Seven." Will this be released in July?

저는 "판타스틱 세븐" 앨범 듣기를 학수고대하고 있습니다. 이것은 7월에 발매될까요?

 **Possible Answer**

Unfortunately, "Fantastic Seven" will not be released in July. I regret to inform you about that and I am sorry for the inconvenience since you will have to wait longer to listen to this Trance album due to the delay.

안타깝습니다만 "판타스틱 세븐"은 7월에 발매되지 않을 것입니다. 이 트랜스 앨범을 들으려면 지연 때문에 더 오래 기다리셔야 하므로 불편을 드려 죄송합니다.

 I regret to inform you 알려 주게 되어 유감입니다   inconvenience 불편함

Would you kindly inform me all the details about the special offers for each month?

각 달의 특별 행사에 대해 상세하게 알려 주실 수 있나요?

 **Possible Answer**

Sure. First, it should be noted that the "Monthly Specials" are available for members only. Thus, if you are not a member yet, I suggest you register. That being said, members receive a fifteen percent discount on all New Release purchases in the month of June and will receive one free album after buying three albums during the month of July. August's "Monthly Special" will be announced in July.

물론입니다. 먼저 "월별 특별 행사"는 회원에게만 해당된다는 것을 주시해 주세요. 따라서 고객님께서 아직 회원이 아니시라면, 등록을 권유해 드립니다. 회원은 6월의 모든 새로운 앨범 구매 시 15% 할인을 받고, 7월에는 앨범 3장 구매 시 1장은 무료입니다. 8월의 "월별 특별 행사"는 7월에 공지될 예정입니다.

 register 등록하다

Question 10   Propose a Solution

Directions: In this part of the test, you will be presented with a problem and asked to propose a solution. You will have 30 seconds to prepare. Then you will have 60 seconds to speak.

이 파트에서 여러분에게 한 가지 문제가 주어집니다. 여러분은 그에 대한 해결책을 제시해주세요. 30초 동안 준비한 뒤 60초 동안 응답하세요.

In your response, be sure to
- show that you recognize the problem, and
- propose a way of dealing with the problem.

여러분의 응답에서
- 여러분이 문제를 인식했다는 것을 보여주세요.
- 그 문제를 대처하는 방법을 제안해주세요.

 Hello. This is Bob from the administration. As you know, I will be making a presentation next Wednesday for our monthly meeting. I was told this meeting will also be televised to our branches in Amsterdam and Germany. The dilemma is that I've never given a presentation in front of such a large group of spectators. I know that you have the experience of being the last presenter. I was wondering if you can give me some advice on how to make a great speech in front of so many people. If you want to contact me, please call 800-3624. Once again, my name is Bob. Thanks.

안녕하세요. 저는 행정관리부에 있는 Bob이라고 합니다. 아시다시피, 저는 다음 주 수요일의 월간 회의에서 프레젠테이션을 할 것입니다. 저는 이 회의가 암스테르담과 독일에 있는 지점으로도 방송될 것이라고 이야기 들었습니다. 문제는 제가 그렇게 많은 청중들 앞에서 프레젠테이션을 한 적이 없다는 것입니다. 귀하께서는 최근에 프레젠테이션을 하신 적이 있다고 알고 있습니다. 많은 사람들 앞에서 좋은 발표를 할 수 있는 방법에 대해서 제게 조금이나마 조언을 해주실 수 있을까요? 저는 Bob이고 800-3624로 연락하실 수 있습니다. 감사합니다.

 **make a presentation** 발표하다   **televise** 텔레비전으로 방송하다   **branch** 지점   **dilemma** 문제, 힘든 점   **spectator** 관객   **contact** 연락하다

 **Possible Answer**

인사	Hello, Bob. This is Claire Mackenzie returning your call.
문제 상황 인식	First, I would like to congratulate you on being the next speaker at our monthly meeting. I am not the only colleague to hear of your success in our company. So, it should be no surprise that our other branches would like to watch your presentation. I understand that you may feel a bit anxious since you have not done any public speaking in front of such a large group of viewers.
해결책 제시	The most important advice that I can give to you is to practice your presentation beforehand until you feel comfortable enough that you don't have to rely on cue cards or notes that much. Also, remember that the people viewing really want to hear what you have to say. They are not there to criticize you. They are your peers, and you should feel honored to share your insights into how you gained success. I am sure you will do a great job.
마무리	If you need any more advice or want to talk more, please don't hesitate to call back. Good luck.

안녕하세요, Bob 씨. 저는 Claire Mackenzie입니다. 전화 주셨다면서요? 우선, 월간 회의에서 다음 발표자로 선정되신 것을 축하드립니다. 저는 회사에서 귀하의 성공 소식을 들은 유일한 동료가 아닙니다. 그러므로 다른 지점에서 귀하의 프레젠테이션을 보길 원하는 것은 놀랄만한 일이 아닙니다. 많은 청중 앞에서 전혀 연설을 해본 적이 없으시므로 다소 걱정을 하실 수 있다는 것을 이해합니다. 제가 해드릴 수 있는 최선의 조언은 큐 카드나 노트에 거의 의존하지 않고 발표하실 수 있을 정도의 충분한 자신감이 생길 때까지 미리 프레젠테이션을 연습해 보시라는 것입니다. 또한 청중은 귀하가 말씀하는 것을 듣고 싶어 한다는 것을 주지하세요. 그들은 귀하를 비판하려고 거기에 있는 것이 아닙니다. 그들은 귀하의 동료이고 귀하는 성공 방법에 대한 식견을 공유함으로써 존중받는 느낌을 받을 것입니다. 저는 귀하가 잘 해낼 것이라고 확신합니다. 조언이 더 필요하거나 더 이야기를 나누길 원하신다면, 망설이지 마시고 연락 주세요. 행운을 빕니다.

colleague 동료   anxious 걱정하는, 불안해하는   pubic speaking 대중 연설   viewer 시청자   practice 연습하다
beforehand 미리, 사전에   rely on 의존하다   cue card 큐 카드(발표자기 말할 내용을 읽을 수 있게 들이 보여주는 가드)
criticize 비평하다   peer 동료   insight 통찰력   gain success 성공을 얻다   hesitate 망설이다, 주저하다

Question 11 Express an Opinion

Directions: In this part of the test, you will give your opinion about a specific topic. Be sure to say as much as you can in the time allowed. You will have 15 seconds to prepare. Then you will have 60 seconds to speak.

이 파트에서 여러분은 특정한 주제에 대한 의견을 말하게 됩니다. 주어진 시간 동안 최대한 많이 말할 수 있도록 하세요. 15초 동안 준비한 뒤 60초 동안 응답하세요.

Do you agree or disagree with the following statement?

The best employees are those who finish their duties in the shortest amount of time.

Give reasons and examples to support your answer.

여러분은 다음 진술에 동의하시나요, 동의하지 않으시나요?

최고의 종업원은 그들의 임무를 최단 시간에 마무리하는 사람이다.

여러분의 의견을 뒷받침하는 이유와 예시를 들어주십시오.

 **Possible Answer 1 (agree)**

의견 제시   I agree with the statement that the best employees are those who finish their duties in the shortest amount of time, for several reasons.

근거 제시 1   First, finishing work in the shortest amount of time demonstrates that employees have the skills to be efficient. They would not waste time on unnecessary tasks and have created more time for other important duties or work.

근거 제시 2   Next, by not prolonging the time to complete their work, employees display to others how they are well-organized. Organization is important when completing an essential task because it ensures the likelihood that details were not overlooked or skipped.

근거 제시 3   Finally, employees who complete their job in the shortest time are very much motivated. In many cases, these motivated workers show their outstanding abilities by completing tasks quickly.

마무리   Thus, workers who finish their tasks in the shortest time are the best employees.

저는 최고의 종업원은 그들의 임무를 최단 시간에 마무리하는 사람이라는 진술에 여러 가지 이유로 동의합니다. 우선, 최단 시간에 일을 끝낸다는 것은 종업원이 효율적인 기술을 가지고 있음을 증명합니다. 종업원은 불필요한 작업에 시간을 낭비하지 않을 것이고 다른 중요한 임무와 일에 더 많은 시간을 할당할 것입니다. 다음으로, 일을 마치는 시간을 연장하지 않음으로써 종업원은 다른 사람들에게 그들이 잘 조직화되어 있다는 것을 보여줍니다. 중요한 작업을 완성하려면 체계성이 중요합니다. 이것이 세부사항이 좌시되고 간과되지 않도록 하기 때문입니다. 마지막으로 그들의 임무를 최단 시간에 마무리하는 종업원은 매우 일에 의욕을 가지고 있을 것입니다. 여러 방면으로, 일에 의욕을 가지고 있는 종업원들은 빨리 임무 완성을 함으로써 그들의 뛰어난 능력을 보여줍니다. 따라서 최고의 종업원들은 그들의 임무를 최단 시간에 마무리하는 사람이라는 진술에 동의합니다.

 in the shortest amount of time 최단 시간으로   efficient 효율적인   unnecessary task 불필요한 일   prolonging the time 시간을 미루는 것   well-organized 매우 조직적인   organization 체계성   essential task 중요한 일   likelihood 가능성   overlook 못 보고 넘어가다, 간과하다   skip 빠뜨리다, 건너뛰다   motivated 의욕을 가진   outstanding 뛰어난   ability 능력   by completing tasks 일을 마침으로써

 Possible Answer 2 (disagree)

의견 제시   I disagree with the statement that the best employees are those who finish their duties in the shortest amount of time, for several reasons.

근거 제시 1   First, it is possible that employees rush through their work to get the job done. However, finishing work in the shortest amount of time does not guarantee that the work was done properly. By working too quickly, small details could be overlooked or missed. As a result, this could cause problems for the workplace at a later time.

근거 제시 2   I also disagree with the statement because I believe that the best employees care to do their best, which is not the same as doing work quickly. Doing the best job certainly takes more time.

예시   For example, certain projects need many specialists who are experts in their fields. To get a project perfectly well done, they will have to attend many meetings and make important decisions, which definitely takes time. Although it takes time, the best employees will ensure that their work performance and the quality of their projects is to the best of their ability.

마무리   Therefore, I don't think the best employees are the ones who finish their duties in the shortest amount of time.

저는 최고의 종업원은 그들의 임무를 최단 시간에 마무리하는 사람이라는 진술에 여러 가지 이유로 동의하지 않습니다. 우선, 종업원이 업무를 마무리하기 위해 그들의 일을 급하게 해 치울 가능성이 있습니다. 그러나 최단 시간에 일을 마무리하는 것은 일을 올바르게 마무리한다는 것을 보장하지 않습니다. 너무 빠르게 일을 진행하면 세세한 사항이 간과되거나 누락될 수 있습니다. 결과적으로, 이것은 차후 직장에 문제를 야기할 수 있습니다. 제가 진술에 동의하지 않는 다른 이유는 최고의 종업원은 최고의 성과를 내려고 한다고 생각하기 때문이며 이것은 일을 빠르게 처리하는 것과 동일하지 않습니다. 일을 잘 히려면 당연히 시간이 필요합니다. 예를 들어, 어떤 일에는 그 분야에서의 전문가나 전문 지식인들이 필요합니다. 그 일을 완벽히 마치기 위해서는 수많은 미팅을 하고 중요한 결정을 내려야 하며 이것들은 당연히 시간을 필요로 합니다. 그렇게 시간이 필요함에도 불구하고, 최고의 종업원은 그들의 업무 성과와 일의 질을 최대한의 능력으로 할 것을 확실히 보장할 것입니다. 따라서 저는 최고의 종업원은 그들의 임무를 최단 시간에 마무리하는 사람이라는 진술에 동의하지 않습니다.

 rush through work 일을 급하게 하다   properly 올바르게   miss 놓치다   cause 일으키다   at a later time 나중에

Questions 1-2 Read a Text Aloud

Directions: In this part of the test, you will read aloud the text on the screen. You will have 45 seconds to prepare. Then you will have 45 seconds to read the text aloud.

이 파트에서 여러분은 스크린의 텍스트를 큰 소리로 읽게 됩니다. 45초의 준비 시간이 주어지고, 그 후 45초 동안 텍스트를 큰 소리로 읽으세요.

TOEIC® Speaking

Question 1 of 11

The Butterfly Spectators' Association is delighted to present Randy Desouza who is currently a professor at Victoria College. Randy has been researching butterflies living in the wilderness for more than 15 years. And now Randy will be joining us to enlighten us about the places to watch the butterflies such as outdoor gardens, zoos other than in urban areas, and nearby parks.

나비 탐구 협회에 현 빅토리아 대학의 교수이신 Randy Desouza님이 참석해 주셔서 영광입니다. Randy 교수님은 15년 이상 야생에 서식하는 나비를 연구했습니다. 이제 Randy 교수님은 도시 지역, 근처 공원 외에 야외 정원, 동물원과 같은 나비를 관찰할 수 있는 장소를 알려 주시고자 저희 팀에 합류하실 것입니다.

 **Speaking Solution**

The **Butterfly Spectators' Association**(고유명사 강세) is **delighted**(감정 강세) to present **Randy Desouza**(고유명사 강세) / (절 앞에 잠시 쉬고) who is **currently** a **professor** at **Victoria College**(고유명사 강세). **Randy** has been **researching butterflies**(중요 의미 강세) / (부가 의미 앞 잠시 끊고) living in the **wilderness**(중요 의미 강세) for **more** than **15 years**(시간/날짜/숫자 강세). And now **Randy**(고유명사 강세) will be joining us to **enlighten** us about the **places** to watch the **butterflies** / (부가 의미 앞 잠시 끊고) such as **outdoor gardens**↗, **zoos**↗ other than in **urban areas**, and **nearby parks**↘(A↗, B↗ and C↘).

 **be delighted to** ~에 기뻐하다 **present** 소개하다 **wilderness** 야생지 **enlighten** 설명하다 **urban** 도시의

Are you planning an event? Marty's Merrymaking Rental Shop has everything you need to make your celebration a sensation. We offer a large assortment of tables, chairs and tents, and even provide free delivery. Whether you are planning a cafe event or a created event, Marty's Merrymaking Rental Shop can be of assistance. Plus this weekend only, we will take twenty percent off our usual prices.

행사를 계획하고 계십니까? Marty's Merrymaking 대여점에는 축하 행사를 감각 있게 꾸미기 위해 여러분께서 필요로 하는 모든 것이 있습니다. 저희는 각종 탁자, 의자 및 텐트를 제공하며 무료 배달서비스도 제공해 드립니다. 여러분께서 계획하시는 이벤트가 카페 이벤트 이든 창의적으로 준비해서 만드는 이벤트 이든, Marty's Merrymaking 대여점이 도움이 될 것입니다. 또한 이번 주말에만 저희는 평소 가격에서 20%를 할인해 드릴 것입니다.

 ## Speaking Solution

Are you **planning** an **event**? / (be동사 의문문 맨 끝) **Marty's Merrymaking Rental Shop**(고유명사) has **everything**(all/every 강조) you need / (부가 외미 앞 잠시 끊고) to **make** your **celebration a sensation**. \ (문장의 맨 끝) We offer a large assortment of tables, ↗ chairs, ↗ and tents \ (A, ↗ B, ↗ and C \), and even provide **free delivery**. \ (문장의 맨 끝) Whether you are planning a **cafe event** or a created **event**. / (계속 의미/쉼표 뒤 짧게 끊고) **Marty's Merrymaking Rental Shop**(고유명사 강세) can be of **assistance**. \ (문장의 맨 끝) **Plus** this weekend **only**(의미상 강조), / (계속 의미/쉼표 뒤 짧게 끊고) we will take **twenty**(숫자 강세) **percent off**(의미 강세) our usual **prices**. \ (문장의 맨 끝)

 **merrymaking** 떠들썩하게 놀기 **celebration** 축하 **sensation** 감각, 대사건 **offer** 제공하다 **a large assortment of** 매우 다양한 **be of assistance** 도움이 되다

Question 3   Describe a Picture

Directions: In this part of the test, you will describe the picture on your screen in as much detail as you can. You will have 30 seconds to prepare your response. Then you will have 45 seconds to speak about the picture.

이 파트에서 여러분은 스크린의 사진을 최대한 자세히 설명하게 됩니다. 대답을 위해 30초의 준비 시간이 주어지고, 그 후 45초 동안 사진에 대해 설명하세요.

 **Possible Answer**

There are five young people sitting at a table in the picture. Three of the people are men, and they are sitting in the middle, and two women are sitting at the ends. They appear to be eating lunch while they are studying. On the table, there are open books and some food. They look happy and are smiling. The woman on the left side of the picture is blonde, while the woman on the right side is a redhead. I think that these young people are students because they are dressed casually.

사진에는 젊은이 다섯 명이 탁자 주변에 앉아 있습니다. 이들 중 세 명은 남성으로 중간에 앉아 있으며 두 여성은 끝에 앉아 있습니다. 공부하면서 점심을 먹고 있는 듯합니다. 탁자에는 펼쳐진 책과 음식이 있습니다. 이들은 행복해 보이고 미소를 짓고 있습니다. 사진의 왼편에 있는 여성은 금발인 반면에 오른편에 있는 여성은 빨강 머리입니다. 젊은이들이 캐주얼하게 입고 있기 때문에 학생이라고 생각합니다.

 **at the end** 끝부분에   **appear** ~인 것 같다   **blonde** 금발인   **redhead** 빨강 머리

Questions 4-6   Respond to Questions

Directions: In this part of the test, you will answer three questions. For each question, begin responding immediately after you hear a beep. No preparation time is provided. You will have 15 seconds to respond to Questions 4 and 5 and 30 seconds to respond to Question 6.

이 파트에서 여러분은 세 가지 질문에 답하게 됩니다. 각 질문에 대해 '삐' 소리가 나면 즉시 대답하세요. 준비 시간은 주어지지 않습니다. 4번과 5번 문제에는 각각 15초, 그리고 6번 문제에는 30초의 응답 시간이 주어집니다.

Imagine that a U.S. marketing firm is doing research in your country. You have agreed to participate in a telephone interview about hair salons.

어느 미국 마케팅 회사가 여러분의 나라에서 조사를 하고 있다고 가정해 봅시다. 여러분은 미용실에 관한 전화 인터뷰 참여를 승낙했습니다.

<table>
<tr><td>TOEIC® Speaking</td></tr>
<tr><td align="center">Question 4 of 11</td></tr>
</table>

When was the last time you went to a barber or hair stylist?

마지막으로 이발사나 미용사를 찾아간 것은 언제입니까?

 **Possible Answer**

The last time I went to get my hair done was four weeks ago. I don't like my hair unkempt, so I get a haircut regularly.

마지막으로 머리 손질을 한 것은 4주 전이었습니다. 저는 단정치 못하고 흐트러진 것을 싫어해서 정기적으로 머리 손질을 합니다.

 **barber** 이발사   **hair stylist** 미용사   **unkempt** 단정하지 못한, 덥수룩한

How far is your home from your barber shop or hair salon?

이발소나 미용실이 집에서 얼마나 멀리 있나요?

 **Possible Answer**

The salon that I usually visit is about twenty kilometers away from my home. It takes me about fifteen minutes to travel there by car or about thirty minutes by bus.

제가 주로 다니는 미용실은 집에서 약 20킬로미터 떨어져 있습니다. 그곳까지 가는데 차로는 약 15분이, 버스로는 약 30분이 걸립니다.

What do you like most about going to your barber shop or hair salon?

현재 다니는 이발소나 미용실의 무엇이 가장 맘에 드시나요?

 **Possible Answer**

The thing that I like most about going to my salon is that my hair stylist knows how to cut and style my hair in a fashionable way. She always does a phenomenal job and never lets me down. That is why I continue to be a loyal customer and return regularly.

제가 다니는 미용실의 가장 맘에 드는 점은 담당 미용사가 제 머리를 유행에 맞게 자르고 스타일을 살리는 법을 안다는 점입니다. 그녀는 늘 멋지게 손질해주며 결코 저를 실망시키지 않습니다. 이것이 제가 주요 단골 고객이 되어 정기적으로 다시 찾아가는 이유입니다.

 in a fashionable way 유행을 따라, 멋지게   phenomenal 굉장한   let down 실망시키다   loyal 충실한
return regularly 정기적으로 다시 찾아 가다

Questions 7-9 Respond to Questions Using Information Provided

Directions: In this part of the test, you will answer three questions based on the information provided. You will have 30 seconds to read the information before the questions begin. For each question, begin responding immediately after you hear a beep. No additional preparation time is provided. You will have 15 seconds to respond to Questions 7 and 8 and 30 seconds to respond to Question 9.

이 파트에서 여러분은 주어진 정보에 기초하여 세 가지 질문에 대답하게 됩니다. 문제가 시작하기 전에 30초 동안 정보를 읽게 됩니다. 각 질문에 대해 '삐' 소리가 나면 즉시 대답하세요. 준비 시간은 주어지지 않습니다. 7번과 8번 문제에는 각각 15초, 그리고 9번 문제에는 30초의 응답 시간이 주어집니다.

Questions 7-9 of 11

Exhibition for Cafés
at the Convention Center

Preparation Checklist for Expo

Due dates	Materials to be submitted
☐ January 11	Display booth application (available on homepage or at Convention Center)
☐ February 15	Signed display booth contract
☐ March 3	Outline of your company for program brochure
☐ March 31	Advertisement for program brochure (non-compulsory)
☐ April 1	Payment closing date
☐ April 19	Leaflet inserts for program brochure (non-compulsory)

I'd like to open a café, and I really want to have a display booth at the exhibition. I'd like to know what I need to do.

Exhibition for Cafés at the Convention Center	카페를 위한 전시 컨벤션 센터에서
Preparation Checklist for Expo	*엑스포 준비 체크리스트*

Due dates	Materials to be submitted
☐ January 11	Display booth application (available on homepage or at Convention Center)
☐ February 15	Signed display booth contract
☐ March 3	Outline of your company for program brochure
☐ March 31	Advertisement for program brochure (non-compulsory)
☐ April 1	Payment closing date
☐ April 19	Leaflet inserts for program brochure (non-compulsory)

마감일	자료 제출
☐ 1월 11일	전시 부스 신청서 (홈페이지 또는 컨벤션 센터에서 신청 가능)
☐ 2월 15일	전시 부스 계약 체결
☐ 3월 3일	프로그램 책자를 위한 귀사의 개요
☐ 3월 31일	프로그램 책자를 위한 광고 (비의무)
☐ 4월 1일	지불 마감일
☐ 4월 19일	프로그램 책자를 위한 전단지 삽입 광고 (비의무)

I'd like to open a café, and I really want to have a display booth at the exhibition. I'd like to know what I need to do.

저는 카페를 열고 싶습니다. 그리고 전시회에서 전시 부스를 갖고 싶어요. 제가 해야 할 일을 알고 싶습니다.

 exhibition 전시 materials to be submitted 제출되어야 할 서류 display booth application 전시 부스 신청서 contract 계약서 outline 개요 non-compulsory 의무적이지 않은 payment closing date 지불 마감일 leaflet 광고지, 전단지 insert 삽입 광고

Where can I find an application, and when do I need to send it there?

어디에서 신청서를 찾을 수 있을까요? 그리고 언제 신청서를 보내야 하나요?

 **Possible Answer**

You can find an application on the Convention Center's homepage. In addition, you can visit the Convention Center and pick up an application form. Please send the application in by January 11th.

귀하는 컨벤션 센터의 홈페이지에서 신청서를 찾을 수 있습니다. 또한, 컨벤션 센터에 방문하여 신청서를 수령하실 수 있습니다. 1월 11일까지 신청서를 보내주시기 바랍니다.

 application 신청서 pick up 직접 가져가다

Do I need to include my payment with the display booth application?

전시 부스 신청서 제출 시 지불해야 하나요?

 **Possible Answer**

It is not necessary to include your payment with the application. However, the payment closing date is April 1st.

신청서 제출 시 지불하실 필요는 없습니다. 그러나 지불 마감일은 4월 1일입니다.

I want to make sure that there's a lot of information about my café in the program brochure. What can I do?

프로그램 책자에 저의 카페 관련 정보가 많이 실리도록 하고 싶습니다. 제가 무엇을 할 수 있을까요?

 **Possible Answer**

To ensure that there is enough information about your café in the program brochure, please supply an outline of your business by March 3rd. In addition, you have the option to have advertisements printed for the program brochure, which needs to be done by the end of March. Finally, the program brochure can be accompanied by leaflet inserts about your café as long as they are ready by April 19th. Please note that the leaflets are non-compulsory like the advertisements.

프로그램 책자에 귀하의 카페 관련 정보가 많이 실리게 하려면 3월 3일까지 귀하의 비즈니스의 개요를 제출하세요. 또한 프로그램 책자에 인쇄 광고를 낼 수 있는 선택도 가능하며, 3월 말까지 광고 신청을 할 필요가 있습니다. 마지막으로, 4월 19일까지 준비된다면 귀하의 카페에 관련한 전단지 삽입 광고가 동반될 수 있습니다. 광고와 마찬가지로 전단지는 의무가 아닙니다.

 **supply** 제공하다   **be accompanied by** 함께 첨부하다   **as long as** ~하는 한   **Please note that** 유념해주세요

Question 10   Propose a Solution

Directions: In this part of the test, you will be presented with a problem and asked to propose a solution. You will have 30 seconds to prepare. Then you will have 60 seconds to speak.

이 파트에서 여러분에게 한 가지 문제가 주어집니다. 여러분은 그에 대한 해결책을 제시해주세요. 30초 동안 준비한 뒤 60초 동안 응답하세요.

In your response, be sure to
- show that you recognize the problem, and
- propose a way of dealing with the problem.

여러분의 응답에서
- 여러분이 문제를 인식했다는 것을 보여주세요.
- 그 문제를 대처하는 방법을 제안해주세요.

TOEIC® Speaking

Question 10 of 11

 Hi. This is Alfred Madison. I'm calling to thank your group for the marvelous results of the sales for our smart phones this month. To show my appreciation, I would like to reward all of your sales group members. Yet, I don't have any knowledge about the group and what would be good for them in return for their hard work. Because you are the sales manager, I guess you should know best about each of your group members. Therefore, I was wondering if you could give me some suggestions about this reward I'm planning. Please think about it and let me know. Thanks!

안녕하세요. 저는 Alfred Madison입니다. 이번 달 스마트 폰 판매의 뛰어난 성과에 대해 귀 부서에 감사 인사차 전화를 드렸습니다. 감사의 표시로 판매부서 사원 모든 분께 포상을 하고 싶습니다. 하지만 저는 부서에 대해서 아는 바가 없고 노고에 대한 포상으로 무엇이 좋을지 모르겠습니다. 귀하는 판매 부장이시므로 부서 사원 각각을 잘 아실 것이라 생각합니다. 따라서 제가 계획 중인 이 포상에 대해 약간의 조언을 주실 수 있으신지요. 고려해보시고 알려주시길 부탁드립니다. 감사합니다!

 **marvelous** 뛰어난   **result** 결과   **appreciation** 감사, 고마움   **reward** 보상하다   **yet** 하지만   **knowledge** 지식, 아는 것   **in return** ~에 대한 보답으로   **therefore** 따라서

 **Possible Answer**

인사	Hello, Mr. Madison. This is Kate, the Sales Manager.
문제 상황 인식	I received your message regarding rewarding my sales group members for their superb sales on smart phones this month. I am thrilled to learn that they will be rewarded for their intense work. I understand that you have not had the opportunity to get to know each of the group members in depth. However, I am more than willing to suggest an idea to reward my team, since I have worked very closely with them and know them very well.
해결책 제시	After much consideration, I believe that the team members would really appreciate a night out together where the company pays for the dinner and drinks. In addition, I think it would be wonderful if the group members were permitted to bring guests to the event, such as their spouse or other loved ones. My group members have worked really hard to increase the smart phone sales and have also worked longer hours than customary.
마무리	Please let me know if this idea is acceptable or not. I look forward to hearing from you.

안녕하세요, Madison 씨. 판매 부장 Kate입니다. 이번 달 스마트 폰 판매에 탁월한 성과를 낸 저희 판매 부서에 포상을 주시려 한다는 메시지를 받았습니다. 그들의 열정적 근무에 대한 포상이 주어진다는 것을 알게 되어 정말 기쁩니다. 귀하가 부서 사원 각각을 좀 더 잘 알 기회가 없었다는 것을 저는 이해합니다. 그러나 저는 그들과 매우 가까이 일해 왔으며 잘 알고 있기 때문에, 제가 기꺼이 포상 아이디어를 제안합니다. 심사숙고 끝에, 저는 회사가 저녁식사와 주류 비용을 지불하는 저녁 회식을 마련해 주신다면 그들이 정말 고마워하리라 생각합니다. 나아가 행사에 배우자나 다른 사랑하는 사람 등의 동반이 허락된다면, 더욱 근사하리라 생각합니다. 제 부서 사원은 스마트 폰 판매의 향상을 위해 참으로 열심히 일했습니다. 그리고 또한 보통의 근무 시간보다 더 긴 시간을 일했습니다. 이 제안이 수락 가능한지 연락 부탁드립니다. 답변을 고대하고 있겠습니다.

regarding ~에 대해서 **superb** 훌륭한, 뛰어난 **thrilled** 흥분된 **intense work** 집중적인 일 **opportunity** 기회 **in depth** 깊이, 상세히 **be willing to** 기꺼이 ~하다 **after much consideration** 상당히 많이 생각한 후에 **appreciate** 감사하다 **be permitted to** ~이 허락되다 **spouse** 배우자 **loved ones** 사랑하는 사람들 **customary** 관례적인 **acceptable** 받아들일 수 있는

Question 11   Express an Opinion

Directions: In this part of the test, you will give your opinion about a specific topic. Be sure to say as much as you can in the time allowed. You will have 15 seconds to prepare. Then you will have 60 seconds to speak.

이 파트에서 여러분은 특정한 주제에 대한 의견을 말하게 됩니다. 주어진 시간 동안 최대한 많이 말할 수 있도록 하세요. 15초 동안 준비한 뒤 60초 동안 응답하세요.

When you go on a trip, do you usually make a precise plan before you leave or do you usually go on a trip without a plan?

Which do you prefer and why?

Give reasons and examples to support your answer.

여행을 떠날 때, 대체로 출발에 앞서 세심한 계획을 짜십니까? 아니면 계획 없이 떠나십니까?

어느 쪽이 바람직하다고 보십니까? 그 이유가 무엇입니까?

여러분의 의견을 뒷받침하는 이유와 예시를 들어주십시오.

Possible Answer 1 (make a precise plan before I leave)

의견 제시	When I go on a trip, I like to make a precise plan before I leave, for several reasons.
근거 제시 1	Most importantly, I do not have much vacation time so I need to maximize my time. I only get five days off a year, so I shouldn't waste my time off researching about interesting things to do.
근거 제시 2	Another reason why I like to make a precise plan is that I have had bad experiences in the past when I did not make any plans.
예시	A few years ago, I went to New York City. I wanted to see some of the shows on Broadway, but a lot of them were sold out. The shows that I could get tickets for only had undesirable seats far from the stage, and I couldn't see the stage that well. I could have bought tickets to better seats for some of the sold-out shows from scalpers, but they were charging almost five times the cost of the original ticket. I just could not afford those prices.
마무리	Thus, I have learned my lesson that it is better to make a precise plan before I leave on a trip than not to make any plans.

저는 여행을 떠날 때 여러 가지 이유로 인해 출발에 앞서 세심한 계획을 짜는 것을 좋아합니다. 가장 중요한 이유는 제 휴가가 길지 않으므로 시간을 최대로 활용해야 한다는 점입니다. 저는 일 년에 단 5일의 휴가를 얻습니다. 따라서 흥미 있는 것을 궁리하느라 시간을 허비해서는 안 됩니다. 제가 세심한 계획을 짜는 것을 좋아하는 또 다른 이유는 아무런 계획을 짜지 않았다가 과거에 좋지 않은 경험을 했었다는 것입니다. 몇 년 전, 저는 뉴욕 시에 갔었습니다. 저는 브로드웨이의 쇼를 보고 싶었습니다. 그러나 거의 대부분 쇼는 매진이었습니다. 제가 그나마 표를 구할 수 있던 쇼는 무대가 잘 보이지 않는 멀리 떨어진 좋지 않은 좌석만 남아 있었습니다. 암표상으로부터 매진된 쇼를 관람할 수 있는 더 좋은 좌석의 표를 구할 수 있었지만 그것은 본래 표보다 거의 다섯 배나 비쌌습니다. 저는 그러한 값을 지불할 형편이 안 되었습니다. 따라서 저는 여행 시 출발에 앞서 세심한 계획을 짜는 것이 아무런 계획을 짜지 않는 것보다 바람직하다는 것을 배웠습니다.

 **maximize** 최대한 활용하다　**day off** 휴가, 쉬는 날　**waste** 낭비하다　**time off** 휴식　**sold out** 매진된　**undesirable** 탐탁지 않은　**scalper** 암표상　**original** 원래의, 처음의　**afford** 여유가 되다

 ## Possible Answer 2 (go on a trip without a plan)

의견 제시　When I go on a trip, I usually do not make any plans.

근거 제시 1　I am a spontaneous kind of person, and I find that I like to be surprised about the interesting places and activities available on my vacation. This has worked well for me in the past.

예시　I went to Cancun, Mexico last spring with a friend of mine. Neither of us made any plans, but we had the best time of our lives. We met up with some other vacationers and joined some of the tours that they had booked. My friend and I did not waste time researching about what to do. We relied on the suggestions of others, and we were never disappointed. I think that personal accounts are more substantial than a brochure or Internet information that would be available if I were to plan my trip precisely beforehand. Also, on some days, I just want to relax and not do anything. I am not sure when I would feel like this so it would be very difficult to plan for it ahead of time.

마무리　Hence, I don't bother making precise plans and prefer to do whatever I feel like doing during my vacation.

여행을 떠날 때 저는 대체로 아무런 계획을 짜지 않습니다. 저는 즉흥적인 사람이며 휴가에서 있을 수 있는 흥미 있는 장소와 활동의 의외성에 놀라는 것을 좋아합니다. 이것은 과거에 제게 있어 잘 맞아 떨어졌습니다. 저는 친구와 지난봄에 멕시코의 칸쿤에 있습니다. 저희 둘 누구도 계획을 짜지 않았으나 저희는 생애 최고의 시간을 가졌습니다. 저희는 낯낯 피서객을 만나 그들이 예약한 관광을 했습니다. 저와 제 친구는 무엇을 할까를 궁리하느라 시간을 낭비하지 않았습니다. 저희는 다른 사람의 추천에 의지했고 실망하지 않았습니다. 만일 제가 미리 세심하게 여행 계획을 짠다면 이용했을 책자나 인터넷 정보보다 다른 사람의 생생한 체험이 더욱 실속이 있다고 생각합니다. 또한 어떤 날엔 푹 쉬면서 아무 것도 하고 싶지 않습니다. 언제 제가 그렇게 느낄지 저도 모르기 때문에 미리 계획을 짜는 것은 매우 힘들 것입니다. 따라서 저는 세심한 계획을 짜지 않고 휴가 동안 하고 싶은 대로 하는 것을 선호합니다.

 **spontaneous** 즉흥적인　**book** 예약하다　**disappoint** 신망하다　**account** 선면, 이야기　**substantial** 상당한　**brochure** 책자　**precisely** 정확하게　**ahead of time** 미리　**hence** 이런 이유로　**I don't bother** 신경 쓰지 않다, 대수롭게 여기지 않다